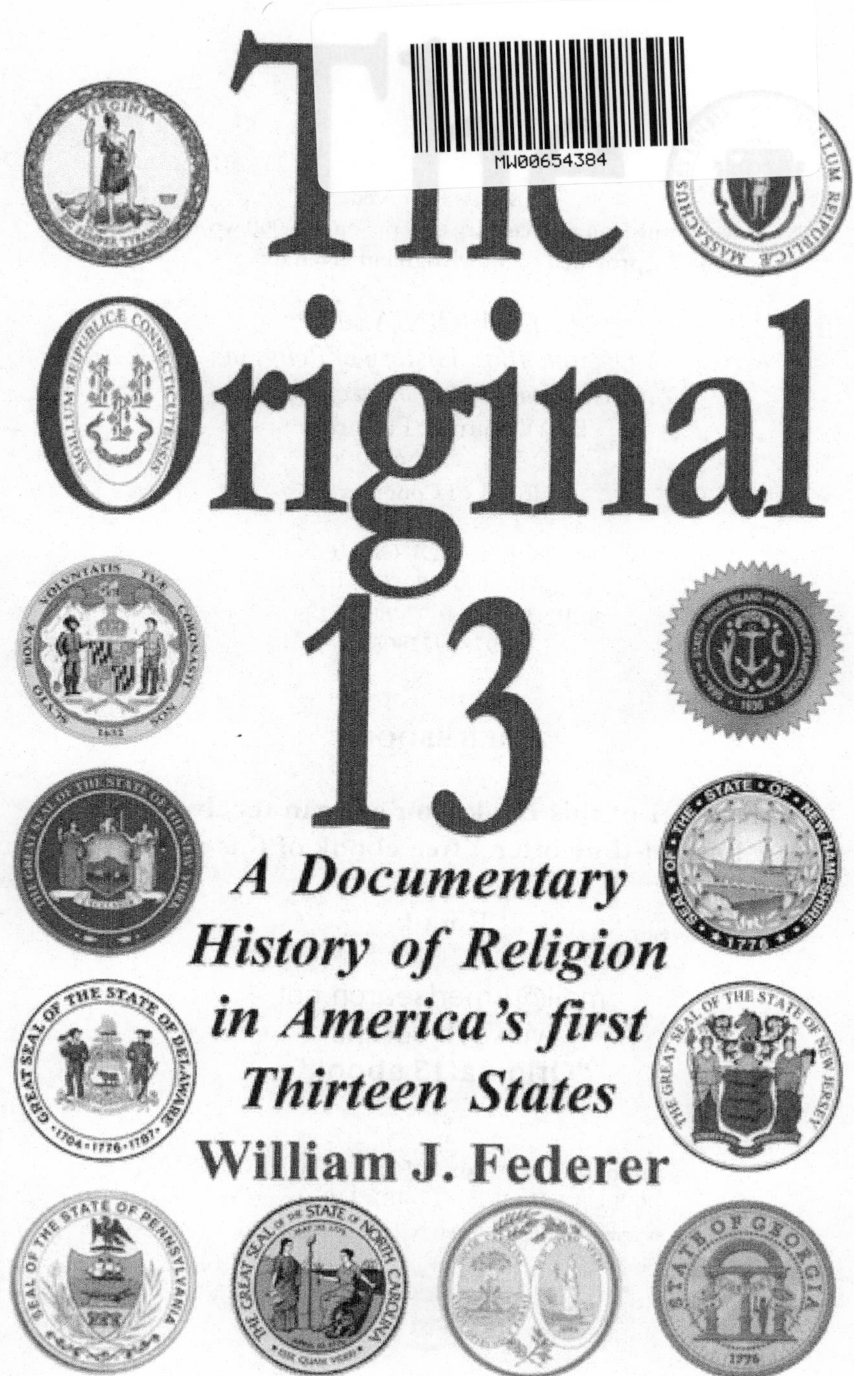

The Original 13

A Documentary History of Religion in America's first Thirteen States

William J. Federer

THE ORIGINIAL 13
-A Documentary History of Religion in America's First Thirteen States
By William J. Federer

Library of Congress

HISTORY / EDUCATION
ISBN 0-9778085-2-1
ISBN13 978-0-9778085-2-6
EAN 9780977808526

FREE EBOOK

As owner of this book, you are can receive as a limited-time offer a free ebook of this title.

Email:

mail@Amerisearch.net
with subject line
"Original13 ebook"

Amerisearch, Inc., P.O. Box 20163, St. Louis, MO 63123,
1-888-USA-WORD, 314-487-4395 voice/fax
www.amerisearch.net, wjfederer@aol.com

CONTENTS

VIRGINIA

MASSACHUSETTS

MAINE

(PART OF MASSACHUSETTS IN 1776)

NEW HAMPSHIRE

VERMONT

(CLAIMED BY NEW HAMPSHIRE IN 1776)

CONNECTICUT

RHODE ISLAND

MARYLAND

NEW YORK

NEW JERSEY

PENNSYLVANIA

DELAWARE

NORTH CAROLINA

SOUTH CAROLINA

GEORGIA

VIRGINIA

QUI TRANSTULIT SUSTINET

EXCELSIOR

DECEMBER 7, 1787

MAY 20TH 1775
N ★ C
APRIL 12TH 1776

STATE OF GEORGIA
1776

INTRODUCTION

> "The whole power over the subject of religion is left exclusively to the **State governments,** to be acted upon according to their own sense of justice and the **State Constitutions.**"
>
> -U.S. Supreme Court Justice Joseph Story, 1833, *Commentaries on the Constitution*

James Madison introduced the First Amendment in the first session in Congress. In 1811, during his term as the fourth President of the United States, Madison appointed Joseph Story to the Supreme Court. Justice Joseph Story served on the Court 34 years and almost single-handedly founded Harvard Law School.

The Constitution of the United States of America-Analysis and Interpretation, prepared by the Legislative Reference Service of the Library of Congress (Edward S. Corwin, editor, U.S. Government Printing Office, Washington, 1953, p. 758), stated:

> In his *Commentaries on the Constitution*, 1833, Justice Joseph Story asserted that the purpose of the First Amendment was not to discredit the then existing **State establishments of religion,** but rather "to exclude from the National Government all power to act on the subject."

Justice Story continued:

> In **some of the States, Episcopalians** constituted the predominant sect; in other, **Presbyterians**; in others, **Congregationalists**; in others, **Quakers;** and in **others** again, there was a close numerical rivalry among contending sects.

> It was impossible that there should not arise perpetual strife and perpetual jealousy on the subject of ecclesiastical ascendancy, if the national government were left free to create a religious establishment.
>
> The only security was in the abolishing the power. But this alone would have been an imperfect security, if it had not been followed up by a declaration of the right of the free exercise of religion...
>
> Thus, **the whole power over the subject of religion is left exclusively to the State governments,** to be acted upon according to their own sense of justice and the **State constitutions**.

Just as today **some States** allow underage drinking and **others** do not; **some States** have smoking bans and **others** do not; **some States** legalized marijuana and **others** did not; **some States** allow gambling and **others** do not; **some States allow** prostitution (Nevada and formerly Rhode Island) and **others** do not; and **some States** allow homosexual marriage and **others** do not; at the time the Constitution was ratified, **some States** allowed more religious freedom (ie. Pennsylvania and Rhode Island) and **others** did not (ie. Massachusetts and Connecticut).

*John Bouvier's Law Dictionary (*Philadelphia: J.B. Lippincott Co., 1889), stated in its definition of Religion:

> The Constitution of the United States provides that 'Congress shall make no law respecting an establishment of religion or prohibiting the free exercise thereof.' **This provision and that relating to religious tests are limitations upon the power of the Congress only ...**
>
> The **Christian religion** is, of course, recognized by the government, **yet ... the preservation of religious liberty is left to the States.**

During North Carolina's Convention to ratify the U.S. Constitution, Governor Samuel Johnston stated, July 30, 1788:

> I know but **two or three States** where there is the least chance of establishing any particular religion. The people of **Massachusetts** and **Connecticut** are mostly **Presbyterians**. In **every other State**, the people are divided into a great number of sects.
>
> In **Rhode Island**, the tenets of the **Baptists**, I believe, prevail. In **New York**, they are divided very much; the most numerous are the **Episcopalians** and the **Baptists**.
>
> In **New Jersey**, they are as much divided as we are. In **Pennsylvania**, if any sect prevails more than others, it is that of the **Quakers**.
>
> In **Maryland**, the **Episcopalians** are most numerous, though there are other sects. In **Virginia**, there are many sects; you all know what their religious sentiments are.
>
> So in **all the Southern States** they differ; as also **New Hampshire**. I hope, therefore, that gentlemen will see **there is no cause of fear that any one religion shall be exclusively established.**

Charles Carroll of Maryland, the only Catholic to sign the Declaration, wrote to Rev. John Stanford, October, 9, 1827:

> Observing **the Christian religion divided into many sects**, I founded the hope that **no one would be so predominant as to become the religion of the State**. That hope was thus early entertained because all of them joined in the same cause.

In 1790, Bishop John Carroll wrote to Rome:

> The thirteen provinces of North America rejected the yoke of England, they proclaimed, at the same time, freedom of conscience...

> Before this great event, **the Catholic faith had penetrated two provinces only, Maryland and Pennsylvania.** In all the others the laws against Catholics were in force.

President John F. Kennedy stated February 9, 1961:

> This country was dedicated to...two propositions: First, a strong **religioius conviction**, and secondly, a recognition that this conviction could flourish only under a system of freedom...
>
> The **Puritans** and the **Pilgrims** of my own section of **New England**, the **Quakers** of **Pennsylvania,** the **Catholics** of **Maryland**, the **Presbyterians** of **North Carolina**, the **Methodists** and **Baptists** who came later, all shared these two great traditions which, like silver threads, have run through the warp and the woof of American History.

Gustave de Beaumont, a contemporary of Alexis de Tocqueville, wrote in *Marie ou L'Esclavage aux E'tas-Unis*, 1835:

> All of the American constitutions exhort the citizens to practice religious worship as a safeguard both to good morals and to public liberties. In the United States, **the law is never atheistic**... All of the American constitutions proclaim freedom of conscience and the liberty and equality of all the confessions.
>
> The Constitution of **Massachusetts** proclaims the freedom of the various faiths in the sense that it does not wish to persecute any of them; but it recognizes within the state **only Christians** and protects **only the Protestants**.
>
> **Maryland**'s Constitution also declares that all of the faiths are free, and that no one is forced to contribute to the maintenance of a particular Church. However, it gives the

legislature the right to establish a general tax, according to the circumstances, for the support of **the Christian religion**.

The Constitution of **Vermont** recognizes **only the Christian faiths**, and says specifically that every congregation of **Christians** should celebrate the Sabbath or the Lord's Day, and observe the religious worship which seems to it most pleasing to the will of God, manifested by revelation.

Sometimes the American constitutions offer religious bodies some indirect assistance: thus, **Maryland** Law declares that, to be admitted to public office, it is necessary to be a **Christian**.

The **Pennsylvania** Constitution requires that one **believe in the existence of God** and in **a future life of punishment or rewards...**

I have just indicated how the law... confirms the power of religion... There is not a single State where public opinion and the customs of the inhabitants do not forcefully constrain an obligation to these beliefs.

Massachusetts Supreme Court stated in *Commonwealth v. Abner Kneeland*, 1838, 37 Mass. (20 Pick) 206, 216-217:

In **New Hampshire**, the constitution of which State has a similar declaration of rights, the open denial of **the being and existence of God or of the Supreme Being** is prohibited by statute, and declared to be blasphemy.

In **Vermont**, with a similar declaration of rights, a statute was passed in 1797, by which it was enacted, that if any person shall publicly deny **the being and existence of God or the Supreme Being**, or shall contumeliously reproach his Providence and government, he shall be deemed a disturber of the peace and

> tranquillity of the State, and an offender against the good morals and manners of society, and shall be punishable by fine....
>
> The State of **Maine** also, having adopted the same constitutional provision with that of **Massachusetts**, in her declaration of rights, in respect to religious freedom, immediately after the adoption of the constitution reenacted, the **Massachusetts** statue against blasphemy....
>
> In **New York** the universal toleration of all religious professions and sentiments, is secured in the most ample manner. It is declared in the constitution... that the free exercise and enjoyment of religious worship, without discrimination or preference, shall for ever be allowed in this State to all mankind...
>
> Notwithstanding this constitutional declaration carrying the doctrine of unlimited toleration as far as the peace and safety of any community will allow, the courts have decided **that blasphemy was a crime at common law** and was not abrogated by the constitution [*People v. Ruggles*].
>
> [The First Amendment] embraces all who believe in **the existence of God**, as well... as **Christians of every denomination....**
>
> **This provision does not extend to atheists, because they do not believe in God** or religion; and therefore... their sentiments and professions, whatever they may be, cannot be called religious sentiments and professions.

U.S. Supreme Court Justice John Paul Stevens wrote in *Wallace v. Jaffree*, 1985:

> The individual's freedom to choose his own creed is the counterpart of his right to refrain from accepting the creed established by the majority.

> At one time it was thought that **this right merely proscribed the preference of one Christian sect over another**, but would not require equal respect for the conscience of the **infidel, the atheist, or the adherent of a non-Christian faith**.

Alexis de Tocqueville wrote in *Democracy in America*, 1840:

> The sects that exist in the United States are innumerable... Moreover, all the sects of the United States are comprised **within the great unity of Christianity, and Christian morality is everywhere the same...**
>
> In the United States **Christian sects** are infinitely diversified and perpetually modified; but **Christianity itself is a fact so irresistibly established**, that no one undertakes either to attack or to defend it."

NYU Professor Emeritus Patricia U. Bonomi, in a National Humanities Center article, titled *The Middle Colonies as the Birthplace of Religious Pluralism*, wrote:

> The colonists were about 98 percent **Protestant**.

John K. Wilson wrote in *Religion Under the State Constitutions 1776-1800* (Journal of Church and State, Volume 32, Autumn 1990, Number 4, pp. 754):

> An **establishment of religion**, in terms of **direct tax aid to Churches**, was the situation in **nine of the thirteen colonies** on the eve of the American revolution.

U.S. Supreme Court Justice Hugo Lafayette Black wrote in *Engel v. Vitale*, 1962:

> When some of the very groups which had most strenuously opposed the established **Church of England** found themselves sufficiently in control of **colonial**

> **governments** in this country to write their own prayers into law, they passed laws **making their own religion the official religion of their respective colonies.**
>
> Indeed, as late as the time of the Revolutionary War, there were **established Churches** in **at least eight of the thirteen former colonies and established religions in at least four of the other five.**
>
> But the successful Revolution against English political domination was shortly followed by intense opposition to the practice of establishing religion by law.
>
> This opposition crystallized rapidly into an effective political force in **Virginia** where the minority religious groups such as **Presbyterians, Lutherans, Quakers** and **Baptists** had gained such strength that the adherents to the established **Episcopal Church** were actually a minority themselves.
>
> In 1785-1786, those opposed to the established Church ... obtained the enactment of the famous **"Virginia Bill for Religious Liberty"** by which **all religious groups were placed on an equal footing.**

Congressman James Meacham (VT) gave a House Judiciary Committee report, March 27, 1854:

> At the adoption of the Constitution, we believe **every State - certainly ten of the thirteen - provided as regularly for the support of the Church** as for the support of the Government: one, **Virginia**, had the system of tithes.
>
> Down to the Revolution, **every colony did sustain religion in some form**. It was deemed peculiarly proper that the religion of liberty should be upheld by a free people.

> **Had the people, during the Revolution, had a suspicion of any attempt to war against Christianity, that Revolution would have been strangled in its cradle.**

The Constitution of the United States of America-Analysis and Interpretation, prepared by the Library of Congress, (U.S. Gov. Printing Office, Washington, 1953, p. 759), stated:

> Justice Story contended, the establishment clause, while it inhibited Congress from giving preference to **any denomination of the Christian faith**, was not intended to withdraw **the Christian religion** as a whole from the protection of Congress.
>
> Justice Joseph Story continued:
>
> Probably **at the time of the adoption of the Constitution,** and of the Amendment to it now under consideration, **the general if not the universal sentiment in America was, that Christianity ought to receive encouragement from the state** so far as was not incompatible with the private rights of conscience and the freedom of religious worship.
>
> Any attempt to level all religions, and make it a matter of state policy to hold all in utter indifference, would have created universal disapprobation, in not universal indignation.

Like a race track with 13 lanes, the original 13 States, by 'successive relaxations', advanced religious tolerance at their own speeds, as James Madison wrote in 1832 to Rev. Jasper Adams, President of the College of Charleston:

> In the colonial state of the country, there were four examples, **Rhode Island, New Jersey, Pennsylvania and Delaware**, and the greater part of **New York** where there were **no religious establishments**; the support of religion being left to the voluntary associations

> and contributions of individuals; and certainly the religious condition of **those Colonies** will well bear **a comparison with that where establishments existed...**
>
> The **New England States have not discontinued establishments of religion** formed under very peculiar circumstances; **but they have by successive relaxations advanced** towards the prevailing example; and without any evidence of disadvantage either to religion or good government.
>
> And if we turn to the **Southern States** where there was, previous to the Declaration of independence, **a legal provision for the support of Religion**; and since that event a surrender of it to a spontaneous support by the people, it may be said that the difference amounts nearly to a contrast in the greater purity & industry of the **Pastors** and **in the greater devotion of their flocks,** in the latter period than in the former.
>
> In **Virginia**...the **abolition of the legal establishment of Religion**...account for the change in the Religious character of the community ... Now more than 50 years since the **legal support of Religion** was withdrawn sufficiently prove that it does not need the support of Government.

In 1868, **the 14th Amendment** was passed to give rights to freed slaves. Congressman John Bingham of Ohio who introduced it, stated: "**I repel the suggestion...that the Amendment will take away from any State any right that belongs to it.**" Yet the process began nonetheless.

When Latter Day Saints wanted to use the First Amendment to practice polygamy, appeals were made to the Federal Judiciary which upheld traditional marriage (*Reynolds v. United States*, 1879 and *Davis V. Beason*, 1890).

Federal Judges gradually began using **the 14th Amendment** to **remove from States' jurisdiction** responsibility for **freedom of speech and press,** *Gitlow v. New York,* 1925 (re: Socialists) and *Fiske v. Kansas,* 1927 (re: Unions); **freedom of press,** *Near v. Minnesota,* 1931 (re: anti-Catholics); and **freedom of assembly,** *DeJonge v. Oregon,* 1937 (re: Communists).

Federal Judges used **the 14th Amendment** to remove responsibility for **religious freedom** from States' jurisdiction in cases regarding Jehovah's Witnesses: *Cantwell v. Connecticut,* 1940; *Minersville School District v. Gobitis,* 1940; *Jones v. Opelika,* 1942; *Taylor v. Mississippi,* 1943; *Martin v. Struthers,* 1943; *United States v. Ballard,* 1944; *Saia v. New York,* 1948; and *Niemotoko v. Maryland,* 1951.

Cases of anti-Catholic discrimination were appealed to the Supreme Court: *Pierce v. Society of Sisters of Holy Names of Jesus and Mary,* 1925, and *Everson v. Board of Education,* 1947. Since then, Federal Courts used a case by case "crucible of litigation" (*Wallace v. Jaffree,* 1985) to evolve the First Amendment into its present interpretation.

Thomas Jefferson predicted this trend in a letter to Charles Hammond in 1821:

> "The germ of dissolution of our federal government is in...**the federal judiciary**... **working like gravity** by night and by day, gaining a little today and a little tomorrow, and advancing its noiseless step like a thief, over the field of jurisdiction, **until all shall be usurped from the States."**

As Justice Joseph Story's 1833 understanding was that the **"power over the subject of religion is left exclusively to the State governments"** and as *Bouvier's Law Dictionary,* 1889, stated **"preservation of religious liberty is left to the States,"** it is necessary to review the **State Constitutions,** and **the Charters that preceded them,** to understand America's progression of religious freedom.

VIRGINIA
SIC SEMPER TYRANNIS

SIGILLUM REIPUBLICÆ MASSACHUSETTENSIS

SEAL OF THE STATE OF RHODE ISLAND AND PROVIDENCE PLANTATIONS
HOPE
1636

SIGILLUM REIPUBLICÆ CONNECTICUTENSIS

SCVTO BONÆ VOLVNTATIS TVÆ CORONASTI NOS
1632

GREAT SEAL OF THE STATE OF DELAWARE
·1704·1776·1787·

THE GREAT SEAL OF THE STATE OF NEW YORK

SEAL OF THE STATE OF PENNSYLVANIA

SEAL · OF · THE · STATE · OF · NEW HAMPSHIRE
★1776★

THE GREAT SEAL OF THE STATE OF NEW JERSEY

THE GREAT SEAL OF THE STATE OF NORTH CAROLINA
MAY 20, 1775
APRIL 12, 1776
★ ESSE QUAM VIDERI ★

1776

NORTH AMERICA

Adam Smith wrote in *The Wealth of Nations,* 1776:

> The **Spaniards**, by virtue of the first discovery, claimed all America as their own, and ... such was ... the terror of their name, that the greater part of the other nations of Europe were afraid to establish themselves in any other part of that great continent...
>
> But ... the defeat ... of their Invincible Armada ... put it out of their power to obstruct any longer the settlements of the other European nations.
>
> In the course of the 17th century... **English, French, Dutch, Danes,** and **Swedes**... attempted to make some settlements in the new world.

The **Spanish** were the first to establish **missions** in North America, but the destruction of the Spanish Armada on July 29, 1588, opened the door for other European countries to successfully settle colonies.

England's claims first began when King Henry VII commissioned explorer John Cabot to discover lands and waterways.

MARCH 5, 1496
PATENT OF KING HENRY VII GRANTED TO JOHN CABOT

Henry, by the **Grace of God**, king of England... Greeting. Be it known that we have given...our well beloved John Cabot citizen of Venice...authority...to sail to all parts, country, and seas of the East, of the West, and of the North, under our banners...to seek out, discover, and find whatsoever isles, countries, regions or provinces of the **heathen and infidels** whatsoever they be, and in what part of the world soever they be, which before this time have been unknown to all **Christians.**

JUNE 11, 1578
PATENT TO SIR HUMPHREY GILBERT

Elizabeth, by the **Grace of God** Queen of England... We...grant to our...well beloved servant Sir Humphrey Gilbert...to discover...such remote, **heathen** and barbarous lands, countries and territories not actually possessed of any **Christian prince or people...**

And...upon the finding out, discovering and inhabiting of such remote lands...it shall be necessary for the safety of all men that shall adventure themselves in those journeys...to determine to live together in **Christian peace** and civil quietness each with other...that the said statutes, laws and ordinances may be as near as conveniently may, agreeable to the form of the laws & policy of England:

And also, that they be not against the **true Christian faith** or **religion** now professed in the **Church of England**, nor in any wise to withdraw any of the subjects or people of those lands or places from the allegiance of us, our heirs or successors, as their immediate Sovereigns under **God**...

We do hereby declare to all **Christian Kings, princes and states**, that if the said Sir Humphrey...act of unjust and unlawful hostility to any of the Subjects of us...the said Sir Humphrey...make such restitution and satisfaction of all such injuries done."

1821, JEFFERSON'S AUTOBIOGRAPHY

The first settlers of Virginia were Englishmen, loyal subjects to their King and Church, and the grant to Sir Walter Raleigh contained an express proviso that their laws **'should not be against the true Christian faith, now professed in the Church of England.'**

In 2006, Pew Research's Religious Landscape Survey identified the United States as:

Evangelical Protestant - 26 percent
Mainline Protestant - 18 percent
Historically Black Protestant - 7 percent
Catholic - 24 percent
Orthodox Christian - 1 percent
Other Christian - <0.5 percent
Mormon - 2 percent
Jehovah's Witnesses - 1 percent
Jewish - 2 percent
Buddhist - 1 percent
Muslim - 1 percent
Hindu - <0.5 percent
Other World Religions - <0.5 percent
Other Faiths - 1 percent
Unaffiliated - 16 percent
Did Not Answer - <0.5 percent

VIRGINIA
SIC SEMPER TYRANNIS

VIRGINIA

Sir Walter Raleigh named Virginia after Virgin Queen Elizabeth. In 1584, he attempted to found the Roanoke Colony, located in present day North Carolina, but it failed. Jamestown was founded by members of the **Church of England**, which was the **established denomination** from 1606 until 1786.

Catholics were prohibited, with even Lord Baltimore, a friend of Charles I, being prohibited from stopping in Virginia in 1628 on his way to found the Colony of Maryland as a refuge for persecuted **Catholics**. The first **Catholic Church** in Virginia, **St. Mary Church,** was not erected until 1795 in Alexandria.

The Civil War in England between Charles I and the **Puritans**, had repercussions in America. Beginning in 1639, "to **tolerate Puritanism** was to resist the king," therefore laws were passed requiring the "governor and council to take care that all **non-conformists** be compelled to depart the colony."

Quakers began arriving in 1655, and the first known **Quaker missionary**, William Robinson, was hung in 1659 in Boston "accused of **heresy** and of being a seducer of the people to faction and committing in open court the felony of denying the humanity of **Christ**." **Quaker** marriages were not recognized.

France's St. Bartholomew's Day massacre and the Revocation of the Edict of Nantes led French **Protestant Huguenots** to immigrate to Virginia.

In 1699, the Virginia **Assembly** adopted William and Mary's first statute for allowing some **toleration** of **Protestant dissenters**. In 1702, there were reported 49 **Anglican parishes** with 34 **ministers**, 3 **Quaker Meetings**, and 3 **Presbyterian congregations**.

In 1729, the Shenandoah Valley, an outlying buffer area from the Indians, was settled by Scotch-Irish **Presbyterians**, German **Lutherans**, **Mennonites**, and **Moravians-Church of the Brethren**. Their decision to settle on the frontier spared them much persecution.

In 1714, a small number of English **Baptists** settled in southeast Virginia and 30 years later a larger number settled in northwest Virginia and in the Blue Ridge region. As their numbers grew rapidly, they were greatly persecuted in the 1760-1770 period preceding the Revolutionary War.

Francis L. Hawks, in his **Ecclesiastical History**, 1836, wrote: "There was a bitterness in the hatred of this **denomination** towards the **established Church**, which surpassed that of all others... No **dissenters** in Virginia experienced for a time harsher treatment than the **Baptists**. They were beaten and imprisoned, and cruelty taxed ingenuity to devise new modes of punishment and annoyance."

Anglican Methodists grew to large numbers beginning in the 1730's due to **George Whitefield's Great Awakening Revival.** When **Anglican Methodist Bishop Francis Asbury** chose to separate the **Methodist Church** from the **Anglican Church**, the **Anglicans** lost their majority, resulting in the **Anglican Church** being **disestablished** in 1786.

Small numbers of **Sephardic Jews** came to Virginia in the late 1650's and a larger number of **Ashkenazic Jews** arrived in the 1830's, fleeing persecution in Germany and Eastern Europe.

The first permanent **synagogue** community, **Kehilah ha Kadosh Beth Shalome**, was founded in 1789 in Richmond, Virginia, with its first permanent building built in 1820.

1584
CHARTER TO SIR WALTER RALEIGH

Elizabeth, by the **Grace of God** of England...**Defender of the Faith**... We give and grant to our trusty and well beloved servant Walter Raleigh...to discover, search, find out, and view such remote, **heathen** and barbarous lands, countries, and territories, not actually possessed of any **Christian** Prince, nor inhabited by **Christian** People...

And...upon...finding...such remote lands...it shall be necessary for the safety of al men, that shall adventure themselves in those...voyages, to determine to live together in **Christian peace**...So always as the said statutes, laws, and ordinances may be as near as conveniently may be agreeable to the form of the laws, statutes, government, or policy of England, and also so as they be not against the **true Christian faith**, now professed in the **Church of England**.

APRIL 10, 1606
FIRST CHARTER OF VIRGINIA

We, greatly commending, and graciously accepting of, their Desires for the Furtherance of so noble a Work, which may, by the **Providence of Almighty God,** hereafter tend to the **Glory of his Divine Majesty,** in propagating of **Christian Religion** to such People, as yet live in Darkness and miserable Ignorance of the **true Knowledge and Worship of God**, and may in time bring the **Infidels** and

Savages, living in those parts, to human Civility, and to a settled and quiet Government.

NOVEMBER 20, 1606
VIRGINIA ASSEMBLY

And we do especially ordain... the said... councils... that they, with all diligence, care, and respect, do provide, that the **true word,** and **service of God** and **Christian faith** be **preached**, planted, and used, not only within every of the said several colonies, and plantations, but also as much as they may amongst the savage people which do or shall adjoin unto them, or border upon them, according to the **doctrine, rights, and Religion now professed and Established within our Realm of England.**

APRIL 26, 1607
MEMORIAL TO REVEREND ROBERT HUNT

After landing at Cape Henry, settlers erected a wooden cross and commenced a **prayer** meeting, led by the **Reverend** Robert Hunt. Later that year, after his death, the settlers wrote:

To the **Glory of God** and in memory of the **Reverend Robert Hunt, Presbyter**, appointed by the **Church of England**. **Minister** of the Colony which **established** the **English Church** and English Civilization at Jamestown, Virginia, in 1607. His people, members of the Colony, left this testimony concerning him. He was an honest, **religious** and courageous **Divine**. He preferred the **Service of God** in so good a voyage to every thought of ease at home.

He endured every privation, yet none ever heard him repine. During his life our factions were often healed, and our greatest extremities so comforted that they seemed easy in comparison with what we endured after his memorable death.

We all received from him the **Holy Communion** together, as a pledge of reconciliation, for we all loved him for his exceeding goodness. He planted the first **Protestant Church** in America and laid down his life in the foundation of America.

MAY 23, 1609
SECOND CHARTER OF VIRGINIA

James, by the **Grace of God**, King of England...**Defender of the Faith**... Greeting. Whereas, at the humble...Request of sundry our loving and well-disposed Subjects, intending to deduce a Colony, and to make Habitation and Plantation of sundry our People in that Part of America, commonly called VIRGINIA, and other Parts...not actually possessed of any **Christian** Prince or People...

Now, forasmuch as divers and sundry of our loving Subjects...which have already engaged themselves in furthering the Business of the said Colony...intend, by the Assistance of **Almighty God**, to prosecute the same to a happy End...in the said Discovery and Plantation of the said Country...

We greatly affecting the effectual Prosecution and happy success of the said Plantation, and commending their good desires therein, for their further Encouragement in accomplishing so excellent a Work, much pleasing to **God**, and profitable to our Kingdom...

And forasmuch as it shall be necessary for all such our loving Subject as shall inhabit within the said Precincts of Virginia aforesaid, to determine to live together in the **Fear and true Worship of Almighty God, Christian Peace** and Civil Quietness each with other...

And lastly, because the principal Effect which ever can desire or expect of this Action, is the **Conversion and Reduction of the People in those Parts unto the true Worship of God and Christian Religion**, in which Respect we should be loath that any Person should be permitted to pass that we suspected to affect the **Superstitions of the Church of Rome**, we do hereby declare, that it is our Will and Pleasure that none be permitted to pass in any Voyage from Time to Time to be made into the said Country, but such as first shall have taken the **Oath of Supremacy**.

MARCH 12, 1611
THIRD CHARTER OF VIRGINIA

James, by the **Grace of God**, King of England...**Defender of the Faith**...Greeting. Whereas at the humble Suit of divers and sundry our loving Subjects, as well Adventurers as Planters of the first Colony in Virginia, and for the **Propagation of Christian Religion,** and Reclaiming of People barbarous, to Civility and Humanity, We have...granted unto them...the first Colony in Virginia...

We therefore tendering the good and happy Success of the said Plantation, both in Regard of the General Weal of human Society, as in Respect of the Good of our own Estate and Kingdoms, and being willing to give Furtherance unto all good Means that may advance the Benefit of the said Company, and which may secure the Safety of our loving Subjects planted in our said Colony, under the **Favor and Protection of God Almighty**, and of our Royal Power and Authority, have...granted...all...Islands whatsoever situate and being in any Part of the Ocean Seas bordering upon the Coast of our said first Colony in Virginia...Provided always, that the said Islands or any Premises herein mentioned...be not actually possessed or inhabited by any other **Christian Prince or Estate...**

And furthermore, whereas We have been certified, That divers lewd and ill disposed Persons, both Sailors, Soldiers, Artificers, Husbandmen, Laborers...having there misbehaved themselves by Mutinies, Sedition, or other notorious Misdemeanors... in Virginia, have endeavored by most vile and slanderous Reports...to bring the said

Voyage and Plantation into Disgrace and Contempt...a great Number of other, our loving and well-disposed Subjects, otherwise well affected and inclined to join and adventure in so noble, **Christian**, and worthy an Action, have been discouraged from the same; but also the utter overthrow and Ruin of the said Enterprise hath been greatly endangered, which cannot miscarry without some Dishonor to Us, and our Kingdom.

1618
ARTICLES SENT TO COUNSEL OF ENGLAND BY PILGRIM LEADERS JOHN ROBINSON AND WILLIAM BREWSTER, REQUESTING APPROVAL TO SETTLE IN VIRGINIA:

Article III. The King's Majesty we acknowledge for Supreme Governor in his Dominion...but in all things obedience is due unto him if the thing commanded be not against **God's Word**...Article VII. And lastly, we desire to give unto all Superiors due honor to preserve the unity of the **Spirit,** with all who fear **God**, to have peace with all men what in us lieth, and wherein we err to be instructed by any.

JULY 30, 1619
NARRATIVES OF VIRGINIA HOUSE OF BURGESSES, JOHN PORY, SPEAKER

But, forasmuch as men's affairs do little prosper when **God's service** is neglected, all the Burgesses took their places in the Quire till **prayer** was said by Mr. Bucke, the **Minister**, that it would please **God** to guide and sanctify all our proceedings to **His own glory**, and the good of this plantation. **Prayer** being ended, to the intent that as we had begun at **God Almighty** so we might proceed awful and due respect toward his lieutenant...

Be it enacted by this present **Assembly** that for laying a surer foundation for the **conversion of the Indians** to **Christian religion**, each town, city, borough, and particular plantation do obtain unto themselves, by just means, a certain number of the natives' children to be educated by them in **true religion** and a civil course of life; of which children the mostly toward boys in wit and graces of nature to be brought up by them in the first elements of literature, so as to be fitted for the college intended for them; that from thence they may be sent to that work of **conversion**...

All **ministers** shall duly read **Divine servic**e and exercise their **ministerial** function according to the **ecclesiastical laws** and orders of the **Church of England**, and every **Sunday** in the afternoon shall **catechize** such as are not yet ripe to come to the **Communion**.

And whosoever of them shall be found negligent or faulty in this kind shall be subjected to the censure of the governor and Council of Estate.

AUGUST 4, 1619
NARRATIVE OF VIRGINIA ASSEMBLY

All **ministers** shall duly read **Divine service**, and exercise their **ministerial function** according to the **Ecclesiastical laws** and orders of the **Church of England**, and every **Sunday** in the afternoon shall **Catechize** such as are not yet ripe to come to the **Communion**. And whosoever of them shall be found negligent or faulty in this kind shall be subject to the censure of the Governor and Council of Estate.

The **Ministers** and **Churchwardens** shall seek to present all **ungodly** disorders, the committers whereof if, upon good admonitions and mild reproof, they will not forebear the said scandalous offenses, as suspicions of whoredoms, dishonest company keeping with women and such like, they are to be presented and punished accordingly.

If any person after two warnings, do not amend his or her life in point of evident suspicion of incontinency or of the commission of any other enormous sins, that then he or she be presented by the **Churchwardens** and suspended for a time from the **Church** by the **minister**. In which Interim if the same person do not amend and humbly submit him or herself to the **Church**, he is then fully to be **excommunicate** and soon after a writ or warrant to be sent from the Governor for the apprehending of his person and seizing on all his goods...

All persons whatsoever upon the **Sabbath day** shall frequent **Divine service** and **sermons** both forenoon and afternoon, and all such as bear arms shall bring their pieces, swords, powder and shot. And every one that shall transgress this law shall forfeit three shillings a time to the use of the **Church**, all lawful and necessary impediments excepted. But if a servant in this case shall willfully neglect his Master's command he shall suffer bodily punishment

DECEMBER 4, 1619
COLONISTS AT BERKELEY HUNDRED

In a place called Berkeley Hundred, thirty-eight colonists landed and enacted:

We ordain that the day of our ship's arrival...in the land of Virginia shall be yearly and perpetually kept **Holy** as a **day of Thanksgiving to Almighty God.**

JULY 24, 1621
VIRGINIA ASSEMBLY ORDINANCE

Know Ye, that we, the said Treasurer, Council, and Company, taking into our careful Consideration the present State of the said Colony of Virginia, and intending, by the **Divine Assistance**, to settle such a Form of Government there, as may be to the greatest Benefit and Comfort of the People.

AUGUST 3, 1621
ORDINANCES FOR VIRGINIA

III. The Council of State...shall be chosen...Persons...which said Counselors and Council we earnestly **pray** and desire, and in his Majesty's Name strictly charge and command...they bend their Care and Endeavors to assist the said Governor; first and principally, in the **Advancement of the Honor and Service of God**, and the **Enlargement of his Kingdom** amongst the **Heathen** People; and next, in erecting of the said Colony in due obedience to his Majesty, and all lawful Authority from his Majesty's Directions; and lastly, in maintaining the said People in Justice and **Christian Conversation** amongst themselves, and in Strength and Ability to withstand their Enemies.

MARCH 22, 1622
JAMESTOWN ISLAND, INDIAN ATTACK AVERTED

Church marker stated: In memory of Chanco, an Indian youth **converted** to **Christianity,** who resided in the household of Richard Pace across the river from Jamestown and who, on the eve of the Indian massacre of March 22, 1622, warned Pace of the murderous plot thus enabling Pace to cross the river in a canoe to alert and save the Jamestown settlement from impending disaster.

1623
VIRGINIA ASSEMBLY REQUIRED MAGISTRATES:

To see that the **Sabbath** was not profaned by working or any employments, or journeying from place to place.

MARCH 5, 1624
VIRGINIA ASSEMBLY

1. That there shall be in every plantation, where the people use to meet for the **worship of God**, a house or room sequestered for that purpose, and not to be for any temporal use whatsoever, and a place...sequestered only to the burial of the dead.

2. That whosoever shall absent himself from **Divine** service any **Sunday** without an allowable excuse shall forfeit a pound of tobacco, and he that absenteth himself a month shall forfeit 50 pound of tobacco.

3. That there be an **uniformity** in **our Church** as near as may be to the **Canons in England**; both in substance and circumstance, and that all persons yield ready obedience unto them under pain of censure.

4. That the 22d of March (in commemoration of the Anglo-Indian conflict of 1622) be yearly solemnized as holiday, and all other holidays (except when they fall two together) betwixt the **feast of the annunciation of the blessed virgin** and **St. Michael the archangel**, then only the first to be observed by reason of our necessities.

5. That no **minister** be absent from his **Church** above two months in all the year upon penalty of forfeiting half his means, and whosoever shall absent above four months in the year shall forfeit his whole means and cure.

6. That whosoever shall disparage a **minister** without bringing sufficient proof to justify his reports whereby the minds of his **parishioners** may be alienated from him, and his **Ministry** prove less effectual by their prejudication, shall not only pay 500 pound weight of tobacco but also ask the **minister** so wronged forgiveness **publicly** in the **congregation**.

7. That no man dispose of any of his tobacco before the **minister** be satisfied, upon pain of forfeiture double his part of the **minister's** means, and one man of every

plantation to collect his means out of the first and best tobacco and corn.

OCTOBER 16, 1629
VIRGINIA ASSEMBLY

It is ordered that there be an especial care taken by all commanders and others that the people do repair to their **Churches** on the **Sabbath day**, and to see that the penalty of one pound of tobacco for every time of absence and 50 pound for every months absence set down in the act of the General Assembly 1623, be levied and the delinquents to pay the same, as also to see that the **Sabbath day** be not ordinarily profaned by working in any employments or by journeying from place to place.

It is thought fit that all those that work in the ground of what quality or condition soever, shall pay **tithes** to the **ministers.**

FEBRUARY 24, 1632
VIRGINIA ASSEMBLY

It is ordered, That there be a **uniformity** throughout this colony both in substance and circumstance to the **cannons** and **constitution of the Church of England**...and that every person yield ready obedience unto them upon penalty of the pains and forfeitures in that case appointed.

That the statutes for coming to **Church** every **Sunday** and holidays be duly executed. That is to say; that the **Church wardens** do levy one shilling for every time of any person's absence from the **Church** having no lawful or reasonable excuse to be absent. And for due execution hereof the Governor and Council together with the burgesses of this grand **Assembly** do in **God's name** earnestly require and charge all commanders, captains and **Church-wardens** that they shall endeavor themselves to the uttermost of their knowledge that the due and true execution hereof may be done and had through this colony, as they will answer before **God** for such evils and plagues wherewith **Almighty God** may justly punish his people for neglecting this good and wholesome law.

And it is further ordered and thought expedient, according to a former order made, by the governor and council that all **Church-wardens** shall take this oath and that it bee administered before those that are of the commission for monthly courts:

"You shall swear that you shall make presentments of all such persons as shall lead a profane or **ungodly** life, of such as shall be common swearers, drunkards and blasphemers, that shall ordinarily profane the **Sabbath days** or contemn **Gods Holy word** or **sacraments**. You shall also present all adulterers or fornicators, or such as shall abuse their neighbors by slandering tale carrying or back biting, or that shall not behave themselves orderly and soberly in the **Church** during **Divine service**. Likewise they shall present such masters and mistresses as shall be delinquent in the **catechizing** the youth and ignorant persons. **So Help You God!**"

No man shall disparage a **minister** whereby the minds of his **parishioners** may be alienated from him and his **Ministry** prove less effectual upon pain of sever censure of the governor and council.

1632
VIRGINIA ASSEMBLY

It is also thought fit, That upon every **Sunday** the **minister** shall half an hour or more before evening **prayer** examine, **catechize**, and instruct the youth and ignorant persons of his **parish**, in the **Ten Commandments** the **articles of the belief** and in the **Lord's prayer**; and shall diligently hear, instruct and teach the **catechism**, set forth in **book of common prayer,**

And all fathers, mothers, masters and mistresses shall cause their children, servants or apprentices which have not learned the **catechism** to come to the **Church** at the time appointed, obediently to hear, and to be ordered by the **minister** until they have learned the same:

And if any of the said fathers, mothers, masters and mistresses, children, servants or apprentices, shall neglect their duties as the one sort in not causing them to come and the other in refusing to learn as aforesaid, they shall be censured by the courts in those places holden. And this act to take beginning at **Easter** next.

Ministers shall not give themselves to excess in drinking, or riot, spending their time idly by day or night, playing at dice, cards, or any other unlawful game; but at all times convenient they shall hear or read somewhat of the **Holy Scriptures**, or shall occupy themselves with some other honest study or exercise, always doing the things which shall appertain to honesty, and endeavor to profit the **Church of God**, always having in mind that they ought to excel all others in **purity** of life, and should be examples to the people to live well and **Christianly.**

APRIL 28, 1634
ROYAL COMMISSION FOR REGULATING PLANTATIONS

Charles, by the **Grace of God,** of England, Scotland, France, and Ireland, King, **Defender of the Faith**, etc...To the **right reverend father in God,** our right trusty and well beloved counselor, William, by the **Providence of God**, **Archbishop of Canterbury...**

Whereas diverse of the subjects of us and of our late dear father, King James, of famous memory, late, of England, King, by virtue of our royal authority, granted not only to enlarge the territories of our empire, but more especially to **propagate the Gospel of our Lord Jesus Christ**, having, with their exceeding industry and charge, deduced great numbers of the people of England into several colonies in several places of the world, either altogether desert and unpeopled, or enjoyed by savage and barbarous nations, void of all manner of knowledge of **Almighty God**...

And for relief and support of the **clergy**, and the rule and cure of the **souls of our people** living in those parts, and for consigning of convenient maintenance to them by **tithes**, oblations, and other profits accruing, according to your good discretion, with the advice of two or three of our **bishops**, whom you shall think fit to call to your consultations, touching the distribution of such maintenance to the **clergy**, and all other matters **ecclesiastical**, and to inflict punishment on all offenders or violators of constitutions and ordinances, either by imprisonments or other restraints, or by loss of life or members, according as the quality of the offense shall require with power also, our royal assent being first ...obtained, to remove all governors and presidents of the said colonies, upon just cause appearing, from their several places, and to appoint others in their stead.

APRIL 30, 1637
PROCLAMATION AGAINST DISORDERLY TRANSPORTING HIS MAJESTY'S SUBJECTS TO THE PLANTATIONS IN AMERICA

The King's most excellent majesty being informed that great numbers of his subjects have been and are every year transported into those parts of America...amongst which numbers there are also many idle and refractory humors whose only or principal end is to live as much as they can without the reach of authority;

His Majesty...is minded to restrain...such promiscuous and disorderly departing out of the realm, and does therefore straightly charge and command all and every the officers and ministers of his several ports in England, Wales, and Berwick that they do not hereafter permit or suffer any persons...to embark themselves in any of the said ports...for any of the said plantations without...certificate from two justices of the peace living next the place where the party last of all...dwelt, that he has taken the **Oath of Supremacy** and Allegiance, and like testimony from the **minister** of the **parish** of his conversation and **conformity** to the orders and **disciplines**s of the **Church of England**.

MARCH 2, 1643
VIRGINIA ASSEMBLY

Whereas it was enacted at an Assembly in January 1641, that according to a statute made in the third year of the reign of our sovereign Lord King James of blessed memory, and that **no popish recusants** should at any time hereafter exercise the place or places of secret counselors, register or commissioner, surveyors or sheriff, or any other public place, but be utterly disabled for the same..

And it is further enacted by the authority aforesaid that the statute in force against the **popish recusants** be duly executed in this government, And that it should not be lawful under the penalty aforesaid for any **popish priest** that shall hereafter arrive to remain above five days after warning given for his departure by the Governor or commander of the place where he or they shall bee, if wind and weather hinder not his departure...

1643
VIRGINIA ASSEMBLY

For the preservation of the **purity of doctrine** and unity of the **Church**, It is enacted that all **ministers** whatsoever which shall reside in the colony are to be conformable to the orders and constitutions of the **Church of England**, and the laws therein **established**, and not otherwise be admitted to teach or **preach publicly** or privately,

And that the Governor and Counsel do take care that all **nonconformists** upon notice of them shall be compelled to depart the colony with all convenience.

NOVEMBER 3, 1647
VIRGINIA ASSEMBLY

Upon divers information presented to this **Assembly** against several **ministers** for their neglects and refractory refusing after warning given them to read **common prayer** or **Divine service** upon the **Sabbath days** contrary to the **cannons of the Church** and acts of parliament therein **established**, for future remedy hereof:

Be it enacted by the Governor, Council and Burgesses of this Grand Assembly, That all **ministers**...upon every **Sabbath day** read such **prayers** as are appointed and prescribed unto them by the said **book of common prayer**, And be it further enacted as a penalty to such as have neglected or shall neglect their duty herein, That no **parishioner** shall be compelled either by distress or otherwise to pay any manner of **tithes** or duties to any **unconformist** as aforesaid.

DECEMBER 1, 1656
VIRGINIA ASSEMBLY

Whereas many **congregations** in this colony are destitute of **ministers** whereby **religion** and devotion cannot but suffer much impairment and decay, which want of the destitute **congregations** ought to be supplied by all means possible to be used, As also to invite and encourage **ministers** to repair hither and merchants to bring them in,

Be it therefore hereby enacted for the reasons aforesaid, that what person or persons soever shall at his or their proper cost and charge transport a sufficient **minister** into this colony without agreement made with him shall receive for satisfaction of his or their said charges of him the said **minister** or that they shall entertain him for their **minister**, twenty pound sterling by bill of exchange or two thousand pounds of tobacco, and also for what money shall be disbursed for them besides their transportation to be allowed for.

MARCH 13, 1660
VIRGINIA ASSEMBLY

Whereas there is an unreasonable and turbulent sort of people, commonly called **Quakers**, who contrary to the law do daily gather unto them unlawful **Assemblies** and **congregations** of people teaching and publishing, lies, miracles, false visions, **prophecies** and **doctrines**, which have influence upon the communities of men both **ecclesiastical** and civil endeavoring and attempting thereby to destroy **religion**, laws, communities and all bonds of civil society, leaving it arbitrary to every vain and vicious person whether men shall be safe, laws **established**, offenders punished, and Governors rule, hereby disturbing the public peace and just interest, to prevent and restrain which mischief,

It is enacted, That no master or commander of any ship or other vessel do bring into this colony any person or persons called **Quakers**, under the penalty of one hundred pounds sterling to be levied upon him and his estate by order from the Governor and Council or the commissioners in the several counties where such s hips shall arrive,

That all such **Quakers** as have been questioned or shall hereafter arrive shall be apprehended wheresoever they shall be found and they be imprisoned without bail or mainprize till they do adjure this country or putt in security with all speed to depart the colony and not to return again:

And if any should dare to presume to return hither after such departure to be proceeded against as contemners of the laws and magistracy and punished accordingly, and caused again to depart the country,

And if they should the third time be so audacious and impudent as to return hither to be proceeded against as felons.

That no person shall entertain any of the **Quakers** that have heretofore been questioned by the Governor and Council, or which shall hereafter be questioned, nor permit in or near his house any **Assemblies** of **Quakers** in the like penalty of one hundred pound sterling,

That commissioners and officers are hereby required and authorized as they will answer the contrary at their peril to take notice of this act to see it fully effected and executed,

And that no person do presume on their peril to dispose or publish their books, pamphlets or libels bearing the title of their tenets and opinions.

AUGUST 8, 1660
VIRGINIA GOVERNOR, WILLIAM BERKELEY, TO OFFICIALS IN LOWER NORFOLD:

Mr. Richard Conquest, I hear with sorrow that you are very remiss in your office, in not stopping frequent meetings of this most pestilent **sect** of ye **Quakers**, whether this be so or not, I do charge you (by virtue of ye power ye grand assemble has entrusted me with) not to suffer any more of their meetings or **Conventicles** & if any such shall be refractory, that you send them up prisoners to James City. I expect your obedience to this which I send you without enclosing that all may take notice of it.

1662
VIRGINIA COMMONWEALTH ENACTED

Enacted that the **Lord's Day** be kept **Holy**, and no journeys be made on that day, unless upon necessity. And all persons inhabiting in this country, having no lawful excuse, shall, every **Sunday**, resort to the **parish Church** or

chapel, and there abide orderly during the common **prayer**, **preaching**, and **Divine** service.

1663
VIRGINIA HOUSE OF BURGESSES, WILLIAMSBURG

passed: "An Act against Persons that refuse to have their Children **Baptized**."

JUNE 27, 1663
VIRGINIA GOVERNOR, WILLIAM BERKELEY, TO OFFICIALS IN LOWER NORFOLD:

Gentlemen I thank you for your care of ye County & desire you to continue it, & especially to provide that abominated seed of ye **Quakers** spread not in your County...Once more I beseech you gentlemen: to have an exact care of this Pestilent **sect** of ye **Quakers**.

SEPTEMBER 1663
VIRGINIA HOUSE OF BURGESSES, WILLIAMSBURG

passed: "An Act prohibiting the Unlawful Assembling of **Quakers**."

1668
VIRGINIA COMMONWEALTH

The 27th of August appointed for a day of **humiliation, fasting,** and **prayer**, to implore **God's mercy**: if any person by found upon that day gaming, drinking, or working (works of necessity excepted), upon presentment by **Church-wardens** and proof, he shall be fined one hundred pounds of tobacco.

1686
VIRGINIA GOVERNOR FRANCIS HOWARD OF EFFINGHAM AND WILLIAM FITZHUGH

Attempted to persuade French refugee Durand de Dauphine to lead **Protestant Huguenots** to Virginia, as Durand de Dauphine noted:

I would have to settle further back & be among the savages, who, he added, are not greatly to be feared, but there is some inconvenience owing to the fact that only small boats can sail up the rivers in the back country so one could not trade by water. For this reason, as there are vast tracts of land for sale very cheap, very good & among **Christians**, he advised me to buy there, rather than further away.

1686
VIRGINIA GOVERNOR FRANCIS HOWARD OF EFFINGHAM

A promise was made to French **Protestants** that they could have their own **ministers** and not be required to attend **Anglican** services:

As for the **pastors**, provided that from time to time they **preached** in English & **Baptized** & married the other **Christians** who might be among the French settlers, he would give benefices to two or three, & they would be required to read the **book of common prayers** when **preaching**, except when they **preached** to French people only, they could do as they were accustomed in France.

1692
CHARTER OF THE COLLEGE OF WILLIAM AND MARY GRANTED TO JAMES BLAIR

William and Mary, by the **Grace of God**, of England, Scotland, France and Ireland, King and Queen, Defenders of the **Faith**, to all whom these our present Letters shall come, greeting. Forasmuch as our well-beloved and trusty

Subjects, constituting the General **Assembly** of our Colony of Virginia, have had it in their minds, and have proposed to themselves, to the end that the **Church** of Virginia may be furnished with a **Seminary** of **Ministers** of the **Gospel**; And that the Youth may be piously educated in Good Letters and Manners, and that the **Christian Faith** may be **propagated** amongst the Western Indians, to the **Glory of God**.

1705
VIRGINIA ASSEMBLY PASSED THE LAW:

If a person brought up in the **Christian religion** denies the **being of a God**, or the **Trinity**, or asserts there are more Gods than one, or denies the **Christian religion** to be true, or the **Scriptures** to be of **Divine authority**, he is punishable on the first offense by incapacity to hold any office of employment, **ecclesiastical**, civil or military; on the second by disability to sue, to take any gift or legacy, to be guardian, executor, or administrator, and by three years' imprisonment without bail.

1710
GOVERNOR SPOTWOOD REPORTED

This government is in perfect peace and tranquillity, under due obedience to royal authority and a gentlemanly conformity to the **Church of England**.

1756
VIRGINIA ACT FOR DISARMING PAPISTS

Due to the French and Indian War, "**Papists** were dangerous at this time" and required to surrender their arms and ammunition, on penalty of three months imprisonment, the loss of their arms, and fine, and not own a horse "above the value of £5, on pain of forfeiture."

MAY 1765 VIRGINIA HOUSE OF BURGESSES, PATRICK HENRY NOTED ON BACK OF STAMP ACT RESOLVES:

This brought on the war which finally separated the two countries and gave independence to ours. Whether this will prove a **blessing** or a curse, will depend upon the use our people make of the **blessings**, which a **gracious God** hath bestowed on us. If they are wise, they will be great and happy. If they are of a contrary character, they will be miserable. **Righteousness** alone can exalt them as a nation. Reader! Whoever thou art, remember this, and in thy sphere practice virtue thyself, and encourage it in others. (signed) P. Henry

1768 SPOTTSYLVANIA COUNTY, VIRGINIA

The sheriff arrested 3 **Baptist ministers**: John Waller, Lewis Craig, and James Childs, for **preaching** contrary to the **Anglican Church**. After 4 weeks in prison, Lewis Craig was brought to trial. Governor Blair rebuked the sheriff of Spottsylvania County:

"You may not molest these conscientious men, so long as they behave themselves in a manner becoming pious **Christians**. I am told that they differ in nothing from **our Church** but in (the manner of) **Baptism**, and their renewing of the ancient **discipline**, by which they have reformed some **sinners** and brought them to be truly penitent...If this be their behavior, it were to be wished we had some of it among us."

After 8 weeks in prison, John Waller and Lewis Childs were brought to trial for "**preaching** the **Gospel** contrary to law." The prosecuting attorney stated:

"May it please your **worship**, these men are great disturbers of the peace: they can not meet a man upon the road, but they must ram a text of **Scripture** down his throat!"

Attorney Patrick Henry road 50 miles and offered to defend the **Preachers**. He secured the immediate discharge of his clients after presenting his defense:

"May it please your lordships, what did I hear read? Did I hear an expression that these men, whom you **worships** are about to try for misdemeanor, are charged with **preaching** the **Gospel of the Son of God**?"

1770
BAPTIST PREACHERS ARRESTED

William Webber and Joseph Anthony, were thrown into Chesterfield County jail, and there "they did much execution by **preaching** through the grates of their windows." In Middlesex County several **Baptist ministers** were imprisoned and treated as criminals.

1772
A LETTER IN THE VIRGINIA GAZETTE

Article sought to justify the persecution, charging **Baptists** with **heresy** and hateful **doctrines**, with disturbing the peace of **religion**, and denying that they were entitled to the benefit of the **toleration** act.

MAY 24, 1774
VIRGINIA HOUSE OF BURGESSES APPROVED DAY OF FASTING, HUMILIATON & PRAYER DRAFTED BY THOMAS JEFFERSON, PROPOSED BY ROBERT CARTER NICHOLAS, SUPPORTED BY RICHARD HENRY LEE, PATRICK HENRY AND GEORGE MASON

This House, being deeply impressed with apprehension of the great dangers to be derived to British America from the hostile invasion of the city of Boston in our Sister Colony of Massachusetts Bay, whose commerce and harbor are, on the first day of June next, to be stopped by an armed force,

deem it highly necessary that the said first day of June be set apart, by the members of this House, as a **Day of Fasting, Humiliation and Prayer,** devoutly to implore the **Divine interposition**, for averting the heavy calamity which threatens destruction to our civil rights and the evils of civil war;

to give us one heart and mind firmly opposed, by all just and proper means, every injury to American rights; and that the minds of His Majesty and his Parliament, may be inspired from above with wisdom, moderation and justice, to remove from the loyal people of America all cause of danger from a continued pursuit of measures pregnant with their ruin.

[Note: Virginia's Royal Governor, Lord Dunmore, interpreted this Day of Fasting as a public protest against the King, so he dissolved Virginia's House of Burgesses, May 27, 1774, setting the stage for the creation of the Continental Congress.]

JUNE 1, 1774
DAY OF FASTING, HUMILIATON & PRAYER

Virginia's Day of Fasting began at the exact time King George III's navy blockaded Boston's port.

Jefferson's older cousin, Peyton Randolph, Speaker of the House, held the ceremonial mace and led citizens from the Capitol in Williamsburg, down Duke of Gloucester Street, to Bruton Parish Church, to pray for Boston. George Washington wrote in his diary "Went to church, fasted all day." Three months later, Peyton Randolph was elected the first President of the Continental Congress.

1774
THOMAS JEFFERSON'S PAMPHLET "A SUMMARY VIEW OF THE RIGHTS OF BRITISH AMERICANS" AS A PROPOSAL FOR THE COLONY'S DELEGATES TO THE FIRST CONTINENTAL CONGRESS:

The **God** who gave us **liberty** at the same time; the hand of force may destroy, but cannot disjoin them.

JULY 26, 1774
THOMAS JEFFERSON'S "RESOLUTIONS OF FREEHOLDERS OF ALBEMARLE COUNTY"

We will ever be ready to join with our fellow-subjects in every part of the same, in executing all those rightful powers which **God** has given us, for the re-establishment and guaranteeing such their constitutional rights, when, where, and by whomever invaded.

MAY 15, 1776
VIRGINIA CONVENTION PREAMBLE & RESOLUTION

Wherefore, appealing to the **Searcher of hearts** for the sincerity of former declarations expressing our desire to preserve the connection with that nation, and that we are driven from that inclination by their wicked councils, and the eternal law of self-preservation:

Resolved, unanimously, That the Delegates appointed to represent this Colony in General Congress be instructed to propose to that respectable body to declare the United Colonies free and independent States, absolved from all allegiance to, or dependence upon, the Crown or Parliament of Great Britain

JUNE 29, 1776
CONSTITUTION OF VIRGINIA (WRITTEN BY JAMES MADISON AND GEORGE MASON)

BILL OF RIGHTS, June 12, 1776, SECTION 16. That **religion**, or the duty which we owe to **our Creator**, and the manner of discharging it, can be directed only by reason and conviction, not by force or violence; and therefore all men are equally entitled to the **free exercise of religion**, according to the **dictates of conscience**; and that it is the mutual duty of all to practice **Christian forbearance, love, and charity** towards each other.

NOVEMBER 11, 1779
VIRGINIA GOVERNOR THOMAS JEFFERSON ISSUED A PROCLAMATION APPOINTING A DAY OF THANKSGIVING AND PRAYER:

Public and **solemn thanksgiving** and **prayer** to **Almighty God**....That He would in **mercy** look down upon us, pardon all our sins, and receive us into **His favor**; and finally, that **He** would **establish** the independence of these United States upon the basis of **religion** and virtue, and support and protect them in the enjoyment of peace, liberty and safety.

1781
VIRGINIA GOVERNOR THOMAS JEFFERSON, NOTES ON STATE OF VIRGINIA, QUERY XVIII:

God who gave us life gave us liberty.

And can the liberties of a nation be thought secure when we have removed their only firm basis, a conviction in the minds of the people that these liberties are of the **Gift of God**? That they are not to be violated but with **His wrath**?

Indeed, I tremble for my country when I reflect that **God** is just; that **His justice** cannot sleep forever; That a revolution of the wheel of fortune, a change of situation, is among possible events; that it may become probable by **Supernatural influence**! The **Almighty** has no attribute which can take side with us in that event.

1784
VIRGINIA ASSEMBLY, PATRICK HENRY SUPPORTED THE BILL "PROVISION FOR TEACHERS OF THE CHRISTIAN RELIGION"

The general diffusion of **Christian knowledge** hath a natural tendency to correct the **morals** of men, restrain their vices, and preserve the peace of society.

JUNE 20, 1785
MEMORIAL & REMONSTRANCE

James Madison reasoned that a bill instituting a tax "for the support of the **Christian religion**" would put civil judges into the position of having to decide what constituted **Christianity**, a function for which they were unqualified.

In his address **"Religious Freedom-A Memorial and Remonstrance,"** Madison stated:

It is the duty of every man to render to the **Creator** such homage, and such only, as he believes to be acceptable to Him. This duty is precedent both in order of time, and degree of obligation, to the claims of civil society. Before any man can be considered as a member of Civil Society, he must be considered as a subject of the **Governor of the Universe**.

Much more must every man who becomes a member of any particular Civil Society, do it with a saving of his allegiance to the **Universal Sovereign**. We maintain therefore that in **matters of Religion**, no man's right is abridged by the institution of Civil Society, and that **Religion** is wholly exempt from its cognizance.

The policy of the bill is adverse to the diffusion of the light of **Christianity**. The first wish of those who ought to enjoy this precious gift, ought to be, that it may be imparted to the whole race of mankind.

Compare the number of those who have as yet received it, with the number still remaining under the dominions of **false religions**, and how small is the former! Does the policy of the bill tend to lessen the disproportion? No; it at once discourages those who are strangers to the **light of Truth**, from coming into the regions of it.

Whilst we assert for ourselves a freedom to embrace, to profess, and to observe the **Religion** which we believe to be of **Divine** origin, we cannot deny an equal freedom to those whose minds have not yet yielded to the evidence which has convinced us. If this freedom be abused, it is an offense against **God**, not against man: To **God**, therefore, not to man, must an account of it be rendered.

Earnestly **praying**, as we are in duty bound, that the **Supreme Lawgiver of the Universe** by illuminating those to whom it is addressed, may, on the one and, turn their councils from every act which would affront **His Holy prerogative**, or violate the trust committed to them; and, on the other, guide them into every measure which may be worthy of **His blessing**.

"The equal right of every citizen to the **free exercise of his religion** according to the **dictates of his conscience**" is held by the same tenure with all our other rights.

If we recur to its origin, it is equally the gift of nature; if we weight its importance, it cannot be less dear to us; if we consult the "Declaration of those rights which pertain to the good people of Virginia, as the basis and foundation of government," it is enumerated with equal solemnity.

OCTOBER 31, 1785
VIRGINIA, JAMES MADISON'S "BILL FOR PUNISHING DISTURBERS OF RELIGIOUS WORSHIP & SABBATH BREAKERS," PASSED 1789

If any person on **Sunday** shall himself be found laboring at his own or any other trade or calling, or shall employ the apprentices, servants or slaves in labor, or other business, except it be in the ordinary household offices of daily necessity, or other work of necessity or charity, he shall forfeit the sum of ten shillings for every such offense, deeming every apprentice, servant, or slave so employed, and every day he shall be so employed as constituting a distinct offense.

OCTOBER 31, 1785
VIRGINIA, JAMES MADISON'S BILL APPOINTING DAYS OF PUBLIC FASTING & THANKSGIVING

The Bill included: Forfeiting fifty pounds for every failure, not having a reasonable excuse.

1786
VIRGINIA ASSEMBLY PASSED JEFFERSON'S NOTES ON THE STATE OF VIRGINIA AS PART OF AN ACT ESTABLISHING RELIGIOUS FREEDOM:

Our rulers can have no other authority over such natural rights, only as we have submitted to them (in a social compact). The **rights of conscience** we never submitted, we could not submit. We are answerable for them to **our God**.

JANUARY 16, 1786
VIRGINIA ASSEMBLY, THOMAS JEFFERSON AND COMMITTEE ON RELIGION DRAFTED:

An Act for **establishing Religious Freedom.** I. Well aware...that **Almighty God** hath created the mind free, and manifested **His Supreme Will** that free it shall remain by making it altogether insusceptible of restraints; that all attempts to influence it by temporal punishments, or burdens, or by civil incapacitations, tend only to begat habits of hypocrisy and meanness, and are a departure from the plan of the **Holy Author of religion,** who being **Lord both of body and mind**, yet chose not to **propagate** it by coercions on either, as was in **his Almighty power** to do, but to extend it by its influence on reason alone.

JANUARY 16, 1786
VIRGINIA STATUTE OF RELIGIOUS LIBERTY

Well aware that **Almighty God** hath created the mind free; that all attempts to influence it by temporal punishments or burdens, or by civil incapacitations, tend not only to beget habits of hypocrisy and meanness, and are a departure from the plan of the **Holy Author of our Religion**, who, being **Lord both of the body and mind**, yet chose not to **propagate** it by coercion on either, as was in **His Almighty power** to do:

Be it, therefore, enacted by the General Assembly That no man shall be compelled to frequent or support any **religious worship**, place, or **Ministry**, whatsoever, nor shall be enforced, restrained, molested, or burdened in his body or goods, nor shall otherwise suffer, on account of his **religious opinions** or **belief**; but that all men shall be free to profess and by argument to maintain their opinions in **matters of religion**, and that the same shall in no wise diminish, enlarge, or affect their civil capacities.

JUNE 7, 1789
VIRGINIA DELEGATE JAMES MADISON INTRODUCED WORDING FOR THE FIRST AMENDMENT TO THE U.S. CONSTITUTION:

The Civil Rights of none shall be abridged on account of **religious belief** or **worship**, nor shall any national

religion be **established**, nor shall the full and equal **rights of conscience** be in any manner, nor on any pretext infringed.

1789
VIRGINIA DELEGATE GEORGE MASON PROPOSED WORDING FOR THE FIRST AMENDMENT:

All men have an equal, natural and unalienable right to the **free exercise of religion**, according to the **dictates of conscience**; and that no particular **sect** or **society** of **Christians** ought to be favored or **established** by law in preference to others.

MAY 10, 1789
PRESIDENT GEORGE WASHINGTON WROTE TO THE UNITED BAPTISTS OF VIRGINIA

Gentlemen - I request that you will accept my best acknowledgments for your congratulations on my appointment to the first office in the nation...

After we had, by the **smiles of Heaven** on our exertions, obtained the object for which we contended, I retired at the conclusion of the war, with an idea that my country would have no farther occasion for my services, and with the intention of never entering again into public life.

But when the exigence of my country seemed to require me once more to engage in public affairs, an honest conviction of duty superseded my former resolution, and became my apology for deviating from the happy plan which I had adopted.

If I could have entertained the slightest apprehension that the Constitution framed by the Convention, where I had the honor to preside, might possibly endanger the **religious rights of any ecclesiastical**

Society, certainly I would never have placed my signature to it;

If I could now conceive that the general Government might ever be so administered as to render **liberty of conscience** insecure, I beg you will be persuaded that no one would be more zealous than myself to **establish** effectual barriers against the horrors of **spiritual** tyranny, and every species of **religious persecution**;

For you doubtless remember I have often expressed my sentiments, that any man, conducting himself as a good citizen, and being **accountable** to **God** alone for his **religious opinions**, ought to be protected in **worshipping** the **Deity** according to the **dictates of his own conscience**.

While I recollect with satisfaction that the **religious society** of which you are members, have been, throughout America, uniformly, and almost unanimously, the firm friends to civil liberty, and the preserving promoters of our glorious revolution;

I cannot hesitate to believe that they will be the faithful supporters of a free, yet efficient general government. Under this pleasing reflection I rejoice to assure them that they may rely on my best wishes and endeavors to advance their prosperity.

Be assured, Gentlemen, that I entertain a proper sense of your **fervent supplications** to **God** for my temporal and **eternal happiness**.

AUGUST 19, 1789
GEORGE WASHINGTON TO BISHOPS, CLERGY & LAITY OF THE PROTESTANT EPISCOPAL CHURCH OF VIRGINIA, NEW YORK, NEW JERSEY, PENNSYLVANIA, DELAWARE, MARYLAND & NORTH CAROLINA:

Gentlemen: I sincerely thank you for your affectionate congratulations on my election to the chief magistracy of the United States...On this occasion it would ill become me to conceal the joy I have felt in perceiving the fraternal affection, which appears to increase every day among friends of **genuine religion.** It affords edifying prospects, indeed, to see **Christians** of different **denominations** dwell together in more charity, and conduct themselves in respect to each other with a more **Christian-like** spirit than every they have done in any former age, or in any other nation.

I receive with the greater satisfaction your congratulations on the establishment of the new constitution of government, because I believe its mild yet efficient operations will tend to remove every remaining apprehension of those with whose opinions it may not entirely coincide, as well as to confirm the hopes of its numerous friends; and because the moderation, patriotism, and wisdom of the present federal Legislature seem to promise the restoration of order and our ancient virtues, the extension of **genuine religion**, and the consequent advancement of our respectability abroad, and of our substantial happiness at home.

I request, most **reverend** and respected Gentlemen, that you will accept my cordial thanks for your devout supplications to the **Supreme Ruler of the Universe** in behalf of me. May you, and the people whom you represent, be the happy subjects of the **Divine benedictions** both here and hereafter.

OCTOBER 1789
GEORGE WASHINGTON TO QUAKERS' YEARLY MEETING FOR VIRGINIA, PENNSYLVANIA, NEW JERSEY, DELAWARE, & MARYLAND

Government being, among other purposes, instituted to protect the persons and **consciences** of men from oppression, it certainly is the duty of rulers, not only to abstain from it themselves, but according to their stations, to prevent it in others.

The liberty enjoyed by the People of these States of **worshipping Almighty God** agreeable to their **consciences** is not only among the choicest of their **blessings**, but also of their rights.

While men perform their social duties faithfully, they do all that society or the state can with propriety demand or expect; and remain responsible only to their **Maker** for the **religion**, or **modes of faith**, which they may prefer or profess.

Your principles and conduct are well known to me; and it is doing the people called **Quakers** no more than justice to say, (except their declining to share with others the burden of the common defense) there is no **denomination** among us, who are more exemplary and useful citizens.

1792
REQUIREMENTS OF THE COLLEGE OF WILLIAM AND MARY

The students shall attend **prayers** in **chapel** at the time appointed and there demean themselves with that decorum which the **sacred duty of public worship** requires.

1813
UNIVERSITY OF VIRGINIA CURRICULUM, WRITTEN BY THOMAS JEFFERSON:

The want of instruction in the various **creeds** of **religious faith** existing among our citizens presents...a chasm in general instruction of the useful sciences...

A remedy, however, has been suggested of promising aspect, which, while it excludes the public authorities from the domain of **public religious freedom**, will give to the **sectarian schools of divinity** the full benefit of **public provisions** made for instruction in the other branches of science...

It has, therefore, been in contemplation, and suggested by some pious individuals, who perceive the advantages of associating other studies with those of **religion**, to **establish** their **religious schools** on the confines of the University, so as to give to their students ready and convenient access and attendance on the scientific lectures of the University; and to maintain, by that means, those destined for **religious professions** on as high a standing of science, and of personal weight and respectability, as may be obtained by others from the benefits of the University.

Such establishments would offer the further and greater advantage of enabling the students of the University to attend **religious exercise[s]** with the professor of their particular **sect,** whether in rooms of the building still to be erected, and destined to that purpose under impartial regulations, as proposed in the same report of the commission, or in the lecturing room of such professor...

Such an arrangement would complete the circle of the useful sciences embraced by this institution, and would fill the chasm now existing, in principles which would leave inviolate the constitutional **freedom of religion**.

MARCH 2, 1819
JAMES MADISON ON RELIGION IN VIRGINIA IN A LETTER TO ROBERT WALSH:

That there has been an increase of **religious** instruction since the revolution can admit of no question.

The English **Church** was originally the **established religion**...

Of other **sects** there were but few adherents, except the **Presbyterians** who predominated on the west side of the Blue Mountains.

A little time previous to the Revolutionary struggle, the **Baptists** sprang up, and made very rapid progress.

Among the early acts of the Republican Legislature, were those abolishing the **Religious establishment**, and putting all **sects** at full liberty and on a perfect level.

At present the population is divided, with small exceptions, among the **Protestant Episcopalians**, the **Presbyterians**, the **Baptists** and the **Methodists**...

I conjecture the **Presbyterians** and **Baptists** to form each about a third, and the two other **sects** together of which the **Methodists** are much the smallest, to make up the remaining third...

Among the other **sects**, **Meeting Houses** have multiplied and continue to multiply...

Religious instruction is now diffused throughout the Community by **Preachers** of every **sect** with almost equal zeal...

The qualifications of the **Preachers**, too among the **new sects** where there is the greatest deficiency, are understood to be improving.

On a general comparison of the present and former times, the balance is certainly and vastly on the side of the present, as to the number of **religious teachers** the zeal which actuates them, the **purity** of their lives and the attendance of the people on their instructions.

OCTOBER 7, 1822
THOMAS JEFFERSON'S MEMORANDUM CLARIFYING THE REGULATIONS OF THE UNIVERSITY OF VIRGINIA:

The relations which exist between man and his **Maker**, and the duties resulting from those relations, are the most interesting and important to every human being, and most incumbent on his study and investigation.

1823
JAMES MADISON, LETTER TO EDWARD EVERETT ON RELIGION IN VIRGINIA:

Prior to the Revolution, the **Episcopal Church** was **established** by law in this State. On the Declaration of Independence it was left with all other **sects**, to a self-support. And no doubt exists that there is much more of **religion** among us now that there ever was before the change; and particularly in the **sect** which enjoyed the legal patronage. This proves...that the law is not necessary to the support of **religion**...

Religion is essentially distinct from Civil Government and exempt from its cognizance...from the partial example in Holland, to its consummation in Pennsylvania, Delaware, N.J., &c, has been found as safe in practice as it is sound in theory.

1824
UNIVERSITY OF VIRGINIA

Thomas Jefferson outlined the responsibilities of the professor of ethics:

The proof of the **being of a God, the Creator, Preserver, and Supreme Ruler of the Universe**, the **author of all the relations of morality**, and the laws and oblations which these infer, will be in the province of the professor of ethics.

1824
UNIVERSITY OF VIRGINIA

Thomas Jefferson not only encouraged the teaching of **religion** by recommending the **establishment** of a school of "**Theology and Ecclesiastical History**," but he also set aside a place inside the Rotunda for **chapel services**:

It is supposed probable, that a building of somewhat more size in the middle of the grounds may be called for in time, in which may be rooms for **religious worship**.

APRIL 7, 1824
UNIVERSITY OF VIRGINIA BOARD OF VISITORS, WITH JAMES MADISON A MEMBER

Approved the regulations prepared by Thomas Jefferson, Rector of the University, which stated:

Should the **religious sects** of this State, or any of them, according to the invitation held out to them, **establish** within or adjacent to, the precincts of the University, schools for instruction in the **religion** of their **sect,** the students of the University will be free, and expected to attend **religious worship** at the **establishment** of their respective **sects**, in the morning, and in time to meet their school in the University at its stated hour...

The students of such **religious** school, if they attend any school of the University, shall be considered as students of the University, subject to the same regulations, and entitled to the same privileges...

The upper circular room of the rotunda shall be reserved for a library. One of its larger elliptical rooms on its middle floor shall be used for annual examinations, or lectures to such schools as are too numerous for their ordinary school room, and for **religious worship**, under the regulations to be prescribed By law.

1830
CONSTITUTION OF VIRGINIA

DECLARATION OF RIGHTS, SECTION 16, That **religion**, or the duty which we owe to **our Creator**, and the manner of discharging it, can be directed only by reason and conviction, not by force or violence; and therefore all men are equally entitled to the **free exercise of religion**, according to the **dictates of conscience**; and that it is the mutual duty of all to practice **Christian forbearance, love, and charity** towards each other...

ARTICLE 3, SECTION 11. No man shall be compelled to frequent or support any **religious worship**, place or **Ministry** whatsoever, nor shall be enforced, restrained, molested or burdened, in his body or goods, nor shall otherwise suffer on account of his **religious opinions** or **belief**: but that all men shall be free to profess, and by argument to maintain, their opinions in **matters of religion**, and that the same shall in no wise diminish, enlarge or affect their civil capacities.

And the legislature shall not prescribe any **religious test** whatsoever; nor confer any peculiar privileges or advantages on any one **sect** or **denomination**; nor pass any law requiring or authorizing any **religious society**, or the people of any district within this commonwealth to levy on themselves or others any tax for the erection or repair of any house for **Public worship** or for the support of any **Church** or **Ministry**, but it shall be left free to every person to select his **religious instructor**, and make for his support such private contract as he shall please.

JUNE 20, 1863
WEST VIRGINIA SEPARATED FROM VIRGINIA
WEST VIRGINIA CONSTITUTION, 1872:

PREAMBLE. Since through **Divine Providence** we enjoy the **blessings** of civil, political and **religious liberty**, we, the people of West Virginia, in and through the provisions of this Constitution, reaffirm **our faith** in and constant reliance upon **God**.

1872
CONSTITUTION OF VIRGINIA

We, therefore, the delegates of the good people of Virginia, elected and in convention assembled, in pursuance of said acts, invoking the favor and guidance of **Almighty God**, do propose to the people the following constitution and form of government for this commonwealth.

ARTICLE 1, SECTION 18. That **religion** or the duty which we owe to **our Creator**, and the manner of discharging it, can be directed only by reason and conviction, not by force or violence; and, therefore, all men are equally entitled to the **free exercise of religion,** according to the **dictates of conscience**; and that it is the mutual duty of all to practice **Christian forbearance, love, and charity** towards each other.

ARTICLE 1, SECTION 19. That neither slavery nor involuntary servitude, except as lawful imprisonment may constitute such, shall exist within this state.

ARTICLE 3, SECTION 6. All persons, before entering upon the discharge of any function as officers of this state, must take and subscribe the following oath or affirmation: "I do solemnly swear (or affirm) that I will support and maintain the Constitution and laws of the United States, and the Constitution and laws of the State of Virginia, that I recognize and accept the civil and political equality of all men before the law, and that I will faithfully perform the duty of....., to the best of my ability. **So Help Me God**."

ARTICLE 5, SECTION 14. No man shall be compelled to frequent or support any **religious worship**, place or **Ministry** whatsoever, nor shall be enforced, restrained, molested, or burdened in his body or goods, nor shall otherwise suffer on account of his **religious opinions** or **belief**; but all men shall be free to profess and by argument to maintain their opinions in **matters of religion**, and the same shall in nowise diminish, enlarge, or affect their civil capacities.

And the General Assembly shall not prescribe any **religious test** whatever, or confer any peculiar privileges or advantages on any **sect** or **denomination**, or pass any law requiring or authorizing any **religious society**, or the people of any district within this Commonwealth, to levy on themselves or others, any tax for the erection or repair of any house of **Public worship**, or for the support of any **Church** or **Ministry**; but it shall be left free to every person to select his **religious** instructor, and to make for his support such private contract as he shall please.

ARTICLE 5, SECTION 17. The general Assembly shall not grant a charter of incorporation to any **Church** or **religious denomination**, but may secure the title to **Church** property to an extant to be limited by law.

CHURCH PROPERTY. The **rights of ecclesiastical** bodies in and to **Church** property, conveyed to them by regular deed of conveyance, shall not be affected by the late and civil, nor by any antecedent or subsequent event, nor by any act of legislature purporting to govern the same...

JUNE 27, 1962
WEST VIRGINIA SENATOR ROBERT BYRD ADDRESSED CONGRESS TWO DAYS AFTER SUPREME COURT STOPPED SCHOOL PRAYER

Inasmuch as our greatest leaders have shown no doubt about **God**'s proper place in the American birthright, can we, in our day, dare do less?...

In no other place in the United States are there so many, and such varied official evidences of deep and abiding **faith** in **God** on the part of Government as there are in Washington...

Every session of the House and the Senate begins with **prayer**. Each house has its own **chaplain**. The Eighty-third Congress set aside a small room in the Capitol, just off the rotunda, for the private **prayer** and meditation of members of Congress. The room is always open when Congress is in session, but it is not open to the public. The room's focal point is a stained glass window showing George Washington kneeling in **prayer**. Behind him is etched these words from Psalm 16:1: "Preserve me, O **God**, for in Thee do I put my trust."

Inside the rotunda is a picture of the Pilgrims about to embark from Holland on the sister ship of the Mayflower, the Speedwell.

The ship's revered **chaplain**, Brewster, who later joined the Mayflower, has open on his lap the **Bible**. Very clear are the words, "the **New Testament** according to **our Lord and Savior, Jesus Christ**." On the sail is the motto of the Pilgrims, "**In God We Trust, God With Us**."

The phrase, "**In God We Trust**," appears opposite the President of the Senate, who is the Vice-President of the United States. The same phrase, in large words inscribed in the marble, backdrops the Speaker of the House of Representatives.

Above the head of the Chief Justice of the Supreme Court are the **Ten Commandments**, with the great American eagle protecting them. **Moses** is included among the great lawgivers in Herman A MacNeil's marble sculpture group on the east front. The crier who opens each session closes with the words, "**God save the United States and this Honorable Court.**"

Engraved on the metal on the top of the Washington Monument are the words: "Praise be to **God**." Lining the walls of the stairwell are such **biblical** phrases as **"Search the Scriptures," "Holiness to the Lord," "Train up a child in the way he should go, and when he is old he will not depart from it."**

Numerous quotations from **Scripture** can be found within its [the Library of Congress] walls. One reminds each American of his responsibility to his **Maker: "What doth the Lord require of thee, but to do justly and love mercy and walk humbly with thy God"(Micah 6:8).**

Another in the lawmaker's library preserves the **Psalmist's** acknowledgment that all nature reflects the order and beauty of the **Creator, "The heavens declare the Glory of God, and the firmament showeth His handiwork"** (Psalm 19:1).

And still another reference: **"The light shineth in darkness, and the darkness comprehendeth it not"** (John 1:5).

Millions have stood in the Lincoln Memorial and gazed up at the statue of the great Abraham Lincoln. The sculptor who chiseled the features of Lincoln in granite all but seems to make Lincoln speak his own words inscribed into the walls. "...That this Nation, under **God**, shall have a new birth of freedom, and that government of the people, by the people, for the people, shall not perish from the earth."

At the opposite end, on the north wall, his Second Inaugural Address alludes to "**God**," the "**Bible**," "**Providence**," "the **Almighty**," and "**Divine** attributes." It then continues: As was said 3000 years ago, so it still must be said, **"The judgments of the Lord are true and righteous altogether."**

On the south banks of Washington's Tidal Basin, Thomas Jefferson still speaks: "**God** who gave us life gave us liberty. Can the liberties of a nation be secure when we have removed a conviction that these liberties are the **gift of God**? Indeed I tremble for my country when I reflect that **God** is just, that his justice cannot sleep forever."

Jefferson's words are a forceful and explicit warning that to remove **God** from this country will destroy it.

1971
CONSTITUTION OF VIRGINIA

ARTICLE 1, SECTION 16. That **religion** or the duty which we owe to **our Creator**, and the manner of discharging it, can be directed only by reason and conviction, not by force or violence; and, therefore, all men are equally entitled to the **free exercise of religion**, according to the **dictates of conscience**; and that it is the mutual duty of all to practice **Christian forbearance, love, and charity** towards each other.

No man shall be compelled to frequent or support any **religious worship**, place or **Ministry** whatsoever, nor shall be enforced, restrained, molested, or burdened in his body or goods, nor shall otherwise suffer on account of his **religious opinions** or **belief**; but all men shall be free to profess and by argument to maintain their opinions in **matters of religion**, and the same shall in nowise diminish, enlarge, or affect their civil capacities.

And the General Assembly shall not prescribe any **religious test** whatever, or confer any peculiar privileges or advantages on any **sect** or **denomination**, or pass any law requiring or authorizing any **religious society**, or the people of any district within this Commonwealth, to levy on themselves or others, any tax for the erection or repair of any house of **Public worship**, or for the support of any **Church** or **Ministry**; but it shall be left free to every person to select his **religious instructor**, and to make for his support such private contract as he shall please.

ARTICLE 2, SECTION 7. All officers elected or appointed under or pursuant to this Constitution shall, before they enter on the performance of their public duties, severally take and subscribe the following oath or affirmation:

"I do solemnly swear (or affirm) that I will support the Constitution of the United States, and the Constitution of the Commonwealth of Virginia, and that I will faithfully and impartially discharge all the duties incumbent upon me as....according to the best of my ability (**So Help Me God**)."

1983
U.S. DISTRICT COURT, WESTERN DISTRICT OF VIRGINIA, CROCKETT V. SORENSON, 568 F. SUPP. 1422, 1425-1430 (W.D. VA. 1983):

The First Amendment was never intended to insulate our **Public** institutions from any mention of **God**, the **Bible** or **religion**. When such insulation occurs, another **religion**, such as **secular humanism**, is effectively **established**.

Clearly, the **Establishment Clause** can be violated in this regard without a showing of outright hostility to traditional **theistic religions**. Though in the context of the British university, the following quote is instructive for the situation in our **public schools**:

On the fundamental **religious** issue, the modern university intends to be, and supposes that it is, neutral, but it is not. Certainly it neither implicates nor expressly repudiates **belief** in **God**. But it does what is far more deadly than open rejection; it ignores **Him**....It is in this sense that the university today is **atheistic**....It is a fallacy to suppose by omitting a subject you teach nothing about it. On the contrary, you teach that it is to be omitted, and that it is therefore a matter of secondary importance. And you teach this not openly and explicitly, which could invite criticism, you simply take it for granted and thereby insinuate it silently, insidiously, and albeit irresistibly.

Moberly, The Crisis in the University, 55-56 (1949) (quoted in Whitehead and Conlin, The Establishment of Religion of Secular Humanism and Its First Amendment Implications, 10 Tex. Tech. L. Rev. 1, 19 n. 104 (1978)).

In art, one cannot truly appreciate such great works as da Vinci's **Last Supper,** Michelangelo's work in the **Sistine Chapel**, or Albrecht Durer's woodcuts without some basic understanding of what the **Bible** contains. Without some introduction to the book of **Isaiah**, Handel's **Messiah** loses much of its force and importance. Literature is replete with **biblical allusion**. Some of the better known works which rely heavily on **allusions** from the **Bible** include Milton's Paradise Lost; the plays of Shakespeare, especially Measure for Measure; Blake's Marriage of **Heaven and Hell**; Melville's Moby Dick; Faulkner's Absalom, Absalom; T.S. Eliot's The Wasteland; and C.S. Lewis' The Screwtape Letters.

Our language and popular culture are also replete with **biblical allusions**. The symbol for the American

Medical Association, a staff with a serpent on it, is drawn from an episode in the **book of Numbers**, when **Moses**, at **God**'s suggestion, raised a bronze serpent on a staff and all the **children of Israel** who looked upon it were healed of snakebites. The phrase "handwriting on the wall" comes from a passage in the **book of Daniel** in which handwriting on the wall foretold rough time ahead for Babylonian King Belshazzar. The popular phrase "the apple of my eye" is used in the **Old Testament** as one of **God**'s descriptions for His people **Israel**. And, of course, the term **"Armageddon"** is the site where the battle will take place which will mark the end of the age, as described in the **Book of Revelations.**

Anglo-American law as we know it today is also heavily indebted to the **principles** and **concepts** found in the **Bible**. William Blackstone, one of the most influential figures in the development of the common law, explained:

"The **doctrine** thus delivered we call the **revealed** or **Divine Law** and they are to be found only in the **Holy Scriptures**....Upon these two foundations, the law of nature and the **law of revelation**, depend all human laws, that is to say, no human law should be suffered to contradict these."

Blackstone posited that the law of nature as well as the **law of revelation**, was derived from **God**.

Further, **biblical** influences pervade many specific areas of the law. The **"good Samaritan"** laws use a phrase lifted directly out of one of **Jesus**' parables.

The concept of the "fertile octogenarian," applicable to the law of wills and trusts, is in a large part derived from the **book of Genesis** where we are told that **Sarah**, the wife of the patriarch **Abraham**, gave birth to **Isaac** when she was "past age." In addition, the **Ten Commandments** have had immeasurable effect on Anglo-American legal development.

Moreover, we as Americans, should especially be aware of the influence that the **Bible** and its **principles** have had on the founding and development of our nation.

In this regard it is significant that Former President Ronald Reagan, on February 3, 1983, issued a proclamation declaring 1983 the "year of the **Bible**" in recognition of the **Bible**'s fundamental and enduring influence on our country.

Secular education imposes immediate demands that the student have a good knowledge of the **Bible**. Two defense exhibits vividly illustrate this point. Defendants Exhibit 14 is a summary of references to the **Bible** in a 1980 edition of the Scholastic Aptitude Manual, used by high school students to prepare for the Scholastic Aptitude Test (SAT)....

Defendants' Exhibit 15, a summary of **Bible** references found in textbooks used in the Bristol **public schools**, is based on selected books from elementary, junior high and high school classes...

In light of the above, it becomes obvious that a basic background in the **Bible** is essential to fully appreciate and understand both Western culture and current events.

JULY 12, 1995
PRESIDENT BILL CLINTON AT JAMES MADISON HIGH SCHOOL, VIENNA, VIRGINIA:

The First Amendment does not require students to leave their **religion** at the schoolhouse door....It is especially important that parents feel confident that their children can **practice religion**...

We need to make it easier and more acceptable for people to express and to celebrate their **faith**...If students can wear T-shirts advertising sports teams, rock groups or politicians, they can also wear T-shirts that promote **religion**...

Religion is too important to our history and our heritage for us to keep it out of our schools...It shouldn't be demanded, but as long as it is not sponsored by school officials and doesn't interfere with other children's rights it mustn't be denied...

Nothing in the First Amendment converts our public schools into **religion-free zones** or requires all **religious expression** to be left behind at the schoolhouse door...

While the government may not use schools to coerce the **consciences** of our students, or to convey official endorsement of **religion**, the government's schools also may not discriminate against private **religious expression** during the school day.

VIRGINIA RELIGIOUS AFFILICATION

The Encyclopedia Britannica, 11th edition, published in 1911, stated:

Out of the total of 793,546 members of **religious denominations** in 1906, more than half, 415,987, were **Baptists**; the **Methodists** numbered 200,771; and there were 39,628 **Presbyterians**, 28,700 **Roman Catholics**, 28,487 **Protestant Episcopalians**, 26,248 **Disciples of Christ**, and 15,010 **Lutherans**

http://www.1911encyclopedia.org/Virginia#Population

The Catholic Encyclopedia, Volume XV, Copyright 1912 by Robert Appleton Company, stated as of 1906, a census listed **Virginia's Church** membership as 793,546, consisting of:

Baptists - 415,987 members
Methodists - 200,771 members
Presbyterians - 39,628 members

Catholics - 28,700 members
Protestant Episcopal - 28,487 members
Disciples - 26,248 members
Lutherans - 15,010 members

Dunkers, Christians, and other **denominations** had small percentages, such as **Quakers**, who were the first to call for an end to slavery. An 1810 Census of Virginia eastern shore identified 131 free black males living in Northampton County, slaves freed by **Quaker** convert Ann Brickhouse. The 1860 Federal census revealed 963 free Negro residents.

In 1836, **Catholic** population was 3,000 members. In 1912, **Catholic** population was 41,000 members, composed of Irish, Germans, Italians, Bohemians, Poles, Slavs, and Syrians, with a few French, Belgians, Native Americans and other nationalities.

http://www.newadvent.org/cathen/15451a.htm

The Wikipedia Online Encyclopedia, as of 2006, listed **Virginia** as:

Christian - 84 percent, consisting of:
- **Baptist** - 32 percent
- **Methodist** - 8 percent
- **Episcopal** - 3 percent
- **Presbyterian** - 3 percent
- **Other Protestant** - 23 percent
- **Catholic** - 14 percent
- **Other Christian** - 1 percent

Other Religions - 2 percent
Non-Religions/ Non-Reporting - 12 percent

http://en.wikipedia.org/wiki/Virginia#Religion

The U.S. Religious Landscape Survey, conducted by The Pew Forum on Religion & Public Life, 2007, published in the USA Today, listed **Virginia** as:

Christian - 76.5 percent, consisting of:
- **Evangelical Protestant** - 31 percent
- **Mainline Protestant** - 20 percent
- **Black Protestant** - 10 percent
- **Catholic** - 14 percent
- **Orthodox** - 1 percent
- **Other Christian** - 0.5 percent

Mormon - 1 percent
Jehovah's Witnesses - <0.5 percent
Jewish - 2 percent
Muslim - 1 percent
Buddhist - 1 percent
Hindu - <0.5 percent
Other World Religions - <0.5 percent
Other Faiths - 1 percent
Unaffiliated - 16 percent
Did not answer - 1 percent

www.pewforum.org
www.usatoday.com/news/graphics/pew-religion-08/flash.htm

SIGILLUM REIPUBLICÆ MASSACHUSETTENSIS

MASSACHUSETTS

Persecution of **dissenting religious** groups by the monarchs in Europe contributed to large scale migrations to America. The Plymouth Colony was founded by persecuted **Pilgrim Separatists**, who settled in 1620, and the Massachusetts Bay Colony was founded **Puritans dissenters** of the **Church of England**, who settled in 1629.

Once in Massachusetts, **Puritans** did not **tolerate dissenting Baptists**, **Congregationalists** and **Quakers**, who fled to found Rhode Island, Connecticut and Pennsylvania, respectively. Legislation was passed against **Baptists** in 1644-1678, and there was specific persecution of **Quakers** between 1656-1662.

The King annulled Massachusetts' charter in 1684. Later, Sir Edmund Andros was sent over with a commission to unite New York and New England under his rule. He met opposition in his efforts to stop town meetings and enforce the **Anglican Church** as the **established Church**. After news arrived in the colonies that James II was deposed in 1689 and that William and Mary were now ruling England, citizens of Boston rose in revolution, imprisoned Andros, and **re-established** their old colonial form of government.

In 1691, the Plymouth Colony and the Colony of Maine were combined with the Massachusetts Bay Colony. The new charter softened **religious testss** to hold office and vote, expanding "**liberty of conscience**," except to **Roman Catholics**. From its founding till 1780, Massachusetts had **established** the **Puritan Congregational**

Church, which was nominally part of the **Church of England**.

The Massachusetts Constitution of 1780, written by John Adams and still in effect, though with numerous amendments, **established** the **Congregational Church** and supported it with state taxes.

Dissenting citizens were allowed to have their share of taxes designated to the **Protestant Church** of their choice. **Baptist** leader Isaac Backus fought this provision, arguing that citizens should be free to voluntarily give financial support to the **Church** of their choice.

In 1775, the Continental Army was camped at Harvard College and on the Cambridge Commons, a force including **Catholics** from Maryland, Pennsylvania, and Canada. When George Washington heard of plans for the annual Guy Fawkes procession and its "custom of burning the Effigy of the **Pope**," he halted the event, expressing dismay at the lack of decency in such an activity. The old **Cathedral of the Holy Cross** on Franklin Street, completed in 1803, was the only **Catholic Church** in the Boston area for decades.

In 1808, the **diocese of Boston** was created from the **Archdiocese of Baltimore**. **Catholics** were allowed to hold office after an amendment was made to the Massachusetts Constitution in 1821 removing **religious tests** for State office-holders.

Beginning in the 1830's, the Irish Potato Famine led thousands of Irish **Catholics** to immigrate, resulting in a backlash, such as the burning of **Ursuline Convent** in Charlestown in 1834. Soon the immigrants overwhelmed the city, with over a thousand Irish living in East Cambridge in 1840. The **diocese of Boston** was enlarged to an **Archdiocese** in 1875, with jurisdiction over Massachusetts, Maine, New Hampshire and Vermont.

The first **Jewish** settlement in Massachusetts was in 1716, though with little freedom. In the late 1700's a number of prominent **Jews** lived in Boston, such as Moses Michael Hays, a neighbor of Paul Revere, and Abraham and Judah Touro, who helped finance the Massachusetts General Hospital and the Bunker Hill monument.

In the 1840's, large numbers of German **Jews** immigrated to Boston, organizing the first **congregation, Ohabei Shalom**, in 1843. The first **Jewish** burial place was secured in 1844 and Boston's first **synagogue** was built in 1852. When Polish **Jews** immigrated, dissension resulted in another **congregation, Adath Israel**, being formed. In 1858, Polish families started **Mishkan Israel**, the successor of which is the **Conservative temple, Mishkan Tefila** in Chestnut Hill.

In the 1870's, **Rabbi Solomon Schindler** of the German **Adath Israel congregation**, led in the emerging **Reform Judaism**, with such changes as mixed seating of men and women, a choir and organ, English language **worship**, and even **Sunday** meetings. **Rabbi** Isaac Meyer Wise called for an English-language American **prayer** book and helped found the **Hebrew Union College** in Cincinnati in 1875.

In the 1880's, pogroms in Russia and Poland sent a great wave of **orthodox Jewish** immigrants to the United States, during which time Boston's **Jewish** population grew from 3,000 in 1875 to 20,000 in 1895. Russian **Jews** did not recognize **Reform Judaism**. In 1882, one boatload of Russian **Jews** was sent back to Russia and another landed in the "poorhouse" for lack of support from the local community.

Finally German **Jews** organized the **American Federation of Jewish Charities** to assist the new immigrants and by the late 1920's, 80 percent of American **Jews** were from Eastern Europe.

In 1898, **Jews** from Lithuania bought a former **Baptist Church**. By 1910, there were 80,000 **Jews** in Boston and seven Yiddish newspapers. **Jewish** percentage of

Harvard's freshman class rose from 7 percent in 1900 to 21.5 percent in 1920. As of 2006, Boston had a population of 208,000 **Jews**.

As of 1911, Massachusetts had schools of theology at Cambridge (**Protestant Episcopal**), Newton (**Baptist**) and Waltham (**New Church**), in connection with Boston University (**Methodist**), Tufts College (**Universalist**) and Harvard (**non-sectarian**, and the affiliated **Congregational Andover Theological Seminary** at Cambridge).

MARCH 3, 1619
PETITION FOR CHARTER OF NEW ENGLAND BY THE NORTHERN COMPANY OF ADVENTURERS

May it please your most excellent Majesty...to give license for the **establishing** of two colonies in Virginia in America, the one called the First Colony undertaken by certain noblemen, knights, and merchants about London, the other called the Second Colony likewise undertaken by certain knights and merchants of the western parts...

Some...have, at their great charge and extreme hazard, continued to endeavor...to bring to pass so noble a work, in the constant pursuit whereof it has pleased **God** to aid them with **His blessing** so far as, in the confidence of the continuance of **His Grace**, they are resolved to pursue the same with all the power and means they are able to make to **His glory**, your Majesty's honor...

Whereby your Majesty's most humble petitioners do verily hope, by **God's Holy assistance**, to settle their plantation to the employing of many of your Majesty's subjects.

1620
CHARTER OF NEW ENGLAND

James, by the **Grace of God**, King of England, Scotland, France and Ireland, **Defender of the Faith**...Greeting, Whereas, upon the humble Petition of divers of our well disposed Subjects, that intended to make several Plantations in the Parts of America...

We according to our princely Inclination, favoring much their worthy Disposition, in Hope thereby to advance the enlargement of **Christian Religion**, to the **Glory of God Almighty**, as also by that Means to stretch out the Bounds of our Dominions...granted unto Sir Thomas Gates, Sir George Somers, Knights, Thomas Hanson, and Raleigh Gilbert...free Liberty to divide themselves into two several Colonies...

And forasmuch as We have been certainly given to understand by divers of our good Subjects, that have for these many Years past frequented those Coasts and Territories...that there is no other the Subjects of any **Christian King or State**, by any Authority from their Sovereigns...actually in Possession of any of the said Lands...

And also for that We have been further given certainly to know, that within these late Years there hath by **God's Visitation** reigned a wonderful Plague, together with many horrible Slaughters, and Murders, committed amongst the Savages and brutish People there, heretofore inhabiting, in a Manner to the utter Destruction, Devastation, and Depopulation of that whole Territory, so that there is not left for many Leagues together in a Manner, any that do claim or challenge any Kind of Interests therein...

Whereby We in our Judgment are persuaded and satisfied that the appointed Time is come in which **Almighty God in His great Goodness and Bounty** towards Us and our People, hath thought fit and determined, that those large and goodly Territories, deserted as it were by their natural Inhabitants, should be possessed and enjoyed by such of our Subjects and People as heretofore have and hereafter shall by his Mercy and Favor, and by his Powerful Army, be directed and conducted thither.

In Contemplation and serious Consideration whereof, We have thought it fit according to our Kingly Duty, so much as in Us lie, to second and follow **God's sacred Will**, rendering reverend Thanks to **his Divine Majesty** for **his gracious favor** in laying open and revealing the same unto us, before any other **Christian** Prince or State, by which Means without Offense, and as We trust to his Glory, We may with Boldness go on to the settling of so hopeful a Work, which tends to the reducing and **Conversion** of such Savages as remain wandering in Desolation and Distress, to Civil Society and **Christian Religion**, to the enlargement of our own Dominions...

And for as much as it shall be necessary for all our loving Subjects as shall inhabit within the said Precincts of New-England aforesaid, to determine to live together in the **Fear and true Worship of Almighty God, Christian Peace,** and civil Quietness...

We...grant unto the said Council...that they shall...have full and absolute Power and Authority to correct, punish, pardon, govern, and rule...

Of the Premises herein before mentioned, and by these Presents intended and meant to be granted, be not actually possessed or inhabited by any other **Christian Prince or Estate**, nor he within the Bounds, Limits, or Territories, of that Southern Colony Heretofore by us granted to be planted by diverse of our loving Subjects...

And that no Persons which shall be sent and employed in the said Plantation...misbehave themselves by mutinous Seditions, or other notorious Misdemeanors...to bring the said Voyages and Plantation into Disgrace and Contempt...and a great number of our loving and well-disposed Subjects, other ways well affected and inclined to join and adventure in so noble a **Christian** and worthy Action may be discouraged from the same, but also the Enterprise itself may be overthrown, which cannot miscarry without some Dishonor to Us and our Kingdom:

We, therefore, for preventing so great and enormous Abuses and Misdemeanors, Do...grant unto the said President or his Deputy...cause to-be apprehended, all and every such Person and Persons, who shall be noted, or accused, or found at any time or times hereafter to offend or misbehave themselves...

We do hereby declare to all **Christian Kings, Princes, and States,** that if any Person...of the said Colony...shall...rob or spoil, by Sea or by Land, or do any Hurt, Violence, or unlawful Hostility to any of the Subjects of Us...

We...shall make open Proclamation...that the Person...having committed any such Robbery or Spoil, shall...make full Restitution...

And lastly, because the principal Effect which we can desire or expect of this Action, is the **Conversion** and Reduction of the People in those Parts unto the **true Worship** of **God** and **Christian Religion**, in which Respect, We would be loath that any Person should be permitted to pass that We suspected to affect the Superstition of the **Church of Rome**, We do hereby declare that it is our Will and Pleasure that none be permitted to pass, in any Voyage from time to time to be made into the said Country, but such as shall first have taken the Oath of Supremacy.

1620
MAYFLOWER COMPACT
BETWEEN SETTLERS AT PLYMOUTH

In **the Name of God, Amen**. We, whose names are underwritten, the Loyal Subjects of our dread Sovereign Lord King James, by the **Grace of God**, of Great Britain,

France, and Ireland, King, **Defender of the Faith**, &c. Having undertaken for the **Glory of God**, and Advancement of the **Christian Faith**, and the Honor of our King and Country, a Voyage to plant the first Colony in the northern Parts of Virginia;

Do by these Presents, solemnly and mutually, **in the Presence of God** and one another, **covenant** and combine ourselves together into a civil Body Politick, for our better Ordering and Preservation, and Furtherance of the Ends aforesaid: And by Virtue hereof do enact, constitute, and frame, such just and equal Laws, Ordinances, Acts, Constitutions, and Officers, from time to time, as shall be thought most meet and convenient for the general Good of the Colony; unto which we promise all due Submission and Obedience.

In Witness whereof we have hereunto subscribed our names at Cape-Cod the eleventh of November, in the Reign of our Sovereign Lord King James, of England, France, and Ireland, the eighteenth, and of Scotland the fifty-fourth, **Anno Domini**; 1620.

1629
CHARTER OF NEW PLYMOUTH COLONY GRANTED TO WILLIAM BRADFORD

Know ye that the said council...in consideration that William Bradford and his associates have for these nine years lived in New England aforesaid and have there inhabited and planted a town called by the name of New Plymouth at their own proper costs and charges:

And now seeing that by the special **Providence of God**, and their extraordinary care and industry they have increased their plantation to near three hundred people, and are upon all occasions able to relieve any new planters or others his Majesty's subjects who may fall upon that coast...do...grant...unto the said William Bradford, his heirs associates and assignee all that part of New-England in America.

1629
CHARTER OF MASSACHUSETTS BAY

The good and prosperous Success of the Plantation...cannot but chiefly depend, next under the **Blessing** of **Almighty God**, and the support of our Royal Authority upon the good Government of the same...

Whereby our said People, Inhabitants there, may be so **religiously**, peaceably, and civilly governed, as their good Life and orderly Conversation, may win and incite the Natives of Country, to the Knowledge and Obedience of the only **true God** and **Savior of Mankind**, and the **Christian Faith**, which is our Royal Intention, and the Adventurers free Profession, is the principal End of this Plantation.

1629
WILLIAM BREWSTER OF THE PLYMOUTH PLANTATION WROTE OF THE MASSACHUSETTS BAY COLONY AT SALEM:

The **Church** that had been brought over the ocean now saw another **Church**, the first-born in America, holding the same **faith** in the same simplicity of **self-government under Christ alone.**

APRIL 25, 1635
DECLARATION FOR RESIGNATION OF THE CHARTER BY THE COUNCIL FOR NEW ENGLAND

The faithful endeavors of some of us that have sought the advancement of the plantation of New England have not been without frequent and inevitable troubles...from our first discovery of that coast to the present...It pleased **God** about that time to bereave us of the most noble and principal props thereof, as the Duke of Lenox, Marquis Hamilton, and many other strong stays to this work...

These crosses did draw upon us such a disheartened weakness as there only remained a carcass in a manner breathless till the end of the last Parliament when there were certain that desired a patent of some lands in the Massachusetts Bay to plant upon, who, presenting the names of honest and **religious men,** easily obtained their first desires.

But these being once gotten they used other means to advance themselves and step beyond their first proportions to a second grant surreptitiously gotten of other lands also justly past unto Captain Robert Gorges long before, who, being made governor of those parts, went in person and took an absolute seizure and actual possession of that country by a settled plantation he made in the Massachusetts Bay, which afterwards he left to the charge and custody of his servants and certain other undertakers and tenants belonging to some of us, who were thrust out by those intenders...

Whereby they did rend in pieces the first foundation of the building and so framed to themselves both new laws and new conceits of **matters of religion** and forms of **ecclesiastical** and temporal orders and government, punishing diverse that would not approve thereof, some by whipping, others by burning their houses over their heads, and some by banishing and the like, and all this partly under other pretenses, though indeed for no other cause save only to make themselves absolute masters of the country, and unconscionable in your new laws...

We...found matters in so desperate a case as that they saw a necessity for his Majesty to take the whole business into his own hands...It is now resolved that the patent shall be surrendered to his Majesty...and a dutiful obedience of all such as shall come under us to his Majesty's laws and ordinances there to be established and put in execution by such his Majesty's lieutenants or governors as shall be employed for those services to the **glory of Almighty God**, the honor of his Majesty, and **public good** of his faithful subjects.

1635
ACT OF SURRENDER OF THE GREAT CHARTER OF NEW ENGLAND TO HIS MAJESTY

To all **Christian People** to whom this present writing shall come: The President and Council established at Plymouth in the County of Devon, for planting, ruling, and governing of New England in America, send Greeting, in **our Lord God everlasting.**

Whereas our late Sovereign Lord King James...did...grant...the...present Council established at Plymouth...Letters Patents...To have perpetual succession...

Now Know ye that, the said President and Council, for divers good causes...have...yielded up and surrendered...unto our most gracious Sovereign Lord Charles by the **Grace of God**, King of England...the said Letters Patents.

JULY 23, 1637
COMMISSION TO SIR FERDINANDO GORGES AS GOVERNOR OF NEW ENGLAND BY CHARLES I

Forasmuch as we have understood and been credibly informed of the many inconveniences and mischief that have grown and are like more and more to arise amongst our subjects already planted in the parts of New England by reason of the several opinions...We take the whole managing thereof into our own hands and apply thereunto our immediate power and authority...

They have humbly resigned the said charter unto us that thereby there may be a speedy order taken for reformation of the aforesaid errors and mischiefs.

And knowing it to be a duty proper to our royal justice not to suffer such numbers of our people to run to ruin and so **religious** and good intents to languish for want of timely remedy and sovereign assistance, we have, therefore, graciously accepted of the said resignation and do approve of their good affections to a service so acceptable to **God** and us.

MARCH 2, 1640
WILLIAM BRADFORD & ASSOCIATES
SURRENDER OF PLYMOUTH PATENT

Whereas the said William Bradford and divers others the first Instruments of **God** in the beginning of this Great work of Plantation together with such as the All Ordering **God** in his **Providence** added unto them have been at very great charges to procure the said lands privileges and freedoms...now for the better settling of the state of the said land...surrender into the hands of the whole court consisting of the Freemen of this Corporation of New Plymouth...the said Letters Patents...except the said Lands before excepted.

1640
FIRST BOOK PRINTED IN AMERICA

John Eliot, with Richard Mather and Thomas Welch, printed the very first book in America, titled the **Bay Psalm Book.** Using the first printing press in the American colonies, located in Cambridge, Massachusetts, this volume became the approved hymnal of the Massachusetts Bay Colony:

The whole **book of Psalms** faithfully translated into English meter, whereunto is prefixed a discourse declaring not only the lawfulness, but also the necessity of the

heavenly Ordinances of singing **Scripture Psalms** in the **Churches** of **God**.

MAY 19, 1643
ARTICLES OF CONFEDERATION OF UNITED COLONIES OF NEW ENGLAND: MASSACHUSETTS, NEW PLYMOUTH, CONNECTICUT, & NEW HAVEN

Whereas we all came into these parts of America with one and the same end and aim, namely, to advance the **Kingdom of our Lord Jesus Christ** and to enjoy the liberties of the **Gospel** in **purity** with peace; and whereas in our settling (by a wise **Providence of God**) we are further dispersed upon the sea coasts and rivers than was at first intended, so that we can not according to our desire with convenience communicate...

And forasmuch as the natives have formerly committed sundry Insolence and outrages upon several Plantations of the English...We therefore do conceive it our bound duty, without delay to enter into a present Consociation amongst ourselves, for mutual help and strength...

That, as in nation and **religion**...we...fully agreed...and henceforth be called by the name of the United Colonies of New England. The said United Colonies for themselves and their posterities do jointly and severally hereby enter into a firm and perpetual league of friendship and amity for...defense, mutual advice and succor upon all just occasions both for preserving and propagating the truth and liberties of the **Gospel** and for their own mutual safety and welfare.

1644
PLYMOUTH GOV. WILLIAM BRADFORD ON WILLIAM BREWSTER'S DEATH:

About the 18th of April died their **reverend elder**, my dear and loving friend, Mr. William Brewster, a man who had done and suffered much for the **Lord Jesus** and the **Gospel's sake**, and had borne his part in the weal or woe with this poor persecuted **Church** for over thirty-five years in England, Holland, and this wilderness, and had done the **Lord** and them faithful service in his calling. Notwithstanding the many troubles and sorrows he passed through, the **Lord** upheld him to a great age.

1646
CONCORD, MASSACHUSETTS FOUNDER PETER BULKELEY WROTE "THE GOSPEL COVENANT OR COVENANT OF GRACE OPENED," PUBLISHED IN LONDON:

We are as a city set upon a hill, in the open view of all the earth....We profess ourselves to be a people in **covenant** with **God**, and therefore...the **Lord our God**...will cry shame upon us if we walk contrary to the **covenant** which we have promised to walk in.

If we open the mouths of men against our **profession**, by reason of the scandalousness of our lives, we (of all men) shall have the greater sin. Let us study so to walk that this may be our excellency and dignity among the nations of the world among which we live; that they may be constrained to say of us, only this people is wise, and a **Holy** and **blessed** people; that all that see us may see and know that **the name of the Lord** is called upon us; and that we are the seed which the **Lord** hath **blessed**. (Deut. 28:10; Isa. 61:9)

1649
MASSACHUSETTS COURT, REGARDING A SEPHARDIC JEWISH MERCHANT WHO ARRIVED IN THE COLONY

The Massachusetts General Court prounced it would: Allow the said Solomon Franco, the **Jew**, six shillings per week out of the treasury for ten weeks for his subsistence till he could get his passage into Holland.

APRIL 7, 1688
COMMISSION OF SIR EDMUND ANDROS FOR THE DOMINION OF NEW ENGLAND

We do hereby give and grant unto you the said Sir Edmund Andros...full power...to levy arm muster command...all persons...within our said Territory...of New England, and, as occasion shall serve, them to transfers from one place to another for the resisting and withstanding all enemies pirates and rebels, both at land and sea, and to transfers such forces to any of our Plantations in America...for the defense of the same against the invasion or attempt of any of our enemies, and then, if occasion shall require to pursue and prosecute in or out of the limits of our said...Plantations...

And **if it shall so please God**, them to vanquish; and, being taken, according to the law of arms to put to death or keep and preserve alive, at your discretion.

OCTOBER 7, 1691
CHARTER OF MASSACHUESTTS BAY

William & Mary by the **Grace of God** King and Queen of England Scotland France and Ireland **Defenders of the Faith**...Whereas his late Majesty King James the First Our Royal Predecessor...did...Grant unto the Council **established** at Plymouth...for the Planting...of New England in America...Provided always that the said

Lands...were not then actually possessed or Inhabited by any other **Christian Prince**...

We do by these presents...Grant...that forever hereafter there shall be a **liberty of Conscience** allowed in the **Worship** of **God** to all **Christians** (Except **Papists**) Inhabiting or which shall Inhabit or be Resident within our said Province...

Whereby our Subjects inhabitants of our said Province may be **Religiously** peaceably and Civilly Governed Protected and Defended so as their good life and orderly Conversation may win the Indians Natives of the Country to the knowledge and obedience of **the only true God and Savior of Mankind** and the **Christian Faith** which his Royal Majesty...king Charles the first in his said Letters Patents declared was his Royal Intentions And the Adventurers free Profession to be the Principal end of the said Plantation.

1735
HARVARD'S FIRST HEBREW GRAMMAR BOOK

One thousand copies of the first **Hebrew** grammar book, Dikdook Leshon Gnebreet, (Boston: Jonas Green, 1735) were published in America for "use of the students at Harvard-College at Cambridge in New-England," where **Hebrew** was a required subject. The book was authored by faculty member and convert to **Christianity**, Judah Monis (1683-1764).

JUNE 15, 1780
CONSTITUTION OF THE COMMONWEALTH OF MASSACHUSETTS (WRITTEN BY JOHN ADAMS)

We, therefore, the people of Massachusetts, acknowledging, with grateful hearts, the goodness of the **Great Legislator of the Universe**, in affording us, in the course of **His Providence**, an opportunity, deliberately and peaceably, without fraud, violence or surprise, of entering into an original, explicit, and solemn compact with each other; and of forming a new constitution of civil government, for ourselves and posterity; and devoutly imploring His direction in so interesting a design, do agree upon, ordain and **establish** the following Declaration of Rights, and Frame of Government, as the Constitution of the Commonwealth of Massachusetts.

PART THE FIRST - A DECLARATION OF THE RIGHTS OF THE INHABITANTS OF THE COMMONWEALTH OF MASSACHUSETTS

ARTICLE 1. All men are born free and equal, and have certain natural, essential, and unalienable rights; among which may be reckoned the right of enjoying and defending their lives and liberties; that of acquiring, possessing, and protecting property; in fine, that of seeking and obtaining their safety and happiness.

ARTICLE 2. It is the right as well as the duty of all men in society, **publicly**, and at stated seasons to **worship the Supreme Being, the great Creator and Preserver of the Universe.** And no subject shall be hurt, molested, or restrained, in his person, liberty, or estate, for **worshipping God** in the manner and season most agreeable to the **dictates of his own conscience**; or for his **religious profession** or **sentiments**; provided he doth not disturb the public peace, or obstruct others in their **religious worship**.

ARTICLE 3. As the happiness of a people, and the good order and preservation of civil government, essentially depend upon **piety**, **religion** and **morality**; and as these cannot be generally diffused through a community, but by the institution of the **Public worship** of **God**, and of **public instructions** in **piety**, **religion** and **morality**:

Therefore, to promote their happiness and to secure the good order and preservation of their government, the people of this commonwealth have a right to invest their legislature with power to authorize and require, and the legislature shall, from time to time, authorize and require, the several towns, **parishes**, precincts, and other bodies politic, or **religious societies**, to make suitable provision, at their own expense, for the institution of the **public worship of God**, and for the support and maintenance of **public Protestant teachers** of **piety**, **religion** and **morality**, in all cases where such provision shall not be made voluntarily.

And the people of this commonwealth have also a right to, and do, invest their legislature with authority to enjoin upon all the subjects an attendance upon the instructions of the **public teachers aforesaid**, at stated times and seasons, if there be any on whose instructions they can conscientiously and conveniently attend.

Provided, notwithstanding, that the several towns, **parishes**, precincts, and other bodies politic, or **religious societies**, shall, at all times, have the exclusive right of electing their **public teachers**, and of contracting with them for their support and maintenance.

And all moneys paid by the subject to the support of **public worship**, and of the **public teachers aforesaid**, shall, if he require it, be uniformly applied to the support of the **public teacher** or **teachers** of his own **religious sect** or **denomination**, provided there be any on whose instructions he attends; otherwise it may be paid towards the support of the **teacher** or **teachers** of the **parish** or precinct in which the said moneys are raised. (in effect until 1833)

And every **denomination** of **Christians**, demeaning themselves peaceably, and as good subjects of the commonwealth, shall be equally under the protection of the law: and **no subordination of any one sect or denomination to another shall ever be established by law...**

PART THE SECOND - THE FRAME OF GOVERNMENT, CHAPTER 2, EXECUTIVE POWER, SECTION 1, THE GOVERNOR

ARTICLE 2. The governor shall be chosen annually; and no person shall be eligible to this office, unless at the time of his election, he shall have been an inhabitant of this commonwealth for seven years next preceding; and unless he shall at the same time, be seized in his own right, of a freehold within the commonwealth of the value of one thousand pounds; and unless he shall declare himself to be of the **Christian religion**...

CHAPTER 5, THE UNIVERSITY AT CAMBRIDGE, SECTION 1, THE UNIVERSITY

ARTICLE 1. Whereas our wise and pious ancestors, so early as the year one thousand six hundred and thirty-six, laid the foundation of Harvard College, in which university many persons of great eminence have, by the **blessing** of **God**, been initiated in those arts and sciences, which qualified them for public employments, both in **Church** and state:

and whereas the encouragement of arts and sciences, and all good literature, tends to the **honor of God**, the advantage of the **Christian religion**, and the great benefit of this and the other United States of America -

it is declared, that the President and Fellows of Harvard College, in their corporate capacity, and their successors in that capacity, their officers and servants, shall have, hold, use, exercise and enjoy, all the powers, authorities, rights, liberties, privileges, immunities and franchises, which they now have or are entitled to have, hold, use, exercise and enjoy: and the same are hereby ratified and confirmed unto them, the said president and fellows of Harvard College, and to their successors, and to their officers and servants, respectively, forever...

CHAPTER 5, SECTION 2, THE ENCOURAGEMENT OF LITERATURE, ETC.

Wisdom, and knowledge, as well as virtue, diffused generally among the body of the people, being necessary for the preservation of their rights and liberties;

and as these depend on spreading the opportunities and advantages of education in the various parts of the country, and among the different orders of the people,

it shall be the duty of legislatures and magistrates, in all future periods of this commonwealth, to cherish the interests of literature and the sciences, and all **seminaries** of them; especially the university at Cambridge, public schools and grammar schools in the towns;

to encourage private societies and public institutions, rewards and immunities, for the promotion of agriculture, arts, sciences, commerce, trades, manufactures, and a natural history of the country;

to countenance and **inculcate the principles of humanity and general benevolence, public and private charity, industry and frugality, honesty and punctuality in their dealings; sincerity, good humor, and all social affections, and generous sentiments among the people...**

CHAPTER 6, OATHS AND SUBSCRIPTIONS; INCOMPATIBILITY OF AND EXCLUSION FROM OFFICES; PECUNIARY QUALIFICATIONS; COMMISSIONS; WRITS; CONFIRMATION OF LAWS; HABEAS CORPUS; THE ENACTING STYLE; CONTINUANCE OF OFFICERS; PROVISION FOR A FUTURE REVISAL OF THE CONSTITUTION, ETC.

ARTICLE 1. Any person chosen governor, lieutenant governor, counselor, senator or representative, and accepting the trust, shall before he proceed to execute the duties of his place or office, make and subscribe the following declaration, viz.-

"I, A. B., do declare, that I believe the **Christian religion**, and have a firm **persuasion** of its truth; and that I am seized and possessed, in my own right, of the property required by the constitution as one qualification for the office or place to which I am elected."

And the governor, lieutenant governor, and counselors shall make and subscribe the said declaration, in the presence of the two houses of Assembly; and the senators and representatives first elected under this constitution, before the president and five of the council of the former constitution, and forever afterwards before the governor and council for the time being.

And every person chosen to either of the places or offices aforesaid, as also any person appointed or commissioned to any judicial, executive, military, or other office under the government, shall, before he enters on the discharge of the business of his place or office, take and subscribe the following declaration, and oaths or affirmations, viz.-

"I, A. B., do truly and sincerely acknowledge, profess, testify and declare, that the Commonwealth of Massachusetts is, and of right ought to be, a free, sovereign and independent state; and I do swear, that I will bear true faith and allegiance to the said commonwealth, and that I will defend the same against traitorous conspiracies and all hostile attempts whatsoever: and that I do renounce and abjure all allegiance, subjection and obedience to the king, queen, or government of Great Britain, (as the case may be) and every other foreign power whatsoever:

And that no foreign prince, person, prelate, state or potentate, hath, or ought to have, any jurisdiction, superiority, pre-eminence, authority, dispensing or other power, in any matter, civil, **ecclesiastical** or **spiritual**, within this commonwealth, except the authority and power which is or may be vested by their constituents in the congress of the United States:

And I do further testify and declare, that no man or body of men hath or can have any right to absolve or discharge me from the obligation of this oath, declaration, or affirmation;

And that I do make this acknowledgment, profession, testimony, declaration, denial, renunciation and abjuration, heartily and truly, according to the common meaning and acceptation of the foregoing words, without any equivocation, mental evasion, or secret reservation whatsoever - **So Help Me, God**."

"I, A. B., do solemnly swear and affirm, that I will faithfully and impartially discharge and perform all the duties incumbent on me as:...according to the best of my abilities and understanding, agreeably, to the rules and regulations of the constitution, and the laws of this commonwealth - **So Help Me, God**."

Provided always, that when any person chosen or appointed as aforesaid, shall be of the **denomination** of the people called **Quakers**, and shall decline taking the said oath[s], he shall make his affirmation in the foregoing form, and subscribe the same, omitting the words "I do swear," "and abjure," "oath or," "and abjuration" in the first oath; and in the second oath, the words "swear and," and in each of them the words "**So Help Me, God**;" subjoining instead thereof, "This I do under the pains and penalties of perjury."

MAY 1789
GEORGE WASHINGTON TO GENERAL ASSEMBLY OF PRESBYTERIAN CHURCHES, UNITED STATES:

All men within our territories are protected in **worshipping** the **Deity** according to the **dictates of their consciences**.

OCTOBER 28, 1789
GEORGE WASHINGTON TO MINISTERS & ELDERS OF MASSACHUSETTS & NEW HAMPSHIRE CHURCHES OF THE FIRST PRESBYTERY OF EASTWARD, NEWBURYPORT:

I am persuaded that the path of **true piety** is so plain as to require but little political direction. To this consideration we ought to ascribe the absence of any regulation, respecting **religion**, from the Magna-Carta of our country.

To the guidance of the **ministers** of the **Gospel** this important object is, perhaps, more properly committed. It will be your care to instruct the ignorant, and to reclaim the devious. And in the progress of **morality** and science, to which our Government will give every furtherance, we may confidently expect the advancement of **true religion**, and the completion of our happiness.

1838
MASSACHUSETTS SUPREME COURT COMMONWEALTH V. ABNER KNEELAND, 37 MASS. (20 PICK) 206, 216-217

The case involved a Universalist who claimed the right of "freedom of the press" as a defense for publishing libelous and defamatory remarks about **Christianity** and **God**.

The Court delivered its decision, stating "freedom of press" was not a license to print without restraint:

According to the argument...every act, however injurious or criminal, which can be committed by the use of language may be committed...if such language is printed.

Not only therefore would the article in question become a general license for scandal, calumny and falsehood against individuals, institutions and governments, in the form of publication...but all incitation to treason, assassination, and all other crimes however atrocious, if conveyed in printed language, would be dispunishable.

The statute, on which the question arises, is as follows:

"That if any person shall willfully blaspheme the **Holy Name of God**, by denying, cursing, or contumeliously reproaching **God**, his creation, government, or final judging of the world," &....

In general, **blasphemy** [libel against **God**] may be described, as consisting in speaking evil of the **Deity**...to alienate the minds of others from the love and reverence of **God**. It is purposely using words concerning **God**...to impair and destroy the reverence, respect, and confidence due him....

It is a willful and malicious attempt to lessen men's reverence of **God** by denying his existence, of his attributes as an **intelligent Creator, governor and judge of men**, and to prevent their having confidence in **Him**....

But another ground for arresting the judgment, and one apparently most relied on and urged by the defendant, is, that this statute itself is repugnant to the constitution...and therefore wholly void....

[This law] was passed very soon after the adoption of the constitution, and no doubt, many members of the convention which framed the constitution, were members of the legislature which passed this law....

In New Hampshire, the constitution of which State has a similar declaration of [**religious**] rights, the open denial of the **being and existence of God** or of the **Supreme Being** is prohibited by statute, and declared to be **blasphemy**.

In Vermont, with a similar declaration of rights, a statute was passed in 1797, by which it was enacted, that if any person shall **publicly** deny the **being and existence of God** or the **Supreme Being**, or shall contumeliously reproach his **Providence** and government, he shall be deemed a disturber of the peace and tranquillity of the State, and an offender against the good **morals** and manners of society, and shall be punishable by fine....

The State of Maine also, having adopted the same constitutional provision with that of Massachusetts, in her declaration of rights, in respect to **religious** freedom, immediately after the adoption of the constitution reenacted, the Massachusetts statue against **blasphemy**....

In New York the universal **toleration** of all **religious professions** and **sentiments**, is secured in the most ample manner. It is declared in the constitution...that the free exercise and enjoyment of **religious worship**, without discrimination or preference, shall for ever be allowed in this State to all mankind....

Notwithstanding this constitutional declaration carrying the **doctrine** of unlimited **toleration** as far as the peace and safety of any community will allow, the courts have decided that **blasphemy** was a crime at common law and was not abrogated by the constitution [People v. Ruggles].

[The First Amendment] embraces all who believe in the **existence of God**, as well...as **Christians of every denomination**....This provision does not extend to **atheists**, because they do not believe in **God** or **religion**; and therefore...their **sentiments** and **professions,** whatever they may be, cannot be called **religious sentiments** and **professions.**

NOVEMBER 6, 1917
CONSTITUTION OF MASSACHUSETTS, AMENDMENT, ARTICLE 18. SECTION 1.

No law shall be passed prohibiting the **free exercise of religion.**

AMENDMENT, ARTICLE 11. Instead of ARTICLE 3 of the bill of rights, the following modification and amendment thereof is substituted.

As the **public worship of God** and instructions in **piety, religion** and **morality**, promote the happiness and prosperity of a people and the security of a republican government; therefore, the several **religious societies** of this commonwealth, whether corporate or unincorporate, at any meeting legally warned and holden for that purpose, shall ever have the right to elect their **pastors** or **religious teachers**, to contract with them for their support, to raise money for erecting and repairing **houses for public worship**, for the **maintenance of religious instruction**, and for the payment of necessary expenses: and all persons belonging to any **religious society** shall be taken and held to be members, until they shall file with the clerk of such **society**, a written notice, declaring the dissolution of their membership, and thenceforth shall not be liable for any grant or contract which may be thereafter made, or entered into by such **society**: and all **religious sects** and **denominations**, demeaning themselves peaceably, and as good citizens of the commonwealth, shall be equally under the protection of the law; and no subordination of any one **sect** or **denomination** to another shall ever be **established** by law." [See Amendments, Arts. XLVI and XLVIII, The Initiative, section 2, and The Referendum, section 2].

MASSACHUSETTS RELIGIOUS AFFILIATION

The Encyclopedia Britannica, 11th edition, published in 1911, stated:

With foreign immigration, the **Roman Catholic Church** greatly increased, so that by 1906, an estimated 355 out of every 1,000 citizens were members of the **Roman Catholic Church** (a proportion exceeded only in New Mexico and Rhode Island; in Louisiana, 310 out of every 1,000 were **Catholic**). Only 148 out of every 1000 were **communicants** of **Protestant** bodies. In 1906 there were 1,080,706 **Roman Catholics** (out of a total of 1,562,621

communicants of all **denominations**), 119,196 **Congregationalists**, 80,894 **Baptists**, 65,498 **Methodists** and 51,636 **Protestant Episcopalians**.

http://www.1911encyclopedia.org/Massachusetts

The Catholic Encyclopedia, Volume XV, Copyright 1912 by Robert Appleton Company, stated as of 1906, a census of religious bodies listed **Massachusetts'** three million citizens as:

Congregationalist - 7.6 percent
Baptists - 5.2 percent
Methodists - 4.2 percent
Protestant Episcopalians - 3.3 percent
Catholics - 69.2 percent, consisting of Irish, French Canadians, Italians, Portuguese, Poles, Lithuanians, Germans, Syrians, Bravas, African America and Chinese.

http://www.newadvent.org/cathen/10024c.htm

The Wikipedia Online Encyclopedia, as of 2006, listed **Massachusetts** as:

Christian - 78 percent, consisting of:
- **Congregational/Church** of **Christ** - 4 percent
- **Baptist** - 4 percent
- **Episcopal** - 3 percent
- **Methodist** - 2 percent
- **Pentacostal** - 2 percent
- **Other Protestant** - 16 percent
- **Catholic** - 47 percent

Latter-day Saint - 1 percent
Unitarian - 1 percent
Jewish - 2 percent
Other Religions - 1 percent
Non-Religious/Non-Reporting - 17 percent

http://en.wikipedia.org/wiki/
Massachusetts#Religion

The U.S. Religious Landscape Survey, conducted by The Pew Forum on Religion & Public Life, 2007, published in the USA Today, listed **Massachusetts** as:

Christian - 72.5 percent, consisting of:
- **Evangelical Protestant** - 11 percent
- **Mainline Protestant** - 15 percent
- **Black Protestant** - 2 percent
- **Catholic** - 43 percent
- **Orthodox** - 1 percent
- **Other Christian** - 0.5 percent

Mormon - <0.5 percent
Jehovah's Witnesses - <0.5 percent
Jewish - 3 percent
Muslim - <0.5 percent
Buddhist - 1 percent
Hindu - 1 percent
Other World Religions - <0.5 percent
Other Faiths - 2 percent
Unaffiliated - 17 percent
Did not answer - 1 percent

www.pewforum.org
www.usatoday.com/news/graphics/pew-religion-08/
flash.htm

MAINE

MAINE

Maine was part of Massachusetts at the time of the Revolutionary War, but explorers have been visiting the coast of Maine for centuries.

In 990, Biarne sailed from Iceland for Greenland, but driven by storms discovered an unknown land covered with forests. Leif and Thorward Ericson, sons of Eric the Red, made voyages to the coast of "Vineland," followed by other Norsemen.

In 1497, John Cabot and his son Sebastian in 1498, thought they were would find the passage to China-"far-off Cathay." In 1524, Italian explorer Verrazano, sailing for the French Government, visited "on the gulf of Maine." In 1525, Estevan Gomez, sailing for the Spanish Government, explored the coast of Maine and for years Spanish maps called the area the "Country of Gomez."

In 1527, John Rut was the first Englishman to set foot upon American soil there, the territory being called Norumbega. In 1541, Diego Maldonado visited the coast of Maine, searching for Ferdinand De Soto.

In 1556, André Thevet, on board a French vessel, landed with others on the banks of the Penobscot. In 1565, Sir John Hawkins explored the coast, and Sir Humphrey Gilbert perished on the way to establish an English colony at Norumbega on the Penobscot.

In 1602, Bartholomew Gosnold landed near where Portland would later be founded, and in 1603, Martin Pring entered Penobscot Bay.

The French were the first to attempt a colony, with Sieur de Monts being granted a charter to colonize "Acadia" by King Henry IV of France in 1603. In 1604, he sailed with Samuel de Champlain and 120 colonists. In a quickly erected **chapel** on De Monts Island, **Catholic Mass** was offered for the first time on the soil of New England by **Reverend Nicholas Aubry** of Paris. From this little colony the **Gospel** spread among the Abenakis tribe, the first Indians on this part of the continent to embrace the **Christian faith**. The colony was transferred the following year to Port Royal on Annapolis Bay.

English Captain George Weymouth explored the southwest coast of Maine in 1605. He kidnapped five Indians and carried them to England, where three of them lived with Sir Ferdinando Gorges, who later founded Maine. On April 10, 1606, James I of England granted the Charter of Virginia, which included the area of Maine. George Popham and Raleigh Gilbert, son of Sir Humphrey Gilbert, sailed with 120 colonists and settled at the mouth of the Kennebec river. A small colony was **established** at Fort Popham on the Sagadahoc peninsula in 1607. Finding insufficient supplies, most returned to England in a few months and the colony was abandoned.

In 1609 the French **Jesuits, Father** Biard and **Father** Masse, **established** a fortified **mission** on Mount Desert Island. In 1613, Antoinette de Pons sent out an expedition from France which landed on the southeastern shore of Mount Desert. **Missionaries** planted a **cross**, celebrated **Mass**, and gave the place the name of St. Sauveur, but that same year Captain Samuel Argall sailed up from Jamestown, Virginia, in a small man-of-war and destroyed it.

Father Masse and fourteen Frenchmen were set adrift in a small boat, and others were taken prisoner to Virginia. Captain Argall also destroyed the French settlements of the St. Croix and Port Royal colonies, though French **Catholic missionary work** continued among the Indians into the next century.

In 1614, Captain John Smith found a few settlers left on the island of Monhegan and around Pemaquid Bay. Conflicting land claims between French **Catholics** and British **Anglicans** began a long and bloody rivalry in which the **religious** element was ever present.

From 1616 to 1677, Maine's English settlement was led by Sir Ferdinando Gorges, his son Robert, and his nephew. In 1622, Gorges received a royal patent from the English king and the next year sent his son Robert as governor of the Province of Maine. He was accompanied by a **minister** of the **Church of England** and several councilors. In 1629, part of Gorge's land was divided, with Captain John Mason's portion becoming New Hampshire.

Maine's first court was convened at Saco on March 21, 1636. In 1639, the King's charter made the Province of Maine the personal possession of Sir Ferdinando Gorges. French and Indians almost destroyed the English settlements in 1675. After much negotiating with the heirs of Gorges, Maine became part of the Royal Province of Massachusetts Bay in 1691.

French Acadia was conveyed to the Duke of York, King James II of England, the last **Catholic** monarch of England. The English put down the French and Indians, capturing Port Royal in 1690 and Louisburg in 1745. French Acadians fled down the Mississippi to Louisiana, where Acadian came to be pronounced "Cajun."

In 1704, Massachusetts sent expeditions to destroy the **mission** stations in Maine, resulting in **Churches** being burned and **priests** killed. For the next seventy years, the remnant of **Catholic Indians** were **ministered** to by the occasional visits of **Catholic missionaries** from Canada.

At the beginning of the Revolutionary War, the Abenakis Indians sided with the patriots and after that, all persecution ceased. The Council of Massachusetts desired to furnish them a **priest**, but could not find one until **Father Ciquard** went, remaining until 1794. The current **Catholic**

Church in Maine dates from the arrival of **Father Cheverus** from Boston in July of 1797, who took charge of two **Indian missions** at Pleasant Point.

During the War of Independence, Falmouth (now Portland) was burned by the British, and in 1775, Benedict Arnold followed Maine's Kennebec and Dead rivers in an attempt to capture Quebec. Troops from Maine, part of the Massachusetts regiment, fought at Bunker Hill. The first naval battle of the Revolution was at Machias, July 11, 1775, where Jeremiah O'Brien and his five sons captured the British ship, Margaretta. During the War of 1812, the British captured Maine's cities of Eastport, Castine, Hampden, Bangor and Machias.

In 1820, Maine was admitted into the Union as a separate free state as part of the Missouri compromise, Missouri entering as a slave state. Dispute over the exact location of Maine's border with British Canada led to many battles, which were eventually resolved through treaties.

Irish immigration of the 1850's, caused the **Catholic** population in Maine and New Hampshire grow, resulting in its own **Diocese** being formed in 1853. An **anti-Catholic** backlash movement, called Knownothingism, resulted in a **Church** being burned at Bath on July 8, 1854, and the tarring, feathering, and riding on a rail of **Father John Bapst** at Ellsworth, October 15, 1854. The persecution ended only after many **Catholics** of Maine fought courageously for the Union during the Civil War.

As of 2006, Maine had 10 **synagogues**.

1639
GRANT OF THE PROVINCE OF MAINE

All Patronages...of all and every such **Churches** and **Chapels** as shall be made and erected within the said Province...any, of them with full power license and authority to build and erect or cause to be built and erected so many **Churches** and **Chapels** there as to the said Sir Ferdinando Gorges his heirs and assignee shall seem meet and convenient and to dedicate and consecrate the same or cause the same to bee dedicated and consecrated according to the **Ecclesiastical Laws of this our Realm of England**...

And for the better government of such our Subjects and others as at any time shall happen to dwell or reside within the said Province...our will and pleasure is that the **Religion** now professed in the **Church of England and Ecclesiastical Government** now used in the same shall be forever hereafter professed and with as much convenient speed as may be settled and **established** in and throughout the said Province and Premises and every of them...

But We Do nevertheless hereby signify and declare our will and pleasure to be the powers and authorities hereby given to the said Sir Ferdinando Gorges his heirs and assignee for and concerning the Government both **Ecclesiastical** and Civil...

And because in a Country so far distant and seated amongst so many barbarous nations the Intrusions or Invasions as well of the barbarous people as of Pirates and other enemies may be justly feared We Do therefore...grant unto the said Sir Ferdinando Gorges...power...that he...may...raise arms and employee all... persons whatsoever inhabiting...within the said Province...for the resisting or withstanding of such Enemies or Pirates both at Land and at Sea and such Enemies or Pirates...to pursue and prosecute out of the limits of the said Province or Premises and then (**if it shall so please God**) to vanquish...

No interpretation being made of any word or sentence Whereby **God's Holy true Christian Religion now taught professed and maintained the fundamental laws of this Realm** or Allegiance to us our heirs or successors may suffer prejudice or diminution.

OCTOBER 29, 1819
CONSTITUTION OF MAINE

PREAMBLE. We the people of Maine, in order to establish justice, insure tranquillity, provide for our mutual defense, promote our common welfare, and secure to ourselves and our posterity the **blessings of liberty, acknowledging with grateful hearts the goodness of the Sovereign Ruler of the Universe in affording us an opportunity, so favorable to the design;** and, **imploring God's aid and direction** in its accomplishment, do agree to form ourselves into a free and independent State, by the style and title of the State of Maine and do ordain and establish the following Constitution for the government of the same...

ARTICLE 1, SECTION 3. All individuals have a natural and unalienable right to **worship Almighty God according to the dictates of their own consciences**, and no person shall be hurt, molested or restrained in that person's liberty or estate for **worshipping God** in the manner and season most agreeable to the **dictates of that person's own conscience**, nor for that person's **religious professions or sentiments**, provided that that person does not disturb the public peace, nor obstruct others in their **religious worship**;

And all persons demeaning themselves peaceably, as good members of the State, shall be equally under the protection of the laws, and **no subordination nor preference of any one sect or denomination to another shall ever be established by law**, nor shall any **religious test** be required as a qualification for any office or trust, under this State; and all **religious societies** in this State, whether incorporate or unincorporate, shall at all times have the exclusive right of electing their public **teachers**, and contracting with them for their support and maintenance...

1911
MAINE STATUTES IN EFFECT AS OF 1911

LORD'S DAY. Statute provided penalties for "whoever on the **Lord's Day** or at any other time, behaves rudely or indecently within the walls of any **house of public worship**; willfully interrupts or disturbs any **Assembly** for **public worship** within the place of such **Assembly** or out of it"; for one "who on the **Lord's Day**, keeps open his shop, workhouse, warehouse or place of business on that day, except works of necessity or charity"; for an innholder or victualler who, "on the **Lord's Day**, suffers any person, except travelers or lodgers to abide in his house, yard or field, drinking or spending their time idly at play, or doing any secular business except works of charity or necessity."

"No person conscientiously believing that the **Seventh Day of the week** ought to be observed as the **Sabbath**, and actually refraining from secular business and labor on that day, is liable to said penalties for doing such business or labor on the first day of the week, if he does not disturb other persons." Service of civil process on the **Lord's Day** were forbidden, and, in fact made void.

ADMINISTRATION OF OATHS. Oaths were administered by all judges, justices of the peace, and notaries public in the form prescribed by statute as follows: the person to whom an oath is administered shall hold up his right hand, unless he believes that an oath administered in that form is not binding, and then it may be administered in a form believed by him to be binding; one believing any other than the **Christian Religion**, may be sworn according to the ceremonies of his **religion**. Persons conscientiously scrupulous of taking an oath may affirm.

BLASPHEMY & PROFANITY. Statutes provided "whoever blasphemes the **Holy Name of God**, by denying, cursing or contumeliously reproaching **God, His creation, government, final judgment of the world, Jesus Christ, the Holy Ghost, or the Holy Scriptures as contained in**

the canonical books of the Old and New Testament or by exposing them to contempt and ridicule, shall be punished by imprisonment for not more than two years or by fine not exceeding two hundred dollars". A five dollar fine was provided for one who "profanely curses or swears."

USE OF **PRAYER** IN LEGISLATURE. There were no statute on this subject, but since Maine became a state it has been customary for the president of the senate and the speaker of the house...to invite in turn the several **clergymen** of Augusta, Hallowell, and Gardiner, to open each day's session in their respective branches with **prayer**. Until 1891, **Protestant clergymen** alone were invited, but since then **Catholic priests** were invited and officiate in their turn.

RECOGNIATION OF **RELIGIOUS HOLIDAYS**. Statutes provided that "no person shall be arrested in a civil action, or mesne process or execution or on a warrant for taxes, on the day of annual fast or thanksgiving, the thirtieth day of May, the fourth day of July, or **Christmas**."

In 1907, the Legislature passed an act abolishing the **annual fast day**, substituting it with Patriots' Day.

SEAL OF CONFESSION. There was no record of any attempt to obtain from any **priest** information acquired by him through the **confessiona**l.

INCORPORATION OF **CHURCHES**. Statutes provided "any persons of lawful age, desirous of becoming an incorporated **parish** or **religious society**, may apply to a justice of the peace" and full provision is made for their incorporation into a **parish**, and "every **parish** may take by gift or purchase any real or personal property, until the income thereof shall amount to three thousand dollars, convey the same and **establish** by-laws not repugnant to law. By Act of the Legislature approved 27 February, 1887, the **Roman Catholic Bishop of Portland** was created a corporation sole.

EXEMPTION OF **CHURCH** PROPERTY FROM TAXATION. Statutes provided that "**houses of religious worship**, including **vestries a**nd the **pews** and furniture within the same, except for **parochial purposes; tombs and rights of burial**; and property held by a **religious society** as a **parsonage**, not exceeding six thousand dollars in value and from which no rent is received, were exempt from taxation.

But all other property of any **religious society,** both real and personal, was liable to taxation, the same as other property."

EXEMPTION OF **CLERGY** FROM CERTAIN PUBLIC DUTIES. Settled **ministers of the Gospel** were exempt by statute from serving as jurors, and by the constitution '**ministers**' were among those entitled to be exempted from military duty.

MARRIAGE AND DIVORCE. Statutes provided that "every justice of the peace, residing in the State; every o**rdained minister of the Gospel** and every person licensed to **preach** by an association of **ministers, religious seminary** or **ecclesiastical body**, duly appointed and commissioned for that purpose by the governor may solemnize marriages"...Another section safeguarded the rights of those contracting marriage in good faith by making it valid, although not solemnized in legal form, and although there may be a want of jurisdiction or authority in the justice or **minister** performing the ceremony.

Grounds for divorce were: "A divorce from the bonds of matrimony may be decreed by the Supreme Judicial Court in the County where either party resides at the commencement of proceedings for cause of adultery, impotence, extreme cruelty, utter desertion continued for three consecutive years next prior to the filing of the libel, gross and confirmed habits of intoxication, cruel and abusive treatment, or, on the libel of the wife, where the husband being of sufficient ability, grossly or wantonly and cruelly refuses or neglects to provide suitable maintenance for her...But when both parties have been guilty of adultery, or there is collusion between them to procure a divorce, it shall not be granted."

EDUCATION. Under the heading of normal schools was the statute: "Said schools, while teaching the **fundamental truths of Christianity** and the **great principles of morality**, recognized by law, shall be free from all **denominational teachings** and open to persons of different **religious connections** on terms of equality."

1993
CONSTITUTION OF THE STATE OF MAINE AS AMENDED & REVISED BY CHIEF JUSTICE

PREAMBLE. We the people of Maine, in order to **establish** justice, insure tranquillity, provide for our mutual defense, promote our common welfare, and secure to ourselves and our posterity the **blessings** of liberty, **acknowledging with grateful hearts the goodness of the Sovereign Ruler of the Universe** in affording us an opportunity, so favorable to the design; and, **imploring God's aid and direction** in its accomplishment, do agree to form ourselves into a free and independent State, by the style and title of the State of Maine and do ordain and **establish** the following Constitution for the government of the same...

DECLARATION OF RIGHTS, ARTICLE 4, PART 3, SECTION 3. All individuals have a natural and unalienable right to **worship Almighty God** according to the **dictates of their own consciences**, and no person shall be hurt, molested or restrained in that person's liberty or estate for **worshipping God** in the manner and season most agreeable to the **dictates of that person's own conscience**, nor for that person's **religious professions or sentiments**, provided that that person does not disturb the public peace, nor obstruct others in their **religious worship**; - and all persons demeaning themselves peaceably, as good members of the State, shall be equally under the protection of the laws, and no subordination nor preference of any one **sect** or **denomination** to another shall ever be **established** by law, nor shall any **religious test** be required as a qualification for any office or trust, under this State; and all **religious societies** in this State, whether incorporate or unincorporate, shall at all times have the exclusive right of electing their **public teachers**, and contracting with them for their support and maintenance...

SECTION 20. Written petitions for a people's veto...must be filed in the office of the Secretary of State, or, if such 5th day is a Saturday, a **Sunday** or a legal holiday, by 5:00 p.m., on the next day which is not a Saturday, a **Sunday** or a legal holiday...

ARTICLE 7, SECTION 5...Persons of the **denominations** of **Quakers** and **Shakers**, Justices of the Supreme Judicial Court, **Ministers of the Gospel** and persons exempted by the laws of the United States may be exempted from military duty...

ARTICLE 9, SECTION 1. Every person elected or appointed to either of the places or offices provided in this Constitution, and every person elected, appointed, or commissioned to any judicial, executive, military or other office under this State, shall, before entering on the discharge of the duties of that place or office, take and subscribe the following oath or affirmation:

"I,____ do swear, that I will support the Constitution of the United States and of this State, so long as I shall continue a citizen thereof. **So Help Me God.**" Alternative affirmation. "I ______ do swear, that I will faithfully discharge, to the best of my abilities, the duties incumbent on me as ______according to the Constitution and laws of the State. **So Help Me God**."

Provided, that an affirmation in the above forms may be substituted, when the person shall be conscientiously scrupulous of taking and subscribing an oath.

MAINE RELIGIOUS AFFILIATION

The Encyclopedia Britannica, 11th edition, published in 1911, stated:

In 1906, **Roman Catholics** were more numerous than all the **Protestant sects** taken together, having a membership of 113,419 out of a total of 212,988 in all **denominations**.

http://www.1911encyclopedia.org/Maine#Population

The **Catholic** Encyclopedia, Volume XV, Copyright 1912 by Robert Appleton Company, stated as of 1906, a census listed: Out of Maine's population of 694,480 in 1900, the **Catholic** population was 123,547.

http://www.newadvent.org/cathen/09541b.htm

The Wikipedia Online Encyclopedia, as of 2006, listed **Maine** as:

- **Christian** - 82 percent, consisting of:
    - **Baptist** - 16 percent
    - **Methodist** - 9 percent
    - **Pentacostal** - 6 percent
    - **United Church** of **Christ** - 3 percent
    - **Lutheran** - 3 percent
    - **Other Protestant** - 18 percent
    - **Catholic** - 25 percent
    - **Other Christian** - 2 percent
- **Other Religions** - 1 percent
- **Non-Religious/Non-Reporting** - 17 percent

http://en.wikipedia.org/wiki/Maine#Religion

The U.S. Religious Landscape Survey, conducted by The Pew Forum on Religion & Public Life, 2007, published in the USA Today, listed **Maine** as:

Christian - 71.5 percent, consisting of:
- **Evangelical Protestant** - 15 percent
- **Mainline Protestant** - 26 percent
- **Black Protestant** - <0.5 percent
- **Catholic** - 29 percent
- **Orthodox** - <0.5 percent
- **Other Christian** - <0.5 percent

Mormon - 1 percent
Jehovah's Witnesses - 1 percent
Jewish - <0.5 percent
Muslim - <0.5 percent
Buddhist - 1 percent
Hindu - <0.5 percent
Other World Religions - <0.5 percent
Other Faiths - 2 percent
Unaffiliated - 25 percent
Did not answer - <0.5 percent

www.pewforum.org
www.usatoday.com/news/graphics/pew-religion-08/flash.htm

SEAL OF THE STATE OF NEW HAMPSHIRE
1776

NEW HAMPSHIRE

Samuel de Champlain sailed along the New Hampshire coast in 1605, and Captain John Smith wrote of it in his Description of New England. Sir Ferdinando Gorges formed the Council for New England in 1620 and procured a grant from King James I. On March 9, 1622, John Mason, called "the founder of New Hampshire," received a grant.

In August 1622, John Mason and Sir Ferdinando Gorges jointly received a grant. David Thomson, Sir Henry Roswell and Edward Hilton were granted land under the name of New Hampshire. The first settlement was by David Thomson in 1623 at Little Harbor, now in the town of Rye. A fur trade was pursued with the Iroquois Indians. Edward Hilton **established** a settlement on Dover Point.

New Hampshire became a separate colony in 1629. In 1638, **dissenting pastor** John Wheelwright was banished from **Puritan** Massachusetts and founded Exeter, New Hampshire. Massachusetts annexed New Hampshire in 1641, and John Wheelwright fled again to Maine. New Hampshire became a separate colony again in 1679. Beginning in 1676 and continuing to 1759, New Hampshire suffered Indian attacks. From 1686 to 1689, New Hampshire was under Sir Edmund Andros, a **Church of England** supporter.

The State taxed all citizens to support the **Congregational Church**, then later gave citizens the option of designating their taxes to other **Churches**.

Legislation in 1792, 1804, 1805, and 1817 gave exemptions to **Episcopalians**, **Baptists**, **Universalists** and

Methodists, providing each should be "considered as a distinct **denomination**, with privileges as such."

Baptists, Methodists and **Universalists** objected to this and in 1819, State collection and distribution of finances for **Churches** was ended by the "**Toleration Act.**"

All office holders still had to be "of the **Protestant Christian religion**" until 1877, and **religious freedom** was only for **Christians** until 1968.

FEBRUARY 12, 1629 GRANT TO THOMAS LEWIS & RICHARD BONIGHTON BY THE COUNCIL FOR NEW ENGLAND

To all **Christian** people to whom these present writing indented shall come, the Council for the affairs of New England in America send greeting **in our Lord God everlasting**...

Thomas Lewis...has already been at the charge to transport himself and others to take a view of New England in America...in advancing of a plantation, and does now wholly intend by **God's assistance** with his associates to plant there, both for the good of his Majesty's realms and dominions and for the **propagation** of **Christian religion** among those **infidels**, and in consideration...with Captain Richard Bonighton...have undertaken at their own proper costs and charges to transport fifty persons there within seven years next ensuing to plant and inhabit there to the advancement of the general plantation.

NOVEMBER 7, 1629 GRANT OF HAMPSHIRE TO JOHN MASON

This Indenture made ye Seventh Day of November **Anno Domini** 1629 & in ye Fifth year of ye Reign of our

Sovereign Lord Charles by ye **Grace of God** King of England Scotland France & Ireland **Defender of the Faith** &c Between ye President & Council of new England on the one party & Capt John Mason of London Esquire on ye other party.

NOVEMBER 17, 1629
GRANT TO SIR FERDINANDO GORGES & JOHN MASON
BY THE COUNCIL OF NEW ENGLAND

This Indenture made the seventeenth day of November **Anno Domini** 1629, and in the fifth year of the reign of our sovereign lord Charles, by the **Grace of God**, King of England, Scotland, France, and Ireland, **Defender of the Faith**, &c., between the President and Council of New England in the one party and Sir Ferdinando Gorges of London, Knight, and Captain John Mason of London, Esquire, on the other party...the president and council intend to name The Province of Laconia...

And also yielding and paying unto the said president and council and successors yearly the sum of ten pounds of lawful money of England at one entire payment within ten days after the feast of **St. Michael the archangel** yearly.

APRIL 22, 1635
GRANT OF PROVINCE OF NEW HAMPSHIRE TO MR. MASON, BY THE NAME MASONIA

To all **Christian** people unto whom these presents shall come The Council for ye affairs of New England in America send greeting in **our Lord God ever lasting,**

Whereas our late Sovereign Lord King James...Letters patents...granted...unto ye said Council...All ye land of New England in America...Said Council of New England in America...granted...unto Capt John Mason Esquire...part of ye maine land of New England aforesaid being from ye middle part of Naumkeck river...to be called by ye name of Masonia.

APRIL 22, 1635
GRANT OF PROVINCE OF NEW HAMPSHIRE TO MR. MASON BY THE NAME OF NEW HAMPSHIRE

This Indenture made the two and twentieth Day of April in the 11th year of the Reign of Our Sovereign Lord Charles by ye **Grace of God** King of England, Scotland, France, & Ireland **Defender of the Faith** &c Between the Council **Established** at Plymouth in the County of Devon for the planting ordering ruling & Governing of Near England in America of ye one part and Capt John Mason Esquire...

Any part or parcel thereof not otherwise granted to any by Special Name All which part & portion of Lands Islands and premises are from henceforth to be called by the Name of New Hampshire...dated ye Day & year first above written **Anno Domini** 1635.

1639
AGREEMENT OF SETTLERS, EXETER, N.H.

Whereas it hath pleased the **Lord** to move the Heart of our dread Sovereign Charles by the **Grace of God** King &c. to grant License and Liberty to sundry of his subjects to plant themselves in the Westerly parts of America,

We his loyal Subjects **Brethren of the Church in Exeter** situate and lying upon the River Pascataqua with other Inhabitants there, considering with ourselves **the Holy Will of God** and our own Necessity that we should not live without wholesome Laws and Civil Government among us of which we are altogether destitute; do **in the name of Christ and in the sight of God** combine ourselves together to erect and set up among us such Government as shall be to our best discerning agreeable to **the Will of God** professing ourselves Subjects to our Sovereign Lord King Charles according to the Liberties of our English Colony of Massachusetts, and binding of ourselves solemnly by **the Grace and Help of Christ and in His Name** and fear to submit ourselves to such **Godly and Christian Laws as are Established in the Realm of England** to our best Knowledge, and to all other such Laws which shall upon good grounds be made and enacted among us according to **God** that we may live quietly and peaceably together in all **Godliness** and honesty.

1680
COMMISSION OF JOHN CUTT

And ye President & Council...before they be admitted to their...offices...shall also take this Oath following,

You shall swear, well and truly to administer Justice to all his Majesty's good subjects, inhabiting within ye Province of New Hampshire under this Government: & also duly & faithfully to discharge & execute ye Trust in you reposed, according to the best of your knowledge; you shall spare no person for favor or affection; nor any person grieve for hatred or ill will. **So Help You God**...

And above all things we do by these presents will, require & command Our said Council to take all possible care for ye discountenancing of vice & encouraging of virtue & good living; that by such examples ye **infidel** may be invited & desire to partake of ye **Christian Religion**, & for ye greater ease & satisfaction of or said loving subjects in **matters of Religion** We do hereby will, require & command that **liberty of conscience** shall be allowed unto all **Protestants**; & that such especially as shall be conformable to **ye rites of ye Church of England**, shall be particularly countenanced & encouraged.

JANUARY 5, 1776
CONSTITUTION OF NEW HAMPSHIRE

That at any session of the...Assembly neither branch shall adjourn from any longer time than from Saturday till the next Monday without consent of the other.

JUNE 2, 1784
NEW HAMPSHIRE CONSTITUTION

PART I, ARTICLE 1: All men are born equally free and independent; therefore all government of rights originates from the people...

PART 1, ARTICLE 4. Among the natural rights, some are in their very nature unalienable, because no equivalent can be given or received for them. Of this kind are the **Rights of Conscience**.

PART 1, ARTICLE 5. Every individual has a natural and unalienable right to **worship GOD** according to the **dictates of his own conscience**, and reason; and no subject shall be hurt, molested, or restrained in his person, liberty or estate for **worshipping God**, in the manner and season most agreeable to the **dictates of his own conscience**, or for his **religious profession**, **sentiments** or **persuasion**; provided he doth not disturb the public peace, or disturb others, in their **religious worship**.

PART 1, ARTICLE 6. As **morality** and **piety**, rightly grounded on **evangelical principles** will give the best and greatest security to government, and will lay in the hearts of men the strongest obligations to due subjection; and as the knowledge of these, is most likely to be **propagated** through a **society** by the institution of the **public worship** of the **Deity**, and of public instruction in **morality** and **religion**;

Therefore, to promote those important purposes, the people of this state have a right to empower, and do hereby fully empower the legislature to authorize from time to time, the several towns, **parishes**, bodies-corporate, or

religious societies within this state, to make adequate provision at their own expense, for the support and maintenance of public **Protestant teachers of piety, religion and morality:**

Provided notwithstanding, That the several towns, **parishes**, bodies-corporate, or **religious societies**, shall at all times have the exclusive right of electing their own public **teachers**, and of contracting with them for their support and maintenance.

And no person of any one particular **religious sect** or **denomination** shall ever be compelled to pay towards the support of the **teacher** or **teachers** of another **persuasion, sect** or **denomination**.

And **every denomination of Christians** demeaning themselves quietly, and as good subjects of the state, **shall be equally under the protection of the law:** and **no subordination of any one sect or denomination to another, shall ever be established by law.**

And nothing herein shall be understood to affect any former contracts made for the support of the **Ministry**; but all such contracts shall remain, and be in the same state as if this constitution had not been made...

PART 2-THE FORM OF GOVERNMENT, SENATE. That no person shall be capable of being elected a senator who is not of the **Protestant religion**, and seized of a freehold estate in his own rights of the value of two hundred pounds, lying within the State, who is not of the age of thirty years, and who shall not have been an inhabitant of the State for seven years immediately preceding his election, and at the time thereof he shall be an inhabitant of the district for which he shall be chosen.

HOUSE OF REPRESENTATIVES...Every member of the house of representatives shall be chosen by ballot, and for two years at least next preceding his election shall have been an inhabitant of this State, shall have an estate within the district which he may be chosen to represent, of the value of one hundred pounds, one-half of which to be a freehold, whereof he is seized in his own right; shall be at the time of his election an inhabitant of the town, **parish**, or place he may be chosen to represent; shall be of the **Protestant religion**, and shall cease to represent such town, **parish**, or place immediately on his ceasing to be qualified...

EXECUTIVE POWER-PRESIDENT. The President shall be chosen annually; and no person shall be eligible to this office, unless at the time of his election, he shall have been an inhabitant of this state for seven years... and unless he shall be of the age of thirty years and unless he shall at the same time have an estate of the value of five hundred pounds, one-half of which shall consist of a freehold in his own right within this State, and unless he shall be of the **Protestant religion**.

ENCOURAGEMENT OF LITERATURE, ETC. Knowledge and learning generally diffused through a community, being essential to the preservation of a free government; and spreading the opportunities and advantages of education through the various arts of the county being highly conducive to promote this end, it shall be the duty of the legislatures and magistrates, in all future periods of this government, to cherish the interests of literature and the sciences, and all **seminaries** and public schools; to encourage private and public institutions, rewards, and immunities for the promotion of agriculture, arts, sciences, commerce, trade, manufactures, and natural history of the country; to countenance and **inculcate the principles of humanity and general benevolence, public and private charity, industry and economy, honesty and punctuality, sincerity, sobriety, and all social affections and generous sentiments among the people.**

OATHS. Any person chosen President, counselor, senator, or representative, military or civil officer... shall...make and subscribe the following declaration, viz:

I, A.B. do truly and sincerely acknowledge... that the state of New Hampshire is, and of right ought to be, a free, sovereign and independent state; and do swear that I will bear faith and true allegiance to the same, and that I will endeavor to defend it against all treacherous conspiracies and hostile attempts whatever: and I do further testify and declare, that no man or body of men, hath or can have, a right to absolve me from the obligation of this oath...**So Help Me God**."

1792
NEW HAMPSHIRE CONSTITUTION

PART FIRST, ARTICLE 4. Among the natural rights, some are in their very nature unalienable, because no equivalent can be given or received for them. Of this kind are the **rights of conscience**.

ARTICLE 5. Every individual has a natural and unalienable right to **worship God** according to the **dictates of his own conscience** and reason; and no person shall be hurt, molested, or restrained in his person, liberty, or estate for **worshipping God** in the manner most agreeable to the **dictates of his own conscience**, or for his **religious profession**, **sentiments**, or **persuasion**; provided he doth not disturb the public peace or disturb others in their **religious worship**.

ARTICLE 6. As **morality** and **piety**, rightly grounded on **evangelical principles** (changed to "high principles" in 1968), will give the best and greatest security to government, and will lay in the hearts of men the strongest obligations to due subjection; and as a knowledge of these is most likely to be **propagated** through a **society** by the institution of the **public worship** of the **Deity**, and of public instruction in **morality** and **religion**; therefore, to promote those important purposes the people of this State have a right to empower, and do hereby fully empower, the legislature to authorize, from time to time, the several towns, **parishes**, bodies corporate, or **religious societies** within this State, to make adequate provisions, at their own expense, for the support and maintenance of public **Protestant teachers** of **piety**, **religion**, and **morality**.

Provided notwithstanding, That the several towns, **parishes**, bodies corporate, or **religious societies**, shall at all times have the exclusive right of electing their own public **teachers**, and of contracting with them for their support and maintenance.

And no person, or any one particular **religious sect** or **denomination**, shall ever be compelled to pay toward the support of the **teacher** or **teachers** of another **persuasion, sect,** or **denomination**.

And every **denomination** of **Christians**, demeaning themselves quietly and as good subjects of the State, shall be equally under the protection of the law; and no subordination of any one **sect** or **denomination** to another shall ever be **established** by law. And nothing herein shall be understood to affect any former contracts made for the support of the **Ministry**; but all such contracts shall remain and be in the same state as if this constitution had not been made.(**Christian** refereence removed in 1968.)...

PART 2, THE FORM OF GOVERNMENT, HOUSE OF REPRESENTATIVES, SECTION 14. Every member of the house of representatives shall be chosen by ballot, and for two years at least next preceding his election shall have been an inhabitant of this State, shall have an estate within the district which he may be chosen to represent, of the value of one hundred pounds, one-half of which to be a freehold, whereof he is seized in his own right; shall be at the time of his election an inhabitant of the town, **parish**, or place he may be chosen to represent; shall be of the **Protestant religion**, and shall cease to represent such town, **parish**, or place immediately on his ceasing to be qualified as aforesaid...(**Protestant** requirement removed in 1877.)

SENATE, SECTION 29. Provided, nevertheless, That no person shall be capable of being elected a senator who is not of the **Protestant religion**, and seized of a freehold estate in his own rights of the value of two hundred pounds, lying within the State, who is not of the age of thirty years, and who shall not have been an inhabitant of the State for seven years immediately preceding his election, and at the time thereof he shall be an inhabitant of the district for which he shall be chosen...(**Protestant** requirement in effect till 1877.)

GOVERNOR, SECTION 42. The governor shall be chosen annually...And no person shall be eligible to this office unless at the time of his election he shall have been an inhabitant of this State for seven years next preceding, and unless he shall be of the age of thirty years and unless he shall at the same time have an estate of the value of five hundred pounds,, one-half of which shall consist of a freehold in his own right within this State, and unless he shall be of the **Protestant religion**...(**Protestant** requirement in effect till 1877.)

ENCOURAGEMENT OF LITERATURE, ETC. SECTION 83. Knowledge and learning generally diffused through a community, being essential to the preservation of a free government; and spreading the opportunities and advantages of education through the various arts of the county being highly conducive to promote this end, it shall be the duty of the legislatures and magistrates, in all future periods of this government, to cherish the interests of literature and the sciences, and all **seminaries** and public schools; to encourage private and public institutions, rewards, and immunities for the promotion of agriculture, arts, sciences, commerce, trade, manufactures, and natural history of the country; to countenance and **inculcate the principles of humanity and general benevolence, public and private charity, industry and economy, honesty and**

punctuality, sincerity, sobriety, and all social affections and generous sentiments among the people.

OATHS, SECTION 84. Any person chosen governor, counselor, senator, or representative, military or civil officer...shall...make and subscribe the following declaration, viz: "I, A. B., do solemnly swear that I will bear faith and true allegiance to the State of New Hampshire, and will support the constitution thereof **So Help Me God**."

1792, 1804, 1805, 1817
SEPARATE ACTS OF LEGISLATION

Exemptions given to **Episcopalians**, **Baptists**, **Universalists**, and **Methodists**, providing that each should be "considered as a distinct **denomination**, with privileges as such."

JULY 1, 1819
NEW HAMPSHIRE TOLERATION ACT

An Act, in amendment of an Act entitled an Act, for Regulating Towns and the Choice of Town Officers, passed February 8th, Anno Domini 1791,—

SECTION 1. Be it enacted...That the inhabitants of each town in this State...may grant...sums of money...for the support of schools, school houses, the maintenance of the poor, for laying out and repairing highways, for building and repairing bridges...

SECTION 2. And be it further enacted, That the tenth section of the Act, to which this is an amendment, be and the same is hereby repealed. Provided that towns between which and any settled **minister** there is prior to, or at the passing of this act a subsisting contract, shall have a right from time to time to vote, assess, collect and appropriate such sum or sums of money as may be necessary for the fulfillment of such contract and for repairing meetinghouses now owned by such town so far as may be necessary to render them useful for town purposes—

Provided that no person shall be liable to taxation for the purpose of fulfilling any contract between any town and settled **minister** who shall prior to such assessment file with the town clerk of the town where he may reside a certificate declaring that he is not of the **religious persuasion** or **opinion** of the **minister** settled in such town.

SECTION 3. And be it further enacted, that each **religious sect** or **denomination** of **Christians** in this State may associate and form **societies**, may admit members, may **establish** rules and byelaws for their regulation and government, and shall have all the corporate powers which may be necessary to assess and raise money by taxes upon the polls and rateable estate of the members of such associations, and to collect and appropriate the same for the purpose of building and repairing houses of **public worship**, and for the support of the **Ministry**; and the assessors and collectors of such associations shall have the same powers in assessing and collecting, and shall be liable to the same penalties as similar town officers have and are liable to-

Provided that no person shall be compelled to join or support, or be classed with, or associated to any **congregation**, **Church** or **religious society** without his express consent first had and obtain-

Provided also, if any person shall choose to separate himself from such **society, or association** to which he may belong, and shall leave a written notice thereof with the clerk of such **society or association**, he shall thereupon be no longer liable for any future expenses which may be incurred by said **society or association-**

Provided also, that no **association or society** shall exercise the powers herein granted until it shall have assumed a name and style by which such **Society** may be known and distinguished in law.

1877
NEW HAMPSHIRE CONSTITUTION, AMENDED

ARTICLE 14 amended, removing requirement that office holders be Protestant.

1968
NEW HAMPSHIRE CONSTITUTION

ARTICLE 5. Every individual has a natural and unalienable right to **worship God** according to the **dictates of his own conscience**, and reason; and no subject shall be hurt, molested, or restrained, in his person, liberty, or estate, for **worshipping God** in the manner and season most agreeable to the **dictates of his own conscience**; or for his **religious profession**, **sentiments**, or **persuasion**; provided he doth not disturb the public peace or disturb others in their **religious worship**.

ARTICLE 6. As **morality** and **piety**, rightly grounded on **high principles**, will give the best and greatest security to government, and will lay, in the hearts of men, the strongest obligations to due subjection; and as the knowledge of these is most likely to be **propagated** through a **society**, therefore, the several **parishes**, bodies, corporate, or **religious societies** shall at all times have the right of electing their own **teachers**, and of contracting with them for their support or maintenance, or both.

But no person shall ever be compelled to pay towards the support of the schools of any **sect** or **denomination**. And every person, **denomination** or **sect** shall be equally under the protection of the law; and no subordination of any one **sect, denomination** or **persuasion** to another shall ever be **established**. Amended 1968 to remove obsolete **sectarian** references.

ARTICLE 84. Any person chosen governor, councilor, senator, or representative, military or civil officer... shall...make and subscribe the following declaration, viz.

"I, A.B. do solemnly swear, that I will bear **faith** and true allegiance to the United States of America and the state of New Hampshire, and will support the constitution thereof. **So Help Me God**." June 2, 1784, Amended 1792 three times, changing president to governor; shortening oath of allegiance; and dispensing with need to take second oath. Amended 1970 adding allegiance to the United States of America.

AUGUST 18, 1981
OATH, TITLE 51, COURTS, CHP. 500-A:18

I. The oath to be administered to jurors in civil cases shall be as follows...:

You swear that, in all cases between party and party that shall be committed to you, you will give a true verdict, according to law and evidence given you. **So Help You God**.

II. If any person selected as a juror is of a **denomination** called **Quakers** or is scrupulous of swearing, and declines to take the oath, the person shall take and subscribe the oath, omitting the words "swear" and "**So Help Me God**", substituting in place thereof, "affirm...under the pains and penalties of perjury".

SECTION 516:19...No other ceremony shall be necessary in swearing than holding up the right hand, but any other form or ceremony may be used which the person to whom the oath is administered professes to believe more binding upon the **conscience**. Source. RS 188:10. CS 200:10. 1860, 2364. GS 209:10. GL 228:10. PS 224:10. PL 336:21. RL 392:19.

SECTION 516:20...Persons scrupulous of swearing may affirm; the word "affirm" being used in administering the oath, instead of the word "swear," and the words "this you do under the pains and penalties of perjury," instead of the words "**So Help You God**." Source. RS 188:11. CS 200:11. GS 209:11. GL 228:11. PS 224:11. PL 336:22. RL 392:20.

SECTION 516:21...No person who **believes in the existence of a Supreme Being** shall be excluded from testifying on account of his opinions on **matters of religion**. Source. RS 188:9. CS 200:9. GS 209:12. GL 228:12. PS 224:12. PL 336:23. RL 392:21.

TITLE LIX, PROCEEDINGS IN CRIMINAL CASES, GRAND JURIES, SECTION 600:3...Grand jurors before entering upon their duties shall take the following oath: You, as grand jurors, do solemnly swear that you will diligently inquire, and a true presentment make, of all such matters and things as shall be given you in charge...**So Help You God**.

TITLE LX, CORRECTION & PUNISHMENT, CHAPTER 622, STATE PRISONS, SECTION 622:23...Inmates shall have **freedom of religious belief** and freedom to **worship God** according to the **dictates of their consciences**, but this shall not permit anything inconsistent with proper discipline. Source. 1881, 39:1. PS 285:25. PL 400:26. RL 464:24.

TITLE XII, PUBLIC SAFETY AND WELFARE, CHAPTER 169-B, DELINQUENT CHILDREN, SECTION 169-B:33...The court...in placing minors, shall, as far as practicable, place them in the care and custody of some individual holding the same **religious beliefs** as the minor or the parents of said minor...No minor under the supervision of any state institution shall be denied the **free exercise of the minor's own religion** or the **religion** of the parents, whether living or dead, nor the **liberty of worshipping God** according thereto. Source. 1979, 361:2. 1995, 302:21, eff. Jan. 1, 1996.

NEW HAMPSHIRE RELIGIOUS AFFILIATION

The Encyclopedia Britannica, 11th edition, published in 1911, stated:

The **Roman Catholic Church** in 1906 had more members than any other **religious denomination** (119,86 3 out of 190,298 **communicants** of all **denominations**); in the same year there were 19,070 **Congregationalists**, 15,974 **Baptists**, 12,529 **Methodist Episcopalians** (North) and 4,892 **Protestant Episcopalians.**

http://www.1911encyclopedia.org/
New_Hampshire#Population

The Catholic Encyclopedia, Volume XV, Copyright 1912 by Robert Appleton Company, stated as of 1906, a census listed **New Hampshire** as:

Congregationalists - 19,070
Methodists - 12,529
Baptists - 9,741
Free Baptists - 6,210
Unitarians - 3,629
Universalists - 1,993
Advent Christians - 1,608
Christians - 1,303
Presbyterians - 842
Catholics - 126,000 **Catholics**, consisting of French Canadians-66,200, Irish-52,250, Poles-5,000, Lithuanians-1,500, Ruthenians-750, with 118 secular **priests**, and 19 regulars; in 99 **Churches**, 24 **Chapels**, and 34 stations; over 13,000 children in **parochial schools**, 7 orphan asylums caring for 718 orphans, 5 homes for working girls with many other charitable institutions.

In 1903, **Catholics** numbered 100,000 in 91 **Churches**, 24 **chapels**, 36 **stations**, 107 **priests**, 12,00 children in the **parochial schools**, 4 hospitals, 4 homes for aged women. In 1884, **Catholics** numbered 45, 000 in 27 **Churches**, 5 **convents**, 40 **priests**, and 3,000 children in the **parochial schools**.

http://www.newadvent.org/cathen/10785a.htm

The Wikipedia Online Encyclopedia, as of 2006, listed **New Hampshire** as:

Christian - 80 percent, consisting of:
- **Congregational/Church** of **Christ** - 7 percent
- **Baptist** - 7 percent
- **Episcopal** - 4 percent
- **Methodist** - 3 percent
- **Other Protestant** - 22 percent
- **Catholic** - 35 percent
- **Other Christian** - 2 percent

Jewish - 1 percent
Other Religions - 1 percent
Non-Religious/Non-Reporting - 19 percent

http://en.wikipedia.org/wiki/New_Hampshire#Religion

Churches established by early **Puritan** settlers were forerunners of the modern **Congregationalist Churches**. While the **denomination** remains active, **Methodists** and **Baptists** have become the largest **Protestant denominations**. The **Roman Catholic Church** is the largest **religious** group, with about 2/5 of all **Church** members.

http://encarta.msn.com/encyclopedia_761577742_5/New_Hampshire.html

The U.S. Religious Landscape Survey, conducted by The Pew Forum on Religion & Public Life, 2007, published in the USA Today, listed **New Hampshire** as:

Christian - 64.5 percent, consisting of:
- **Evangelical Protestant** - 11 percent

Mainline Protestant - 23 percent
Black Protestant - <0.5 percent
Catholic - 29 percent
Orthodox - <0.5 percent
Other Christian - <0.5 percent

Mormon - 1 percent
Jehovah's Witnesses - <0.5 percent
Jewish - 1 percent
Muslim - <0.5 percent
Buddhist - 1 percent
Hindu - <0.5 percent
Other World Religions - <0.5 percent
Other Faiths - 7 percent
Unaffiliated - 26 percent
Did not answer - <0.5 percent

www.pewforum.org
www.usatoday.com/news/graphics/pew-religion-08/flash.htm

VERMONT
FREEDOM
& UNITY

VERMONT

Vermont, pronounced in French "verts monts," meaning Green Mountain, was part of New Hampshire at the time of America's Revolutionary War. It was originally part of New France, as area explored by Jacque Cartier in 1534.

Samuel de Champlain was sent there in 1603 by French King Henry IV to begin a settlement. Because growth was slow, Cardinal Richelieu, Prime **Minister** for King Louis XIII, founded the Company of One Hundred Associates on April 29, 1627, to bring more colonists, increase fur trade and require all settlers to be **Catholic**.

The first settlement in area of Vermont was Fort Sainte Anne, erected in 1666 on Isle La Motte to fortify Lake Champlain. This was the site of the first **Roman Catholic Mass** in the State. In 1690, **Dutch Reformed** settlers arrived. During the French and Indian War, in 1759, British commander Jeffrey Amherst captured French Fort St. Frédéric and Fort Carillon, renaming the later Fort Ticonderoga. Ethan Allen's Green Mountain Boys captured Fort Ticonderoga in 1775.

Many French survivors were killed a year later by the Mohawks. The colonies of Massachusetts, New Hampshire and New York all claimed the area of Vermont. Massachusetts relinquished its claims and New Hampshire issued land grants to proprietors, who subdivided it into lots. Some of these lots were set aside for the **Society for the Propagation of the Gospel in Foreign Parts, a missionary organization of the Church of England**, some for the **Church of England** itself, and some for the first **clergyman** who would settle in each township.

When the Revolutionary War began, Vermont fought both Britain and New York, resulting in it being its own nation for 14 years, similar to Texas and Hawaii. In 1791, Vermont applied to be the 14th State of the Union, being accepted by President George Washington.

Predominant **denominations** were **Congregationalists, Episcopalians** and **Baptists**, followed by **Methodists, Presbyterians, Free Will Baptists** and **Quakers**. In the early 1800's there were some **Unitarians, Universalists,** and **unconventional sects**, such as **Millerites** and **Perfectionists.**

Beginning in 1820 with the **Second Great Awakening, revivalism** swept Vermont and academies with **religious affiliations** were founded. Anti-slavery sentiment grew strong. In the 1840's the **Catholic Church** increased with French Canadians and Irish immigrants.

In the late 1800's, **Judaism**, Welsh **Presbyterianism**, Swedish **Lutheranism** and **Greek Orthodoxy** made a presence.

MARCH 1534
COMMISSION OF KING FRANCIS I TO JACQUE CARTIER

Other than the line "to discover certain islands and lands where it is said a great quantity of gold and other precious things are to be found," the actual commission has not been found. It reportedly stated the objectives of finding a route to Asia and **establishing Churches among Natives of the New World.**

APRIL 29, 1627
COMPANY OF A HUNDRED ASSOCIATES (COMPAGNIE DES CENT-ASSOCIÉS)

King Henry the Great, our father of glorious memory, did seek and discover the lands and countries of New France, known as Canada, some able dwelling to **establish** a colony there, in order to, **with Divine assistance,** bring the peoples living there to the **knowledge of the true God**, and to organize and instruct in the **Apostolic** and **Roman Catholic faith** and **religion**..."

JULY 8, 1777
CONSTITUTION OF VERMONT

Whereas, all government ought to be instituted and supported, for the security and protection of the community, as such, and to enable the individuals who compose it, to enjoy their natural rights, and **the other blessings which the Author of Existence has bestowed upon man;** and whenever those great ends of government are not obtained, the people have a right, by common consent, to change it, and take such measures as to them may appear necessary to promote their safety and happiness...

And whereas, the inhabitants of this State have (in consideration of protection only) heretofore acknowledged allegiance to the King of Great Britain, and the said King has not only withdrawn that protection, but commenced, and still continues to carry on, with unabated vengeance, a most cruel and unjust war against them; employing therein, not only the troops of Great Britain, but foreign mercenaries, savages and slaves, for the avowed purpose of reducing them to a total and abject submission to the despotic domination of the British parliament, with many other acts of tyranny, (more fully set forth in the declaration of Congress) whereby all allegiance and fealty to the said King and his successors, are dissolved and at an end; and all power and authority derived from him, ceased in the American Colonies.

And whereas, the territory which now comprehends the State of Vermont, did antecedently, of right, belong to the government of New Hampshire; and the former Governor thereof, viz. his Excellency Benning Wentworth, Esq., granted many charters of lands and corporations, within this State, to the present inhabitants and others.

And whereas, the late Lieutenant Governor Colden, of New York, with others, did, in violation of the tenth command, covet those very lands; and by a false representation made to the court of Great Britain...

Therefore, it is absolutely necessary, for the welfare and safety of the inhabitants of this State, that it should be, henceforth, a free and independent State; and that a just, permanent, and proper form of government, should exist in it, derived from, and founded on, the authority of the people only, agreeable to the direction of the honorable American Congress.

We the representatives of the freemen of Vermont, in General Convention met, for the express purpose of forming such a government, **confessing the goodness of the Great Governor of the Universe, (who alone, knows to what degree of earthly happiness, mankind may attain**, by perfecting the arts of government,) in permitting the people of this State, by common consent, and without violence, deliberately to form for themselves, such just rules as they shall think best for governing their future society;

And being fully convinced that it is our indispensable duty, to **establish** such original principles of government, as will best promote the general happiness of the people of this State, and their posterity, and provide for future improvements, without partiality for, or prejudice against, any particular class, **sect,** or **denomination** of men whatever,

Do, by virtue of authority vested in us, by our constituents, ordain, declare, and **establish**, the following declaration of rights, and frame of government, to be the CONSTITUTION of this COMMONWEALTH...

CHAPTER 1, A DECLARATION OF THE RIGHTS OF THE INHABITANTS OF THE STATE OF VERMONT

1. That all men are born equally free and independent, and have certain natural, inherent and unalienable rights, amongst which are the enjoying and defending life and liberty; acquiring, possessing and protecting property, and pursuing and obtaining happiness and safety. Therefore, no male person, born in this country, or brought from over sea, ought to be holden by law, to serve any person, as a servant, slave or apprentice, after he arrives to the age of twenty-one Years, nor female, in like manner, after she arrives to the age of eighteen years, unless they are bound by their own consent, after they arrive to such age, or bound by law, for the payment of debts, damages, fines, costs, or the like.

2. That private property ought to be subservient to public uses, when necessity requires it; nevertheless, whenever any particular man's property is taken for the use of the public, the owner ought to receive an equivalent in money.

3. That all men have a natural and unalienable right to **worship ALMIGHTY GOD**, according to the **dictates of their own consciences** and understanding, regulated by the **word of GOD**; and that no man ought, or of right can be compelled to attend any **religious worship**, or erect, or support any **place of worship**, or maintain any **minister**, contrary to the **dictates of his conscience;**

Nor can any man who professes the **Protestant religion**, be justly deprived or abridged of any civil right, as a citizen, on account of his **religious sentiment,** or peculiar **mode of religious worship**, and that no authority can, or ought to be vested in, or assumed by, any power whatsoever, that shall, in any case, interfere with, or in any manner control, the **rights of conscience**, in the **free exercise of religious worship**: nevertheless, every **sect** or **denomination** of people ought to observe the **Sabbath**, or the **Lord's Day**, and keep up, and support, some sort of **religious worship**, which to them shall seem most agreeable to the **revealed Will of GOD**...

14. That the people have a right to freedom of speech, and of writing and publishing their sentiments; therefore, the freedom of the press ought not be restrained.

15. That the people have a right to bear arms for the defense of themselves and the State; and, as standing armies, in the time of peace, are dangerous to liberty, they ought not to be kept up; and that the military should be kept under strict subordination to, and governed by, the civil power...

CHAPTER 2, PLAN OR FRAME OF GOVERNMENT, SECTION 6. Every man of the full age of twenty-one years, having resided in this State for the space-of one whole year, next before the election of representatives, and who is of a quiet and peaceable behavior, and will take the following oath (or affirmation) shall be entitled to all the privileges of a freeman of this State.

I_____ solemnly swear, by the **ever living God**, (or affirm, in the **presence of Almighty God**,) that whenever I am called to give any vote or suffrage, touching any matter that concerns the State of Vermont, I will do it so, as in arty **conscience**, I shall judge will roost conduce to the best good of the same, as **established** by the constitution, without fear or favor of any man...

SECTION 9. A quorum of the house of representatives shall consist of two-thirds of the whole number of members elected; and having met and chosen their speaker, shall, each of them, before they proceed to business, take and subscribe, as well the oath of fidelity and allegiance herein after directed, as the following oath or affirmation, viz.

"I ____ do solemnly swear, by the **ever living God**, (or, I do solemnly affirm in the **presence of Almighty God**) that as a member of this Assembly, I will not propose or assent to any bill, vote, or resolution, which shall appear to me injurious to the people; nor do or consent to any act or thing whatever, that shall have a tendency to lessen or abridge their rights and privileges, as declared in the Constitution of this State; but will, in all things' conduct myself as a faithful, honest representative and guardian of the people, according to the best of my judgment and abilities."

And each member, before he takes his seat, shall make and subscribe the following declaration, viz.

"I ____ do believe in **one God, the Creator and Governor of the Universe, the Rewarder of the good and Punisher of the wicked.** And I do acknowledge the **Scriptures** of the **Old and New Testament** to be given by **Divine inspiration**, and own and profess the **Protestant religion**."

And no further or other **religious test** shall ever, hereafter, be required of any civil officer or magistrate in this State...

THE OATH OR AFFIRMATION OF ALLEGIANCE

"I ____ do solemnly swear by the **ever living God**, (or affirm in **presence of Almighty God**,) that I will be true and faithful to the State of Vermont; and that I will not, directly or indirectly do any act or thing, prejudicial or injurious, to the constitution or government thereof, as **established** by Convention."

THE OATH OR AFFIRMATION OF OFFICE

"I _____ do solemnly swear by the **ever living God**, (or affirm in **presence of Almighty God**) that I will faithfully execute the office of______and will do equal right and justice to all men, to the best of my judgment and abilities, according to law."...

SECTION 41. Laws for the encouragement of virtue and prevention of vice and immorality, shall be made and constantly kept in force; and provision shall be made for their due execution; and all **religious societies** or bodies of men, that have or may be hereafter united and incorporated, for the advancement of **religion** and learning, or for other pious and charitable purposes, shall be encouraged and protected in the enjoyment of the privileges, immunities and estates which they, in justice, ought to enjoy, under such regulations; as the General Assembly of this State shall direct.

JULY 4, 1786
CONSTITUTION OF VERMONT

Whereas all government ought to be instituted and supported for the security and protection of the community as such, and to enable the individuals, who compose it, to enjoy their natural rights, and the other **blessings** which the **Author of Existence** has bestowed upon man: and whenever those great ends of government are not obtained, the people have a right, by common consent, to change it, and take such measures as to them may appear necessary to promote their safety and happiness...

CHAPTER 1, A DECLARATION OF THE RIGHTS OF THE, INHABITANTS OF THE STATE OF VERMONT

1. THAT all men are born equally free and independent, and have certain natural, inherent and unalienable rights; amongst which are, the enjoying and defending life and liberty-acquiring, possessing and protecting property-and pursuing and obtaining happiness and safety. Therefore, no male person, born in this country, or brought from over sea, ought to be holden by law to serve any person, as a servant, slave, or apprentice, after

he arrives to the age of twenty one Years; nor female, in like manner, after she arrives to the age of eighteen years; unless they are bound by their own consent after they arrive to such age; or bound by law for the payment of debts, damages, fines, costs, or the like...

3. That all men have a natural and unalienable right to **worship Almighty God** according to the **dictates of their own consciences** and understandings, as In their opinion shall be regulated by the **word of God**; and that no man ought, or of right can be compelled to attend any **religious worship**, or erect or support any **place of worship**, or maintain any **minister**, contrary to the **dictates of his conscience**; nor can any man be justly deprived or abridged of any civil right as a citizen, on account of his **religious sentiments**, or peculiar **mode of religious worship**; and that no authority can, or ought to be vested in, or assumed by any power whatsoever, that shall in any case interfere with, or in any manner control the **rights of conscience**, in the **free exercise of religious worship**: Nevertheless, every **sect** or **denomination** of **Christians** ought to observe the **Sabbath** or **Lord's Day**, and keep up some sort of **religious worship**, which to them shall seem most agreeable to the **revealed Will of God**...

15. That the people have a right of freedom of speech and of writing and publishing their sentiments, concerning the transactions of government-and therefore the freedom of the press ought not to be restrained...

18. That the people have a right to bear arms, for the defense of themselves and the State: and as standing armies, in the time of peace, are dangerous to liberty, they ought not to be kept up; and that the military should be kept under strict subordination to, and governed by the civil power...

CHAPTER 2, PLAN OR FRAME OF GOVERNMENT

12. The representatives, having met, and chosen their speaker and clerk, shall each of them, before they proceed to business, take and subscribe, as well the oath or affirmation of allegiance herein after directed (except where they, shall produce certificates of their having heretofore taken and subscribed the same) as the following oath or affirmation, viz.

"You do solemnly swear, (or affirm) that, as a member of this Assembly, you will not propose or assent to any bill, vote, or resolution, which shall appear to you injurious to the people; nor do nor consent to any act or thing whatever, that shall have a tendency to lessen or abridge their rights and privileges as declared by the Constitution of this State; but will, in all things, conduct yourself as a faithful, honest representative and guardian of the people, according to the best of your judgment and abilities. (In case of an oath) **So Help You God**." (And in case of an affirmation) Under the pains and penalties of perjury.

And each member, before he takes his seat, shall make and subscribe the following declaration, viz.

"You do believe in one **God**, the **Creator** and **Governor of the Universe**, the Rewarder of the good, and Punisher of the wicked. And you do acknowledge the **Scriptures** of the **Old and New Testament** to be given by **Divine inspiration**; and own and profess the **Protestant religion**."

And no further or other **religious test** shall ever hereafter be required of any civil officer or magistrate, in this State...

THE OATH OR AFFIRMATION OF ALLEGIANCE

"You __ do solemnly swear (or affirm) that you will be true and faithful to the State of Vermont; and that you will not, directly nor indirectly, do any act or thing injurious to the Constitution or government thereof, as **established** by Convention. (If an oath) **So Help You God**." (If an affirmation) Under the pains and penalties of perjury.

THE OATH OR AFFIRMATION OF OFFICE

"You __do solemnly swear, (or affirm) that you will faithfully execute the office of___ for the___ of___; and will therein do equal right and justice to all men, to the best of your judgment and abilities, according to law. (If an oath) **So Help You God**." (If an affirmation) Under the pains and penalties of perjury...

38. Laws for the encouragement of virtue, and prevention of vice and immorality, ought to be constantly kept in force, and duly executed; and a competent number of schools ought to be maintained in each town for the convenient instruction of youth; and one or more grammar schools be incorporated, and properly supported in each county in this State. And all **religious societies**, or bodies of men, that may be hereafter united or incorporated, for the advancement of **religion** and learning, or for other pious and charitable purposes, shall be encouraged and protected in the enjoyment of the privileges, immunities, and estates, which they in justice ought to enjoy, under such regulations as the General Assembly of this State shall direct.

1793
CONSTITUTION OF VERMONT
(AS AMENDED NOVEMBER 5, 2002)

CHAPTER 1, ARTICLE 1. That all persons are born equally free and independent, and have certain natural, inherent, and unalienable rights, amongst which are the enjoying and defending life and liberty, acquiring, possessing and protecting property...

No person born in this country, or brought from over sea, ought to be holden by law, to serve any person as a servant, slave or apprentice, after arriving to the age of twenty-one years, unless bound by the person's own consent...

CHAPTER 1, ARTICLE 3. That all persons have a natural and unalienable right, to **worship Almighty God**, according to the **dictates of their own consciences** and understandings, as in their opinion shall be regulated by the **word of God**; and that no person ought to, or of right can be compelled to attend any **religious worship**, or erect or support any **place of worship**, or maintain any **minister**, contrary to the **dictates of conscience**, nor can any person be justly deprived or abridged of any civil right as a citizen, on account of **religious sentiments**, or peculiar **mode of religious worship**; and that no authority can, or ought to be vested in, or assumed by, any power whatever, that shall in any case interfere with, or in any manner control the **rights of conscience**, in the **free exercise of religious worship**.

Nevertheless, every **sect** or **denomination** of **Christians** ought to observe the **Sabbath** or **Lord's Day**, and keep up some sort of **religious worship**, which to them shall seem most agreeable to the **revealed Will of God**.

CHAPTER 1, ARTICLE 13. That the people have a right to freedom of speech, and of writing and publishing their sentiments, concerning the transactions of government, and therefore the freedom of the press ought not to be restrained.

CHAPTER 2, SECTION 17. The Representatives having met on the day appointed by law for the commencement of a biennial session of the General Assembly and chosen their Speaker, and the Senators having met, shall, before they proceed to business, take and subscribe the following oath, in addition to the oath prescribed in the foregoing section:

"You _____ do solemnly swear (or affirm) that you did not at the time of your election to this body, and that you do not now, hold any office of profit or trust under the authority of Congress. **So Help You God**. (Or in the case of an affirmation)"

CHAPTER 2, SECTION 56. Every officer, whether judicial, executive, or military, in authority under this State, before entering upon the execution of office, shall take and subscribe the following oath...

"You do solemnly swear (or affirm) that you will be true and faithful to the State of Vermont, and that you will not, directly or indirectly, do any act or thing injurious to the Constitution or Government thereof. (If an oath) **So Help You God**. (If an affirmation) Under the pains and penalties of perjury."

The Oath or Affirmation of Office:

"You do solemnly swear (or affirm) that you will faithfully execute the office of _____ for the _____ of _____ and will therein do equal right and justice to all persons, to the best of your judgment and ability, according to law. (If an oath) **So Help You God**. (If an affirmation) Under the pains and penalties of perjury."

VERMONT RELIGIOUS AFFILIATION

The Encyclopedia Britannica, 11th edition, published in 1911, stated:

Of 147,223 **communicants** of all **Churches** in Vermont in 1906, the largest number, 82,272, were **Roman Catholics;** 22,109 were **Congregationalists;** 17,471 **Methodist Episcopalians;** 8,450 **Baptists;** 1,501 **Free Baptists;** and 5,278 **Protestant Episcopalians**.

http://www.1911encyclopedia.org/
Vermont#Population

The Catholic Encyclopedia, Volume XV, Copyright 1912 by Robert Appleton Company, stated as of 1906, a census listed **Vermont** as:

Catholic - 77,389 members divided between Irish and Canadians, with two Polish **congregations** and a few others, in 97 **Churches** and 25 **missions**
Congregationalists - 20,271 with 186 **ministers** in 197 **Churches**
Methodists - 16,067 members with 161 **ministers** in 182 **Churches**
Baptists - 8,623 members with 111 **ministers** in 105 **Churches**
Free Baptists - 4,000 members in 60 **Churches**
Episcopalians - 3,926 **communicants** with 36 **ministers** in 52 **parishes**
Adventists - 1,750 members in 35 **Churches**

http://www.newadvent.org/cathen/15354b.htm

The Wikipedia Online Encyclopedia, as of 2006, listed **Vermont** as:

Chrisstian - 73 percent, consisting of:
- **Congregational/U.Church of Christ** - 7 percent
- **Methodist** - 7 percent
- **Episcopal** - 5 percent
- **Baptist** - 3 percent
- **Other Protestant** - 12 percent
- **Catholic** - 39 percent
- **Other Christian** - 1 percent

Jewish - 1 percent
Other Religions - 1 percent
Non-Religious/Non-Reporting - 24 percent

http://en.wikipedia.org/wiki/Vermont#Religion

The U.S. Religious Landscape Survey, conducted by The Pew Forum on Religion & Public Life, 2007, published in the USA Today, listed **Vermont** as:

- **Christian** - 74.5 percent, consisting of:
  - **Evangelical Protestant** - 11 percent
  - **Mainline Protestant** - 23 percent
  - **Black Protestant** - <0.5 percent
  - **Catholic** - 29 percent
  - **Orthodox** - <0.5 percent
  - **Other Christian** - <0.5 percent
- **Mormon** - 1 percent
- **Jehovah's Witnesses** - <0.5 percent
- **Jewish** - 1 percent
- **Muslim** - <0.5 percent
- **Buddhist** - 1 percent
- **Hindu** - <0.5 percent
- **Other World Religions** - <0.5 percent
- **Other Faiths** - 7 percent
- **Unaffiliated** - 26 percent
- **Did not answer** - <0.5 percent

www.pewforum.org
www.usatoday.com/news/graphics/pew-religion-08/flash.htm

SIGILLUM REIPUBLICÆ CONNECTICUTENSIS
QUI TRANSTULIT SUSTINET

CONNECTICUT

In 1614, Dutch traders from New Amsterdam sailed up the Connecticut River and in 1623 set up a fort, which was later abandoned. Traders from the Plymouth Colony settled the first English settlement on the Connecticut River in 1635. Thomas Hooker, driven out of England by **Anglican Archbishop** William Laud, became the **pastor** of the eighth **Church** in the colony of Massachusetts. After a dispute with **Puritan** leader John Cotton, Hooker left with one hundred people to found Hartford in 1636.

Thomas Hooker's sermon, in which he **preached** that **Churches** should be independent and each member of the **congregation** should have an equal vote - called **Congregational** - was adapted into the Fundamental Orders and adopted by Hartford, Windsor and Wethersfield on January 24, 1639, as the first written constitution in America. It provided that each citizen would have an equal vote for governor, magistrates, and a General Court with legislative and judicial powers.

In 1661, Governor John Winthrop petitioned King Charles II for a charter, which, when granted in 1664, forcibly combined Hartford with Saybrook and New Haven to form the Commonwealth of Connecticut. The Fundamental Orders were used as the Constitution of Connecticut until a new Constitution was adopted in 1818.

In 1786, Connecticut ceded to the United States its public land in the west, called the "Western Reserve," which later became the State of Ohio.

Though the majority of the population was English **Puritan**, Irish immigration increase before the Revolution, and again after the Irish potato famine of 1846. Other immigrants arrived from Germany, French Canada, Italy and later Russian **Jews**, Scandinavians, Lithuanians, and Greeks.

Citizens of Connecticut furnished more soldiers for the Revolutionary War than Virginia, surpassed only by Massachusetts.

Membership in the **Congregational Church** was a qualification for civil office and for the exercise of civil rights. **Congregationalism** was the **established religion** and supported by public taxation, though other **Christian sects** were gradually given limited **toleration**.

Sunday observance was strictly enforced by law, and, except for works of necessity or **mercy**, statutes charged a fine not exceeding fifty dollars to any person who engaged on **Sunday** in secular business, labor, keeping open a shop, warehouse, manufacturing **establishment**, and exposing any property for sale. Statutes fined any person not more than four dollars who, on **Sunday**, attended a concert of music, danced, engaged in a sport or other public diversion. Saloons and sale of liquor was prohibited on **Sunday**.

Judges, magistrates, clerks of courts and officials were required to take an oath, which universally was raising the right hand in the presence of the magistrate, always beginning with the words "You solemnly swear" and ending with the invocation "**So Help You God**".

Statutes against **blasphemy** and **profanity** existed since the settlement of the colony, with severe punishments. Statutes of 1642 and 1650 provide that one who **blasphemes God, any person of the Holy Trinity, the Christian religion, or the Holy Scriptures**, shall be fined not more than one hundred dollars and imprisoned not more than one year. One who shall use any profane oath or wickedly curse anyone shall be fined one dollar.

It was customary to open daily sessions of both houses of the General Assembly with **prayer** by **chaplains** appointed by each body whose salaries were fixed by law. Supreme and Superior courts were opened with **prayer** by a **clergyman** who was paid an honorarium.

The governor proclaimed a day of thanksgiving in the late autumn to be observed as a **religious holiday**.

Christmas received little recognition among the **Congregationalists** of Connecticut and the other New England States until the latter half of the nineteenth century when **Episcopalians** and **Catholics** population increased, resulting in December 25th being declared by statute a legal holiday.

Earlier settlers proclaimed by legal authority a day in early spring for **fasting** and **prayer**. The governor customarily selected **Good Friday** as the **annual spring fast**. Though **Christmas** and **Good Friday** have been recognized by the civil authority, no statute ever compelled their observance.

In 1835 a census taken by **Bishop** Fenwick of Boston found only 720 **Catholics** in Connecticut, and in 1844 only 4,817 **Catholics**. By 1890, due in large part to Irish immigration, **Catholics** increased to 152,945, outnumbering the **communicants** of all **Protestant denominations**. In 1899, with the immigration of Germans, Italians, French Canadians, and Poles, **Catholic** population in Connecticut exceeded 250,000, and in 1908 reached 395,354, with a remaining non-**Catholic** population of 725,000.

In 1843, Hartford **Jews** petitioned the legislature to amend the State Constitution to permit **public worship** by **Jews**, followed by the prompt enactment of an enabling public act, which set in motion the beginning of **synagogue** building which contributed to the growth of the **Jewish community** as well as to the architecture of the state.

Connecticut, being one of the few states to do so, has inventoried the entire state's historic **Jewish religious** sites, listing 46 historic **synagogue** buildings.

Russian **Jews** settled in Hartford, Connecticut between 1881 and 1930, and after 1975, Soviet **Jews** emigrated.

JANUARY 14, 1639
FUNDAMENTAL ORDERS

For as much as it hath pleased **Almighty God** by the wise disposition of his **Divine Providence** so to order and dispose of things that we the Inhabitants and Residents of Windsor, Hartford and Wethersfield are now cohabiting and dwelling in and upon the River of Connectecotte and the lands thereunto adjoining;

And well knowing where a people are gathered together the word of **God** requires that to maintain the peace and union of such a people there should be an orderly and decent Government **established** according to **God**, to order and dispose of the affairs of the people at all seasons as occasion shall require;

Do therefore associate and conjoin ourselves to be as one Public State or Commonwealth; and do for ourselves and our successors and such as shall be adjoined to us at any time hereafter, enter into Combination and Confederation together, to maintain and preserve the liberty and **purity** of the **Gospel of our Lord Jesus** which we now **profess**, as also, the **discipline** of the **Churches**, which according to the truth of the said **Gospel** is now **practiced** amongst us;

As also in our civil affairs to be guided and governed according to such Laws, Rules, Orders and Decrees as shall be made, ordered, and decreed as followeth...

The Governor, which being chosen and sworn according to an Oath recorded for that purpose, shall have the power to administer justice according to the Laws here **established**, and for want thereof, according to the **Rule of the Word of God**."

JUNE 4, 1639
CONSTITUTION OF THE COLONY OF NEW HAVEN

All the free planters assembled together in a general meeting, to consult about settling civil government, according to **GOD**, and the nomination of persons that might be found, by consent of all, fittest in all respects for the foundation work of a **Church**, which was intended to be gathered in Quinipiack. After **solemn invocation of the name of GOD**, in **prayer for the presence and help of his spirit and grace**, in those weighty businesses, they were reminded of the business whereabout they met, (viz.) for the **establishment** of such civil order as might be most pleasing unto **GOD**, and for the choosing the fittest men for the foundation work of a **Church** to be gathered.

For the better enabling them to discern the mind of **GOD**, and to agree accordingly concerning the **establishment** of civil order, Mr. John Davenport propounded divers queries to them **publicly**, **praying** them to consider seriously in the presence and fear of **GOD**, the weight of the business they met about, and not to be rash or slight in giving their votes to things they understood not; but to digest fully and thoroughly what should be propounded to them, and without respect to men, as they should be satisfied and persuaded in their own minds, to give their answers in such sort as they would be willing should stand upon record for posterity.

This being earnestly pressed by Mr. Davenport, Mr. Robert Newman was entreated to write, in characters, and to read distinctly and audibly in the hearing of all the people, what was propounded and accorded on, that it might appear, that all consented to matters propounded, according to words written by him.

QUERY 1. WHETHER the **Scriptures** do hold forth a perfect rule for the direction and government of all men in all duties which they are to perform to **GOD** and men, as well in families and commonwealth, as in **matters of the Church**? This was assented unto by all, no man **dissenting**, as was expressed by holding up of hands. Afterwards it was read over to them, that they might see in what words their vote was expressed. They again expressed their consent by holding up their hands, no man **dissenting**.

QUERY 2. WHEREAS there was a covenant solemnly made by the whole **Assembly** of free planters of this plantation, the first day of extraordinary **humiliation**, which we had after we came together, that as in matters that concern the gathering and ordering of a **Church**, so likewise in all public officers which concern civil order, as choice of magistrates and officers, making and repealing laws, dividing allotments of inheritance, and all things of like nature, we would all of us be ordered by those rules which the **Scripture** holds forth to US; this covenant was called a plantation covenant, to distinguish it from a **Church** covenant, which could not at that time be made a **Church** not being then gathered, but was deferred till a **Church** might be gathered, according to **GOD**.

It was demanded whether all the free planters do hold themselves bound by that covenant, in all businesses of that nature which are expressed in the covenant, to submit themselves to be ordered by the rules held forth in the **Scripture**...

This also was assented unto by all, and no man gainsayed it; and they did testify the same by holding up their hands, both when it was first propounded, and confirmed the same by holding up their hands when it was read unto them in public. John Clark being absent, when the covenant was made, doth now manifest his consent to it...

QUERY 3. THOSE who have desired to be received as free planters, and are settled in the plantation, with a purpose, resolution and desire, that they may be admitted into **Church fellowship**, according to **CHRIST**, as soon as **GOD** shall fit them "hereunto, were desired to express it by holding up hands. According all did express this to be their desire and purpose by holding up their hands twice (viz.) at the proposal of it, and after when these written words were read unto them.

QUERY 4. All the free planters were called upon to express, whether they held themselves bound to **establish** such civil order as might best conduce to the securing of the **purity** and peace of the ordinance to themselves and their posterity according to **GOD** In answer hereunto they expressed by holding up their hands twice as before, that they held themselves bound to **establish** such civil order as might best conduce to the ends aforesaid.

Then Mr. Davenport declared unto them, by the **Scripture**, what kind of persons might best be trusted with matters of government; and by sundry arguments from **Scripture** proved that such men as were described in **Exod. xviii. 2, Dent. 1. 13,** with **Dent. xvii. A,** and **1 Cor. vi. 1, 6, 7,** ought to be entrusted by them, seeing they were free to cast themselves into that mold and form of commonwealth which appeared best for them in reference to securing the peace and peaceable improvement of **CHRIST,** his ordinances in the **Church** according to **GOD,** whereunto they have bound themselves, as hath been acknowledged.

Having thus said he sat down **praying** the company freely to consider, whether they would have it voted at this time or not. After some space of silence, Mr. Theophilus Eaton answered it might be voted, and some others also spake to the same purpose, none at all opposing it. Then it was propounded to vote.

QUERY 5. Whether free burgesses shall be chosen out of the **Church** members, they that are in the foundation work of the **Church** being actually free burgesses, and to choose to themselves out of the like estate of **Church** fellowship, and the power of choosing magistrates and officers from among themselves, and the power of making and repealing laws, according to the word, and the dividing of inheritances, and deciding of differences that may arise, and all the businesses of like nature are to be transacted by those free burgesses. This was put to vote and agreed unto by lifting up of hands twice, as in the former it was done.

Then one man stood up and expressed his **dissenting** from the rest in part; yet granting,

1. That magistrates should be men fearing **GOD**.

2. That the **Church** is the company where, ordinarily, such men may be expected.

3. That they that choose them ought to be men fearing **GOD**; only at this he stuck, that free planters ought not to give this power out of their hands.

Another stood up and answered, that nothing was done, but with their consent. The former answered, that all the free planters ought to resume this power into their own hands again, if things were not orderly carried. Mr. Theophilus Eaton answered, that in all places they choose committees in like manner. The companies in London choose the liveries by whom the public magistrates are chosen. In this the rest are not wronged, because they expect, in time, to be of the livery themselves, and to have the same power. Some others entreated the former to give his arguments and reasons whereupon he dissented. He refused to do it, and said, they might not rationally demand it, seeing he let the vote pass on freely and did not speak till after it was past, because he would not hinder what they agreed upon.

Then Mr. Davenport, after a short relation of some former passages between them two about this question, **prayed** the company that nothing might be concluded by them on this weighty question, but what themselves were persuaded to be agreeing with the mind of **GOD**, and they had heard what had been said since the voting; he entreated them again to consider of it, and put it again to vote as before. Again all of them, by holding up their hands, did show their consent as before. And some of them confessed that, whereas they did waver before they came to the Assembly, they were now fully convinced, that it is **the mind of GOD.**

One of them said that in the morning before he came reading **Deut. xvii. 15**, he was convinced at home.

Another said, that he came doubting to the **Assembly**, but he blessed **GOD**, by what had been said, he was now fully satisfied, that the choice of burgesses out of **Church members** and to entrust those with the power before spoken of is according to the **mind of GOD revealed in the Scriptures.** All having spoken their apprehensions it was agreed upon, and Mr. Robert Newman was desired to write it as an order whereunto every one, that hereafter should be admitted here as planters, should submit, and testify the same by subscribing their names to the order: Namely, that **Church members** only shall be free burgesses, and that they only shall choose magistrates and officers among themselves, to have power of transacting all the public civil affairs of this plantation; of making and repealing laws, dividing of inheritances, deciding of differences that may arise, and doing all things and businesses of like nature.

This being thus settled, as a fundamental agreement concerning civil government, Mr. Davenport proceeded to propound something to consideration about the gathering of a **Church** and to prevent the blemishing of the first beginnings of the **Church** work, Mr. Davenport advised, that the names of such as were to be admitted might be

publicly propounded, to the end that they who were most approved might be chosen; for the town being cast into several private meetings, wherein they that lived nearest together gave their accounts one to another of **GOD'S gracious world** upon them, and **prayed** together and conferred to their mutual edification, sundry of them had knowledge one of another, and in every meeting some one was more approved of all than any other; for this reason and to prevent scandals, the whole company was entreated to consider whom they found fittest to nominate for this work.

QUERY 6. Whether are you all willing and do agree in this, that twelve men be chosen, that their fitness for the foundation work may be tried; however there may be more named yet it may be in their power who are chosen to reduce them to twelve, and that it be in the power of those twelve to choose out of themselves seven, that shall be most approved of by the major part, to begin the **Church**.

This was agreed upon by consent of all, as was expressed by holding up of hands, and that so many as should be thought fit for the foundation work of the **Church**, shall be propounded by the plantation, and written down and pass without exception, unless they had given public scandal or offense. Yet so as in case of public scandal or offense, every one should have liberty to propound their exception, at that time, **publicly** against any man, that should be nominated, when all their names should be writ down. But if the offense were private, that men's names might be tendered, so many as were offended were entreated to deal with the offender privately, and if he gave not satisfaction to bring the matter to the twelve, that they might consider of it impartially and in the **fear of GOD.**

MAY 19, 1643
ARTICLES OF CONFEDERATION OF THE UNITED COLONIES OF NEW ENGLAND, MASSACHUSETTS, NEW PLYMOUTH, CONNECTICUT, NEW HAVEN

Whereas we all came into these parts of America with one and the same end and aim, namely, to **advance the Kingdom of our Lord Jesus Christ** and to **enjoy the liberties of the Gospel in purity with peace**; and whereas in our settling (by a **wise Providence of God**) we are further dispersed upon the sea coasts and rivers than was at first intended, so that we can not according to our desire with convenience communicate...

And forasmuch as the natives have formerly committed sundry Insolence and outrages upon several Plantations of the English...

We therefore do conceive it our bounder duty, without delay to enter into a present Consociation amongst ourselves, for mutual help and strength...

That, as in nation and **religion**...we...fully agreed...and henceforth be called by the name of the United Colonies of New England.

The said United Colonies for themselves and their posterities do jointly and severally hereby enter into a firm and perpetual league of friendship and amity for offense and defense, mutual advice and succor upon all just occasions both for **preserving and propagating the truth and liberties of the Gospel** and for their own mutual safety and welfare.

NOVEMBER 6, 1643
GOVERNMENT OF NEW HAVEN COLONY

It was agreed and concluded as a fundamental order not to be disputed or questioned hereafter, that none shall be admitted to be free burgesses in any of the plantations within this jurisdiction for the future, but such planters as are members of some or other of the approved **Churches of New England**, nor shall any but such free burgesses have any vote in any election, (the six present freemen aft Milforde enjoying the liberty with the cautions agreed,) nor shall any power or trust in the ordering of any civil affairs, be after any time put into the hands of any other than such **Church members**, though as free planters, all have right to their inheritance & to commerce, according to such grants, orders and laws as shall be made concerning the same.

2. All such free burgesses shall have power in each town or plantation within this jurisdiction to chose fit and able men, from amongst themselves, being **Church** members as before, to be the ordinary judges, to hear and determine all inferior causes, whether civil or criminal, provided that no civil cause to be tried in any of these plantation Courts in value exceed 201, and that the punishment in such criminals, according to the mind of **God, revealed in his word**, touching such offenses, do not exceed stocking and whipping, or if the fine be pecuniary, that it exceed not five pounds...

3...It is provided and agreed, that no plantation shall aft any election be left destitute of a magistrate if they desire one to be chosen out of those in **Church** fellowship with them.

4...If any of them be absent aft one of the clock in the afternoons on Monday aforesaid, when the court shall sift, or if any of them depart the town without leave, while the court sifts, he or they shall pay for any such default, twenty shillings fine, unless some **Providence of God** occasion the same...

5...If any of the said magistrates or Deputies shall either be absent after the first sitting of the said General Court, unless some **Providence of God** hinder...they shall each of them pay twenty shillings fine, with due considerations of further aggravations if there shall be cause;

which General Court shall, with all care and diligence provide for the maintenance of the **purity of religion** and suppress the contrary, according to their best light from the word of **God**, and all wholesome and sound advice which shall be given by the **elders** and **Churches** in the jurisdiction, so fare as may concern their civil power to deal therein.

1662
CHARTER OF CONNECTICUT

Whereby Our said People Inhabitants there, may be so **religiously**, peaceably and civilly governed, as their good Life and orderly Conversation may win and invite the Natives of the Country to the Knowledge and Obedience of the **only true GOD, and He Savior of Mankind**, and the **Christian Faith**, which in Our Royal Intentions, and the adventurers free Possession, is the only and principal End of this Plantation...

Nevertheless, our Will and Pleasure is, and We do hereby declare unto all **Christian Kings, Princes, and States**, that if any Persons which shall hereafter be of the said Company or Plantation, or any other Appointment of the said Governor and Company for the time being, shall at any time or times hereafter rob or spoil by sea or by land, and do any hurt, violence, or unlawful hostility to any of the subjects of us, or heirs...

1776
CONNECTICUT CONSTITUTION
(1662 COLONIAL CHARTER KEPT IN FORCE.)

PREAMBLE. The People of this State being by the **Providence** of **God**, free and independent, have the sole and exclusive Right of governing themselves as a free, sovereign, and independent State; and having from their ancestors derived a free and excellent Constitution of Government whereby the legislature depends on the free and annual election of the people, they have the best security for the preservation of their civil and **religious rights** and Liberties. And forasmuch as the free Fruition of such Liberties and Privileges as Humanity, Civility and **Christianity** call for, as is due to every Man in his Place and Proportion, without impeachment and infringement, hath ever been, and will be the Tranquillity and Stability of **Churches** and Commonwealths; and the Denial thereof, the Disturbance, if not the Ruin of both.

OCTOBER 7, 1801
DANBURY BAPTIST ASSOCIATION'S LETTER TO PRESIDENT THOMAS JEFFERSON:

The address of the **Danbury Baptist Association,** in the State of Connecticut; assembled October 7th 1801. To Thomas Jefferson Esq., the President of the united States of America.

Sir, Among the many millions in America and Europe who rejoice in your Election to office, we embrace the first opportunity which we have enjoyed in our collective capacity, since your Inauguration, to express our great satisfaction, in your appointment to the chief Magistracy in the United States:

And though our mode of expression may be less courtly and pompous than what many others clothe their addresses with, we beg you, Sir to believe, that none are more sincere.

Our **Sentiments** are uniformly on the side of **Religious Liberty** - That **Religion** is at all times and places a Matter between **God** and Individuals - That no man ought to suffer in Name, person or effects on account of his **religious Opinions** - That the legitimate Power of civil Government extends no further than to punish the man who works ill to his neighbor:

But Sir our constitution of government is not specific. Our ancient charter, together with the Laws made coincident therewith, were adopted as the Basis of our government at the time of our revolution; and such had been our laws & usages, & such still are; that **Religion is considered as the first object of Legislation**; & therefore what **religious privileges** we enjoy (as a minor part of the State) we enjoy as favors granted, and not as inalienable rights: and these favors we receive at the expense of such degrading acknowledgments, as are inconsistent with the rights of freemen.

It is not to be wondered at therefore; if those who seek after power & gain under the pretense of government & **Religion** should reproach their fellow men - should reproach their chief Magistrate, as an enemy of **religion,** Law & good order because he will not, dares not assume the prerogative of **Jehovah** and make Laws to govern the **Kingdom of Christ**.

Sir, we are sensible that the President of the united States is not the national Legislator & also sensible that the national government cannot destroy the Laws of each State; but our hopes are strong that the **sentiments** of our beloved President, which have had such genial Effect already, like the radiant beams of the Sun, will shine & prevail through all these States and all the world till Hierarchy and Tyranny be destroyed from the Earth.

Sir, when we reflect on your past services and see a glow of philanthropy and good will shining forth in a course of more than thirty years we have reason to believe that **America's God** has raised you up to fill the chair of State out of that good will which he bears to the Millions which you preside over.

May **God** strengthen you for the arduous task which **Providence** & the voice of the people have called you to sustain and support you in your Administration against all the predetermined opposition of those who wish to rise to wealth & importance on the poverty and subjection of the people.

And may the **Lord** preserve you safe from every evil and bring you at last to his **Heavenly Kingdom** through **Jesus Christ our Glorious Mediator.** Signed in behalf of the Association,

Signed - The Committee, Neh'h Dodge, Eph'm Robbins, Stephen S. Nelson

JANUARY 1, 1802
PRESIDENT THOMAS JEFFERSON SENT A PERSONAL LETTER TO DANBURY BAPTIST ASSOCIATION LEADERS, NEHEMIAH DODGE, EPHRAIM ROBBINS, AND STEPHEN NELSON:

Gentlemen: The affectionate **sentiments** of esteem and approbation which you are so good as to express towards me, on behalf of the **Danbury Baptists Association**, give me the highest satisfaction.

My duties dictate a faithful and zealous pursuit of my constituents and in proportion as they are persuaded of my fidelity to those duties, the discharge of them becomes more and more pleasing.

Believing with you that **religion** is a matter which lies solely between man and his **God**, that he owes account to none other for **faith** or his **worship**, that the legislative powers of government reach actions only, and not opinions, I contemplate with solemn reverence that act of the whole American people which declared that their legislature should "make no law respecting an **establishment of religion**, or prohibiting the free exercise thereof," thus building a **wall of separation** between **Church and State.**

Adhering to this expression of the supreme will of the nation in behalf of the **rights of conscience**, I shall see with sincere satisfaction the progress of those **sentiments** which tend to restore man to all his natural rights, convinced he has no natural right in opposition to his social duties.

I reciprocate your kind **prayers** for the **protection and blessing of the common Father and Creator of man**, and tender you for yourselves and your **religious association**, assurances of my high respect and esteem. (Reference to letter of Rhode Island **Baptist** founder Roger Williams to John Cotton in 1644. See page 194.)

1818
CONSTITUTION OF CONNECTICUT

PREAMBLE. The people of Connecticut acknowledging with gratitude, the good **Providence of God**, in having permitted them to enjoy a free government, do, in order more effectually to define, secure, and perpetuate the liberties, rights and privileges which they have derived from their ancestors, hereby, after a careful consideration and revision, ordain and **establish** the following constitution and form of civil government...

ARTICLE 1, DECLARATION OF RIGHTS, SECTION 3. The exercise and enjoyment of **religious profession** and **worship**, without discrimination, shall forever be free to all persons in this state; provided, that the right hereby declared and **established** shall not be so construed as to excuse acts of licentiousness, or to justify practices inconsistent with the peace and safety of the State...

ARTICLE 1, SECTION 4. No preference shall be given by law to any **Christian sect** or **mode of worship**.

ARTICLE 7, OF **RELIGION**, SECTION 1. It being the duty of all men to **worship** the **Supreme Being, the great Creator and Preserver of the Universe**, and their right to render that **worship**, in the mode most consistent with the **dictates of their consciences**; no person shall by law be compelled to join or support, nor be classed with, or associated to, any **congregation**, **Church** or **religious association**.

But every person now belonging to such **congregation**, **Church**, or **religious association**, shall remain a member thereof, until he shall have separated himself therefrom, in the manner hereinafter provided.

And each and every **society** or **denomination** of **Christians** in this state, shall have and enjoy the same and equal powers, rights and privileges; and shall have power and authority to support and maintain the **ministers** or **teachers** of their respective **denominations**, and to build and repair houses for **public worship**, by a tax on the members of any such **society** only, to be laid by a major vote of the legal voters assembled at any **society meeting**, warned and held according to law, or in any other manner.

ARTICLE 7, OF **RELIGION**, SECTION 2. If any person shall choose to separate himself from the **society** or **denomination** of **Christians** to which he may belong, and shall leave a written notice thereof with the clerk of such **society**, he shall thereupon be no longer liable for any future expenses which may be incurred by said **society**...

ARTICLE 10, GENERAL PROVISIONS, SECTION 1. Members of the General Assembly and all officers, executive and judicial, shall before they enter on the duties of their respective offices, take the following oath or affirmation, to wit: You do solemnly swear (or affirm, as the case may be) that you will support the constitution of the United States, and the constitution of the state of Connecticut, so long as you continue a citizen thereof; and that you will faithfully discharge, according to the law, the duties of the office of......to the best of your abilities. **So Help You God**.

AMENDMENTS TO 1818 CONSTITUTION

ARTICLE 1. From and after the first Wednesday [of May], in **the Year of Our Lord** one thousand eight hundred and thirty, the Senate of this state shall consist of not less than eighteen, nor more than twenty-four members, and be chosen by districts...

ARTICLE 40...In case the governor shall not transmit the bill to the secretary, either with his approval or with his objections, within five calendar days, **Sundays** and legal holidays excepted, after the same shall have been presented to him, it shall be a law...

ARTICLE 13, SECTION 1. The general Assembly may provide by law for voting in the choice of any officer to be elected or upon any question to be voted on at an election by qualified voters of the state who are unable to appear at the polling place on the day of election because of absence from the city or town of which they are inhabitants or because of sickness or physical disability or because the **tenets of their religion** forbid secular activity. (Art. 12. Adopted November 24, 1964.)

1843
PETITION OF HARTFORD JEWS

Resulted in Jews being permitted the right to public worship. The State's first synagogue was built on Charter Oak Avenue. Methodists were permitted to the right to public worship the same year.

1844
JEWTT V. THOMAS BANK, 16 CONN. 511.

All **ecclesiastical** bodies are private rather than public corporations, thus they cannot access state action to compel compliance with **Church** regulations and **discipline**.

1965
CONSTITUTION OF CONNECTICUT

PREAMBLE. The People of Connecticut acknowledging with gratitude, the good **Providence** of **God**, in having permitted them to enjoy a free government; do, in order more effectually to define, secure, and perpetuate the liberties, rights and privileges which they have derived from their ancestors; hereby, after a careful consideration and revision, ordain and **establish** the following constitution and form of civil government...

ARTICLE 1, SECTION 3. The exercise and enjoyment of **religious profession** and **worship**, without discrimination, shall forever be free to all persons in the state; provided, that the right hereby declared and **established**, shall not be so construed as to excuse acts of licentiousness, or to justify practices inconsistent with the peace and safety of the state...

ARTICLE 1, SECTION 20. No person shall be denied the equal protection of the law nor be subjected to segregation or discrimination in the exercise or enjoyment of his civil or political rights because of **religion**, race, color, ancestry or national origin...

ARTICLE 6, SECTION 7. The general **Assembly** may provide by law for voting in the choice of any officer to be elected or upon any question to be voted on at an election by qualified voters of the state who are unable to appear at the polling place on the day of election because of absence from the city or town of which they are inhabitants or because of sickness, or physical disability or because the tenets of their **religion** forbid secular activity...

ARTICLE 6, SECTION 8. The general **Assembly** may provide by law for the admission as electors in absentia of members of the armed forces, the United States merchant marine, members of **religious** or welfare groups or agencies attached to and serving with the armed forces and civilian employees of the United States, and the spouses and dependents of such persons...

ARTICLE 7, OF **RELIGION**. It being the right of all men to **worship** the **Supreme Being, the Great Creator and Preserver of the Universe**, and to render that **worship** in a mode consistent with the **dictates of their consciences**, no person shall by law be compelled to join or support, nor be classed or associated with, any **congregation**, **Church** or **religious association**. No preference shall be given by law to any **religious society** or **denomination** in the state. Each shall have and enjoy the same and equal powers, rights and privileges, and may support and maintain the **ministers** or **teachers** of its **society** or **denomination**, and may build and repair houses for **public worship**.

ARTICLE 11, GENERAL PROVISIONS, SECTION 1. Members of the General Assembly and all officers, executive and judicial, shall, before they enter on the duties of their respective offices, take the following oath or affirmation, to wit: You do solemnly swear (or affirm, as the case may be) that you will support the constitution of the United States, and the constitution of the state of Connecticut, so long as you continue a citizen thereof; and that you will faithfully discharge, according to law, the duties of the office of.......to the best of your abilities. **So Help You God**...

AMENDMENTS, ARTICLE 5. SECTION 20 of ARTICLE 1 of the constitution is amended to read as follows: No person shall be denied the equal protection of the law nor be subjected to segregation or discrimination in the exercise or enjoyment of his or her civil or political rights because of **religion**, race, color, ancestry, national origin or sex...

AMENDMENTS, ARTICLE 21. ARTICLE 5 of the amendments to the constitution is amended to read as follows:

No person shall be denied the equal protection of the law nor be subjected to segregation or discrimination in the exercise or enjoyment of his or her civil or political rights because of **religion**, race, color, ancestry, national origin, sex or physical or mental disability.

MAY 3, 1925
CALVIN COOLIDGE, LAYING CORNER STONE OF THE JEWISH COMMUNITY CENTER, WASHINGTON, D.C.:

A common **spiritual inspiration** was potent to bring and mold and weld together into a national unity the many and scattered colonial communities that had been planted along the Atlantic seaboard....

There were well-nigh as many divergencies of **religious faith** as there were of origin, politics and geography...From its beginning, the new continent had seemed destined to be the home of **religious tolerance**. Those who claimed the right of individual choice for themselves finally had to grant it to others.

Beyond that - and this was one of the factors which I think weighed heaviest on the side of unity - the **Bible** was the one work of literature that was common to all of them.

The **Scriptures** were read and studied everywhere. There are many testimonies that their teachings became the most important intellectual and **spiritual force** for unification.

I remember to have read...in the writings of the historian Lecky, the observation that "**Hebraic mortar** cemented the foundations of American democracy."

Lecky had in mind this very influence of the **Bible** in drawing together the feelings and sympathies of the widely scattered communities.

All the way from New Hampshire to Georgia, they found a common ground of **faith** and reliance in the **Scriptural writings**...

This **biblical** influence was strikingly impressive in all the New England colonies, and only less so in the others. In the CONNECTICUT CODE OF 1650, the **Mosaic model** is adopted. The magistrates were authorized to administer justice "according to the laws here **established**, and, for want of them, according to the word of **God**."

In the NEW HAVEN CODE OF 1655, there were 79 topical statutes for the Government, half of which contained references to the **Old Testament**.

The founders of the New Haven, John Davenport and Theophilus Eaton, were expert **Hebrew scholars**. The extent to which they leaned upon the **moral** and administrative system, laid down by the **Hebrew lawgivers,** was responsible for their conviction that the **Hebrew language and literature** ought to be made as familiar as possible to all the people. So it was that John Davenport arranged that in the first public school in New Haven the **Hebrew language** should be taught.

CONNECTICUT RELIGIOUS AFFILIATION

The Encyclopedia Britannica, 11th edition, published in 1911, stated:

> In the early part of the 19th century the **Congregational Church** had the largest membership, but in 1906, three-fifths of the **Church** population was **Roman Catholic** and one third of the remainder was **Congregationalists**, and next ranked **Episcopalians, Methodists** and **Baptists**.

http://www.1911encyclopedia.org/
Connecticut#Population

The Catholic Encyclopedia, Volume XV, Copyright 1912 by Robert Appleton Company, stated as of 1906, **Connecticut's Protestant denominations** as:

Congregationalists - 59,154
Protestant Episcopalians - 26,652
Methodists - 29,411

Baptists - 22,372
Presbyterians - 1,680

http://www.newadvent.org/cathen/04253b.htm

The Wikipedia Online Encyclopedia, as of 2006, listed **Connecticut** as:

Christian - 83 percent, consisting of:
- **Baptist** - 10 percent
- **Episcopal** - 6 percent
- **Methodist** - 4 percent
- **Lutheran** - 4 percent
- **Congregational/U.Church of Christ** - 2 percent
- **Other Protestant** - 22 percent
- **Catholic** - 34 percent
- **Other Christian** - 1 percent

Jewish - 3 percent
Other Religions - 1 percent
Non-Religious/Non-Reporting - 13 percent

http://en.wikipedia.org/wiki/Connecticut#Religion

The U.S. Religious Landscape Survey, conducted by The Pew Forum on Religion & Public Life, 2007, published in the USA Today, listed **Connecticut** as:

Christian - 71.5 percent, consisting of:
- **Evangelical Protestant** - 10 percent
- **Mainline Protestant** - 13 percent
- **Black Protestant** - 4 percent
- **Catholic** - 43 percent
- **Orthodox** - 1 percent
- **Other Christian** - <0.5 percent

Mormon - <0.5 percent
Jehovah's Witnesses - 1 percent
Jewish - 1 percent

Muslim - <0.5 percent
Buddhist - 1 percent
Hindu - <0.5 percent
Other World Religions - <0.5 percent
Other Faiths - 2 percent
Unaffiliated - 23 percent
Did not answer - 1 percent

www.pewforum.org
www.usatoday.com/news/graphics/pew-religion-08/flash.htm

SEAL OF THE STATE OF RHODE ISLAND AND PROVIDENCE PLANTATIONS
HOPE
1636

RHODE ISLAND

On December 1, 1630, Roger Williams, a Puritan Minister, fled England as he believed the government of the King should not control the church. In 1635, he fled Massachusetts, as he believed the government of the Massachusetts' General Court should not control the church. In the Spring of 1636, Rev. Roger Williams was granted a tract of land by the Narragansett chiefs Canonicus and Miantonmoh, and he founded **Providence** Plantation and the first **Baptist Church** in America.

In 1639, Rev. John Clarke was driven out of **Puritan** Massachusetts and founded Newport, Rhode Island, where he began the second **Baptist Church** in America. Theses settlements were combined by Charles II in the Charter of 1663 to become the Colony of Rhode Island and Providence Plantation.

The colony was predominately **Baptist**, and as such, believed **conversion** and genuine **religion** should be voluntary from the inside out, not forced by the government from the outside in.

John Clarke wrote: "No such **believer**, or servant of **Christ Jesus**, has any liberty, much less authority from his **Lord**, to smite his fellow servant, nor yet with outward force, or arm of flesh, to constrain or restrain his **Conscience**."

Roger Williams wrote: "In holding an enforced **uniformity** of **religion** in a civil state, we must necessarily disclaim our desires and hopes of the **Jews' conversion** to **Christ**."

Rhode Island was unique among the colonies in allowing complete **religious** freedom.

In 1658, **Jewish** immigrants Mordecai Campanal and Moses Pacheco arrived in Rhode Island, from Barbados. Soon 15 families relocated there, and by the American Revolution the **Jewish** community of Newport Rhode Island had grown to over 30 families.

Congregation Yeshuat Israel was formed in 1702, and its first leader was Isaac Touro. In 1763, Touro **Synagogue** was dedicated in Newport. It is the oldest standing permanent **Jewish** House of **Worship** in North America.

In 1739 there were 33 **Churches** in the colony; 12 **Baptist**, 10 **Quaker**, 6 **Congregational** or **Presbyterian**, and 5 **Episcopalian**. In 1680, there was not one **Catholic** in the colony, but a hundred years later, a 1777 map of Newport, Rhode Island, published in London, showed houses of **worship** for **Baptists**, **Congregationalists**, **Quakers**, **Jews** and **Catholics**.

In 1828 there were less than 1,000 **Catholics** in the state. **Bishop** Fenwick of Boston assigned **Rev.** Robert Woodley to a "**parish**" which included the entire State of Rhode Island. **Father** Woodley purchased a building in Newport to use for a **Church** and school. In 1829, a **Church** was built in Pawtucket. In 1830, **Rev.** John Corry built a **Church** in Taunton.

The first **Catholic Church** in **Providence** was built in 1837. In 1844, the **Diocese** of Hartford was created which included Rhode Island and Connecticut. There were only six **priests** in the two states. After the 1846 Irish potato famine, Irish **Catholic** immigrants increased to the largest segment of the population.

Following the Civil War, the growing cotton industry drew large numbers of Canadian **Catholics**. Later **Catholics** immigrated from Italy, Poland, Portugal, Armenia and Syria.

SEPTEMBER 6, 1640
PLANTATION AGREEMENT AT PROVIDENCE

We agree, as formerly hath been the liberties of the town, so still, to hold forth **liberty of Conscience**...

MARCH 19, 1641
GOVERNMENT OF RHODE ISLAND

The General Court of Election began and held at Portsmouth, from the 16th of March, to the 19th of the same month, 1641.

1. It was ordered and agreed, before the Election, that an engagement by oath should be taken of all the officers...To the Execution of this office, I Judge myself bound before **God** to walk **faithfully** and this I profess in ye **presence of God**...

3. It is ordered and unanimously agreed upon, that the Government which this Body Politic doth attend unto in this Island, and the Jurisdiction thereof, in favor of our Prince is a DEMOCRACIE, or Popular Government; that is to say, It is in the Power of the Body of Freemen orderly assembled, or the major part of them, to make or constitute Just Laws, by which they will be regulated, and to depute from among themselves such **Ministers** as shall see them faithfully executed between Man and Man.

MARCH 14, 1643
PATENT FOR PROVIDENCE PLANTATIONS

The said Laws, Constitutions, and Punishments, for the Civil Government of the said Plantations, be conformable to the Laws of England, so far as the Nature and Constitution of the place will admit...for the better transacting of their public Affairs to make and use a public Seal as the known Seal of Providence-Plantations, in the Narraganset-Bay, in New-England.

In Testimony whereof, the said Robert Earl of Warwick...the Fourteenth Day of March, in the Nineteenth Year of the Reign of our Sovereign-Lord King Charles, and in **the Year of Our Lord God**, 1643.

1644
ROGER WILLIAMS REPLIED TO MASSACHUSETTS PURITAN LEADER JOHN COTTON IN HIS WORK "THE BLOODY TENET OF PERSECUTION FOR CONSCIENCE SAKE" & "MR. COTTON'S LETTER, LATELY PRINTED, EXAMINED AND ANSWERED," PUBLISHED IN LONDON

Mr. Cotton...hath not duly considered these following particulars.

First, the faithful labors of many witnesses of **Jesus Christ**, existing in the world, abundantly proving, that the **Church of the Jews under the Old Testament in the type** and **the Church of the Christians under the New Testament in the antitype**, were both **separate from the world**; and that when they have **opened a gap** in the **hedge**, or **wall of separation,** between **the garden of the Church and the wilderness of the world, God hath ever broken down the wall** itself, **removed the candlestick**, &c. and **made his garden a wilderness**, as at this day.

And that therefore if **He** will ever please to **restore His garden and paradise again**, it must of necessity be **walled in** peculiarly unto **Himself** from the **world**, and that all that shall be saved out of the world are to be transplanted out of the **wilderness of the world** and added unto **His Church or garden**...a **separatio**n of **Holy** from **unHoly**, penitent from impenitent, **Godly** from **unGodly**.

Rev. Roger Williams alluded to:

Isaiah 5:1-7 My well-beloved hath a **vineyard** in a very fruitful hill: And he **fenced it**, and gathered out the stones thereof, and planted it with the choicest vine, and built a tower in the midst of it, and also made a winepress therein: and he looked that it should bring forth grapes, and it brought forth wild grapes.

And now, O inhabitants of Jerusalem, and men of Judah, judge, I pray you, betwixt me and my **vineyard**. What could have been done more to my **vineyard** that I have not done in it? Wherefore, when I looked that it should bring forth grapes, brought it forth wild grapes?

And now go to; I will tell you what I will do to my **vineyard**: **I will take away the hedge thereof,** and it shall be eaten up; **and break down the wall thereof,** and it shall be trodden down...

For the **vineyard** of the Lord of hosts **is the house of Israel, and the men of Judah his pleasant plant:** and he looked for judgment, but found oppression."

Mark 12:1 A certain man planted a **vineyard**, and set an **hedge** about it, and digged a place for the wine vat, and built a tower, and let it out to husbandmen, and went into a far country.

Proverbs 24:30-31 I went by the field of the slothful, and by the **vineyard** of the man void of understanding; And, lo, it was all grown over with thorns, and nettles had covered the face thereof, and **the stone wall thereof was broken down.**

Revelation 2:1-5 Unto the angel of the Church of Ephesus write...thou hast left thy first love. Remember therefore from whence thou art fallen and **repent...or** else I will come unto thee quickly and **will remove thy candlestick.**

1651
JOHN CLARKE, AFTER THE WHIPPING OF BAPTIST OBADIAH HOLMES IN LYNN, MASSACHUSETTS, WROTE: "ILL NEWS FROM NEW ENGLAND OR A NARRATIVE OF NEW ENGLAND'S PERSECUTION"

No such **believer**, or servant of **Christ Jesus**, has any liberty, much less authority from his **Lord**, to smite his fellow servant, nor yet with outward force, or arm of flesh, to constrain or restrain his **Conscience**, no nor yet his outward man for **Conscience sake**, or **worship of his God**, where injury is not offered to the person, name, or estate of others."

JULY 15, 1663
CHARTER OF RHODE ISLAND AND PROVIDENCE PLANTATIONS

Charles the Second, by the **Grace of God**, King of England, Scotland, France and Ireland, **Defender of the Faith**...greeting: Whereas we have been informed, by the humble petition of our trusty and well beloved subject, **John Clarke**, on the behalf of Benjamin Arnold, William Brenton, William Codington, Nicholas Easton, William Boulston, John Porter, John Smith, Samuell Gorton, John Weeks, **Roger Williams**, Thomas Olnie, Gregorie Dexter, John Cogeshall, Joseph Clarke, Randall Holden, John Greene, John Roome, Samuell Wildbore, William Ffield, James Barker, Richard Tew, Thomas Harris, and William Dyre, and the rest of the purchasers and free inhabitants of our island, called Rhode-Island, and the rest of the colony of Providence Plantations, in the Narragansett Bay, in New-England, in America,

That they, pursuing, with peaceable and loyal minds, their sober, serious and **religious intentions,** of **Godly edifying themselves**, and one another, in the **Holy Christian faith** and **worship** as they were persuaded;

Together with the gaining over and **conversion** of the poor ignorant Indian natives, in those parts of America, to the sincere **profession** and obedience of the same **faith** and **worship**, did, not only by the consent and good encouragement of our royal progenitors, transport themselves out of this kingdom of England into America, but also, since their arrival there, after their first settlement amongst other our subjects in those parts,

For the avoiding of discord, and those manic evils which were likely to ensue upon some of those our subjects not being able to bear, in these remote parties, their different apprehensions in **religious concernements,** and in pursuance of the aforesaid ends, did once again leave their desirable stations and habitations, and with excessive labor and travel, hazard and charge, did transplant themselves into the midst of the Indian natives, who, as we are informed, are the most potent princes and people of all that country; where, by the good **Providence of God**, from whom the Plantations have taken their name, upon their labor and industry, they have not only been preserved to admiration, but have increased and prospered,

And are seized and possessed, by purchase and consent of the said natives, to their full content, of such lands, islands, rivers, harbors and roads, as are very convenient, both for plantations and also for buildings of ships, supply of pypestaves, and other merchandise; and which lies very commodious, in many respects, for commerce, and to accommodate our southern plantations, and may much advance the trade of this our realm, and greatly enlarge the territories thereof; they having, by near neighborhood to and friendly society with the great body of the Narragansett Indians, given them encouragement, of their own accord, to subject themselves, their people and lands, unto us; whereby, as is hoped, there may, in due time, by the **blessing** of **God** upon their endeavors, be laid a sure foundation of happiness to all America:

And whereas, in their humble address, they have freely declared, that it is much on their hearts (if they may be permitted), to hold forth a lively experiment, that a most flourishing civil state may stand and best be maintained, and that among our English subjects, with a full liberty in **religious concernements**; and that **true piety** rightly grounded upon **Gospel principles**, will give the best and greatest security to sovereignty, and will lay in the hearts of men the strongest obligations to true loyalty:

Now know ye, that we being willing to encourage the hopeful undertaking of our said loyal and loving subjects, and to secure them in the free exercise and enjoyment of all their civil and **religious rights**, appertaining to them, as our loving subjects; and to preserve unto them that liberty, in the **true Christian faith** and **worship** of **God**, which they have sought with so much travail, and with peaceable minds, and loyal subjection to our royal progenitors and ourselves, to enjoy; **and because some of the people and inhabitants of the same colony cannot, in their private opinions, conforms to the public exercise of religion, according to the liturgy, forms and ceremonies of the Church of England,** or take or subscribe the oaths and articles made and **established** in that behalf; and for that the same, by reason of the remote distances of those places, will (as we hope) be no breach of the unity and **uniformity established** in this nation:

Have therefore thought fit, and do hereby publish, grant, ordain and declare, That **our royal will and pleasure is, that no person within the said colony, at any time hereafter, shall be any wise molested, punished, disquieted, or called in question, for any differences in opinion in matters of religion**, and do not actually disturb the civil peace of our said colony; but that all and every person and persons may, from time to time, and at all times hereafter, freely and fully have and enjoy his and their own judgments and **consciences**, in **matters of religious**

concernments, throughout the tract of land hereafter mentioned; they behaving themselves peaceably and quietly, and **not using this liberty to licentiousness and profaneness,** nor to the civil injury or outward disturbance of others; any law, statute, or clause, therein contained, or to be contained, usage or custom of this realm, to the contrary hereof, in any wise, notwithstanding.

And that they may be in the better capacity to defend themselves, in their just rights and liberties against all the enemies of the **Christian faith**, and others, in all respects, we have further thought fit, and at the humble petition of the persons aforesaid are graciously pleased to declare, That they shall have and enjoy the benefit of our late act of indemnity and free pardon, as the rest of our subjects in other our dominions and territories have; and to create and make them a body politic or corporate, with the powers and privileges hereinafter mentioned...

Whereby our said people and inhabitants, in the said Plantations, may be so **religiously**, peaceably and civilly governed, as that, by their good life and orderly conversations, they may win and invite the native Indians of the country to the knowledge and obedience of the only **true God**, and **Savior of mankind...**

Also our will and pleasure is, and we do hereby declare unto all **Christian Kings, Princes and States**, that if any person, which shall hereafter be of the said Company or Plantations...rob or spoil, by sea or land, or do any hurt, unlawful hostility to any of the subjects of us...the person or persons committing any such robbery or spoil shall...make full restitution

APRIL 1664
ROGER WILLIAMS WROTE OF SIR HENRY VANE, COMMISSIONER WHO SIGNED THE CHARTER FOR PROVIDENCE PLANTATION:

Under **God**, the great anchor of our ship is Sir Henry.

1763
RHODE ISLAND COLLEGE, RENAMED BROWN UNIVERSITY AFTER BENEFACTORS NICHOLAS AND MOSES BROWN, IS THE SEVENTH OLDEST COLLEGE IN AMERICA. FOUNDED IN PROVIDENCE, RHODE ISLAND, WITH THE MOTTO "IN DEO SPERAMUS" (IN GOD WE TRUST)

The Charter stated: And that the number of the trustees shall, and may be thirty-six; of which twenty-two shall forever be elected of the **denomination** called **Baptists**, or **AntipedoBaptists**; five shall forever be elected of the **denomination** called **Friends**, or **Quakers**; four shall forever be elected of the **denomination** called **Congregationalists**; and five shall forever be elected of the **denomination** called **Episcopalians**.

MAY 28, 1773
FIRST JEWISH SERMON PUBLISHED IN AMERICA

Preached at the Touro **Synagogue** in Newport, Rhode Island, by an emissary from the **Holy Land**, Haim Isaac Karigal, to celebrate **Shavu'ot**, one of the three **Jewish pilgrimage festivals**. The sermon was **preached** in Spanish interspersed with **Hebrew**, and translated into English by Abraham Lopez.

JANUARY 4, 1776
GENERAL NATHANIEL GREENE, LATER RHODE ISLAND LEGISLATOR, WROTE TO SAMUEL WARD, RHODE ISLAND DELEGATE TO CONGRESS:

Permit me, then, to recommend from the sincerity of my heart, ready at all times to bleed in my country's cause, a declaration of independence; and call upon **the world, and the great God who governs it**, to witness the necessity, propriety and rectitude thereof...Let us, therefore, act like men inspired with a resolution that nothing but the frowns of **Heaven** shall conquer us.

MARCH 9, 1781
GENERAL WASHINGTON WROTE FROM NEWPORT, R.I., TO WILLIAM GORDON:

We have, as you very justly observe, abundant reasons to thank **Providence** for its many favorable interpositions in our behalf. It has at times been my only dependence, for all other resources seemed to have failed us.

MAY 29, 1790
RATIFICATION OF THE CONSTITUTION BY THE STATE OF RHODE ISLAND

4. That **religion**, or the duty which we owe to **our Creator**, and the manner of discharging it, can be directed only by reason and conviction, and not by force or violence, and therefore all men, have an equal, natural and unalienable right to the **free exercise of religion**, according to the **dictates of conscience**, and that no particular **religious sect** or **society** ought to be favored, or **established** by law in preference to others.

AMENDMENTS

17. As a traffic tending to **establish** or continue the slavery of any part of the human species, is disgraceful to the cause of liberty and humanity, that Congress shall, as

soon as may be, promote and **establish** such laws and regulations, as may effectually prevent the importation of slaves of very description into the United States.

AUGUST 17, 1790 GEORGE WASHINGTON WROTE TO THE HEBREW CONGREGATION IN NEWPORT, RHODE ISLAND:

It is now no more that **toleration** is spoken of as if it were the indulgence of one class of people that another enjoyed the exercise of their inherent natural rights, for, happily, the Government of the United States, which gives to bigotry no sanction, to persecution no assistance, requires only that they who live under its protection should demean themselves as good citizens in giving it on all occasions their effectual support...

May the **children of the stock of Abraham** who dwell in this land continue to merit and enjoy the good will of the other inhabitants - while every one shall sit in safety under his own vine and fig tree and there shall be none to make him afraid. May **the Father of all mercies** scatter light, and not darkness, upon our paths, and make us all in our several vocations useful here, and in **His** own due time and way **everlastingly** happy.

1797 SEAL OF THE STATE OF RHODE ISLAND HAS INSCRIBED THE MOTTO:

In **God** We Hope

NOVEMBER 5, 1842 RHODE ISLAND CONSTITUTION

PREAMBLE. We, the people of the State of Rhode Island and Providence Plantations, grateful to **Almighty God** for the civil and **religious liberty** which **He** hath so long permitted us to enjoy, and looking to **Him** for a **blessing** upon our endeavors to secure and to transmit the same, unimpaired, to succeeding generations, do ordain and **establish** this Constitution of government...

ARTICLE 1, SECTION 3. Whereas **Almighty God** hath created the mind free, and all attempts to influence it by temporal punishment, or burdens, or by civil incapacitations, tend to beget habits of hypocrisy and meanness; and whereas a principal object of our venerated ancestors, in their migration to this country and their settlement of this State, was, as they expressed it, to hold forth a lively experiment that a flourishing civil state may stand and be best maintained with full liberty in **religious concernments**;

We therefore declare, that no man shall be compelled to frequent or to support any **religious worship**, place, or **Ministry** whatever, except in fulfillment of his own voluntary contract; nor enforced, restrained, molested, or burdened in his body or goods; nor disqualified from holding any office; nor otherwise suffer on account of his **religious belief**; and that every man shall be free to **worship God** according to the **dictates of his own conscience**, and to profess, and by argument to maintain, his opinion in **matters of religion**; and that the same shall in no wise diminish, enlarge, or affect his civil capacity.

ARTICLE 1, SECTION 4. Slavery shall not be permitted in this state...

ARTICLE 3, SECTION 3. All general officers shall take the following engagement before they act in their respective offices, to wit: You being by the free vote of the electors of this state of Rhode Island and Providence Plantations, elected unto the place of do solemnly swear (or, affirm) to be true and faithful unto this state, and to support the Constitution of this state and of the United States; that you will faithfully and impartially discharge all the duties of your aforesaid office to the best of your abilities, according to law: **So Help You God**. Or: This affirmation you make and give upon the peril of the penalty of perjury...

ARTICLE 12, SECTION 1: The diffusion of knowledge, as well as of virtue, among the people being essential to the preservation of their rights and liberties, it shall be the general Assembly to promote public schools, and to adopt all means which they deem necessary and proper to secure to the people the advantages and opportunities of education.

1988
RHODE ISLAND CONSTITUTION

PREAMBLE. We, the people of the State of Rhode Island and Providence Plantations, grateful to **Almighty God** for the civil and **religious liberty** which He hath so long permitted us to enjoy, and looking to Him for a **blessing** upon our endeavors to secure and to transmit the same, unimpaired, to succeeding generations, do ordain and **establish** this Constitution of government...

ARTICLE 1, SECTION 3. Whereas **Almighty God** hath created the mind free; and all attempts to influence it by temporal punishments or burdens, or by civil incapacitations, tend to beget habits of hypocrisy and meanness; and whereas a principal object of our venerable ancestors, in their migration to this country and their settlement of this state, was, as they expressed it, to hold forth a lively experiment that a flourishing civil state may stand and be best maintained with full liberty in **religious concernments**;

We, therefore, declare that no person shall be compelled to frequent or to support any **religious worship**, place, or **Ministry** whatever, except in fulfillment of such person's voluntary contract; nor enforced, restrained, molested, or burdened in body or goods; nor disqualified from holding any office; nor otherwise suffer on account of such person's **religious belief**; and that every person shall be free to **worship God** according to the **dictates of such person's conscience**, and to profess and by argument to maintain such person's opinion in **matters of religion**; and that the same shall in no wise diminish, enlarge, or affect the civil capacity of any person...

ARTICLE 3, SECTION 3. All general officers shall take the following engagement before they act in their respective offices, to wit: You being by the free vote of the electors of this state of Rhode Island and Providence Plantations, elected unto the place of do solemnly swear (or, affirm) to be true and faithful unto this state, and to support the Constitution of this state and of the United States; that you will faithfully and impartially discharge all the duties of your aforesaid office to the best of your abilities, according to law: **So Help You God**.

RHODE ISLAND RELIGIOUS AFFILIATION

The Encyclopedia Britannica, 11th edition, published in 1911, stated:

> In 1906 there were in the state 264,712 **communicants** of various **religious denominations**, and of these 1 99,951 were **Roman Catholics**. Second in strength were the **Baptists**, who founded the colony; in 1906 they numbered 19,878, of whom 14,304 were of the Northern Convention. There were 15,443 **Protestant Episcopalians;** 9,858 **Congregationalists;** 7,892 **Methodists**. The **Friends**, whose influence was so strong in the early history of **Providence**, numbered in 1906 only 648 in the whole state.

http://www.1911encyclopedia.org/Rhode_Island

The Catholic Encyclopedia, Volume XV, Copyright 1912 by Robert Appleton Company, stated as of 1906, a census listed **Rhode Island** as:

Protestant Episcopal: 15,441 (68 **Churches**)
Baptist: 14,761 (75 **Churches**)
Methodist Episcopal: 5,725 (45 **Churches**)
Congregationalist: 9,738 (42 **Churches**)
Lutheran: 2,217 (12 **Churches**)
Free Baptist: 3,306 (30 **Churches**)
Presbyterian: 993 (4 **Churches**)
Universalist: 1,166 (9 **Churches**)
Unitarian: 1,000 (4 **Churches**)
Seventh Day Baptist: 1,040 (5 **Churches**)
Friends: 915 (7 **Churches**)
Catholic: 200,000 (76 **Churches**)

Included in the **Catholic** population are approximately 65,000 Canadians and French, 40,000 Italians, 10,000 Portuguese, 8,000 Poles, and 1,000 Armenians and Syrians. According to a special government report on the census of **religious** bodies of the United States, 76.5 per cent, of the population of the City of **Providence** are **Catholics**. There are 199 **priests** in the **diocese**, including about 47 Canadian and French **priests**, 8 Italian **priests**, and 5 Polish **priests**.

http://www.newadvent.org/cathen/13020a.htm

The Wikipedia Online Encyclopedia, as of 2006, listed **Rhode Island** as:

Christian - 81 percent, consisting of:
- **Episcopal** - 8 percent
- **Baptist** - 6 percent
- **Other Protestant** - 14 percent
- **Catholic** - 52 percent
- **Other Christian** - 1 percent

Jewish - 2 percent
Other Religions - 1 percent

Non-Religious/Non-Reporting - 16 percent

http://en.wikipedia.org/wiki/Rhode_Island#Religion

The U.S. Religious Landscape Survey, conducted by The Pew Forum on Religion & Public Life, 2007, published in the USA Today, listed **Rhode Island** as:

Christian - 71.5 percent, consisting of:
- **Evangelical Protestant** - 10 percent
- **Mainline Protestant** - 13 percent
- **Black Protestant** - 4 percent
- **Catholic** - 43 percent
- **Orthodox** - 1 percent
- **Other Christian** - <0.5 percent

Mormon - <0.5 percent
Jehovah's Witnesses - 1 percent
Jewish - 1 percent
Muslim - <0.5 percent
Buddhist - 1 percent
Hindu - <0.5 percent
Other World Religions - <0.5 percent
Other Faiths - 2 percent
Unaffiliated - 23 percent
Did not answer - 1 percent

www.pewforum.org
www.usatoday.com/news/graphics/pew-religion-08/flash.htm

SCVTO BONÆ VOLVNTATIS TVÆ CORONASTI NOS
FATTI MASCHII PAROLE FEMINE
1632

MARYLAND

Maryland was founded as a colony for persecuted **Catholics** in 1632 by Cecil Calvert and his brother Leonard Calvert. It was named for King Charles I's wife, Henrietta Maria, who was a French **Catholic**. **Religious** tensions of that era were such that the **Puritans** of Boston would not allow Calvert into their port after his transatlantic voyage.

In 1644, during the Civil War in England, Virginia **Anglicans** Richard Ingle and William Claiborne led an attack on Maryland's St. Mary's City, burned the **Church**, took control of government and imprisoned the **Catholic** leaders. Leonard Calvert returned with a small force, drove out the marauders and re-**established** his authority. The population of Maryland in 1645 was between 4,000 and 5,000, with three-fourths being **Catholics**. There were 4 **Franciscan priests**, followed by 4 **Jesuit priests**.

After Leonard Calvert died in 1647, Cecil appointed **Protestant** Governor William Stone in 1648. Cecil granted the **Tolerance Act of 1649,** which allowed any **Christian** to hold office. This was the first instance of freedom of conscience in colonial America.

A few years earlier, Virginia's House of Burgesses passed a law requiring all persons to conform to the **Church of England**. Virginia's Governor strictly enforced this law, resulting in many **Puritans** and **Quakers** fleeing. Governor William Stone invited these refugees to Maryland and gave them a large tract of land where they founded Annapolis.

The **Puritans** complained that their **consciences** would not allow them to submit to a **Catholic** government, so in

1650, they seized the Colony's government and repealed the **Toleration Act.**

They defeated Governor William Stone's forces at the Battle of the Severn and declared **Catholics** ineligible to hold office. Their act "**Concerning Religion**" stated: "That none who profess and exercise the **Papistic**, commonly known as the **Roman Catholic religion**, can be protected in this province." During this **Puritan** usurpation, gangs broke into **Catholic chapels** and **mission houses** and destroyed their property. Three of the four **Jesuit priests** fled to Virginia where they lived in hiding for several years.

A second civil war in England resulted in **Puritan** Commissioners of the English Parliament controlling Maryland from 1652 to 1655. In 1658 the government of the province was restored to Lord Baltimore and the **Toleration Act** of 1649 was put back into effect.

Philip Calvert, brother of Cecil, was governor from 1660 to 1662, then he was succeeded by Charles Calvert, the son Cecil. Charles married and settled in Maryland and there was an era of prosperity. By 1665, the population grew to 16,000, and by 1671 the population was 20,000, of which 5,000 were **Catholic**, served by 5 **priests**.

In 1672, George Fox, founder of the **Quakers-Religious Society of Friends, preached** in Anne Arundel County, Maryland, and the **Friends** formed the Maryland Yearly Meeting. In 1682, **Quakers** began building the **Third Haven Meeting House** in Talbot County.

After the death of his father Cecil in 1675, Charles took the title of third Lord Baltimore. In 1676, attempts were made to force him to provide public support for **clergymen** of the **Church of England**, which he resisted. Several **Protestants** denounced him and assembled in arms in Calvert County to overthrow the government. Governor Thomas Notley suppressed the movement and hanged two of the ringleaders.

John Coode and Colonel Jowles formed "**The Protestant Association** in arms to defend the **Protestant**

religion." Charles Calvert's government was overthrown, Deputy Governor Notley was forced out of office, and a "Committee of Public Safety" was installed. This Committee appealed to and was granted recognition by England's new sovereigns, William and Mary.

Lord Baltimore never regained the government, though he was allowed to retain his lands, which kept Maryland from being absorbed into Virginia or Pennsylvania.

In 1683, Colonel William Stevens of Rehobeth, Maryland, invited **Reverend Francis Makemie** to be a **Presbyterian missionary** in the colonies. Francis Makemie, born in 1658 in County Donegal, Ireland, was educated at Glasgow University and ordained in 1682. In 1684, he built the first **Presbyterian Church** in America at Snow Hill. At Rehobeth in Somerset County, Maryland, he built a **Church** which remains as the oldest standing **Presbyterian Church** in America. Makemie **preached** in a meeting house on the Buckingham Plantation, which became Buckingham **Presbyterian Church** in Berlin, Maryland. He founded Beaver Dam **Presbyterian Church** and Pitts Creek **Presbyterian Church** in Pocomoke City, Maryland. Near a ferry site on the Pocomoke River, the **congregation** erected a log meeting house. Unfriendly residents threw the logs into the river, but members retrieved the logs and rebuilt the meeting house. As early as 1724, **worship** services were held at West Nottingham **Church** in Colora, Maryland.

Rev. Makemie organized the first meeting of **Presbyterian** leaders in America, called a "Presbytery," in the city of Philadelphia, and by 1716 there were four Presbyteries in America: Snow Hill, New York, Philadelphia and New Castle, Delaware. In 1717, these four united to form the Synod of Philadelphia.

In 1691, William and Mary made Maryland a royal colony and appointed Lionel Copley as governor. In 1692, they issued the "**Act of Religion**" which **established** the **Church of England**, even though members of the **Church**

of England were a minority. This Act was very obnoxious to **Catholics**, **Quakers** and other **Dissenters**. The **Test Oath** of 1692 debarred **Catholic** attorneys from practicing in provincial courts.

In 1702, an Act exempted **Puritans**, **Quakers** and other **Dissenters** from the provisions of this law, but not **Catholics**.

By the Act of 1704, **Catholics** were prohibited from practicing their **religion**, **priests** could not exercise their functions, **Catholic** parents were forbidden to teach their children **religion**, and children were encouraged to refuse obedience to the authority of their **Catholic** parents.

Charles Calvert died February 20, 1715. In 1718, a more stringent law was passed barring **Catholics** from holding any office in the province. Another law was adopted stating that if a **Protestant** should die leaving a widow and children, and such a widow should marry a **Catholic**, it should be the duty of the governor and council to remove the children out of the custody of such parents. Re-enacted in 1729, this law gave judges authority to remove **Catholic** children and place them wherever they pleased, without regard to sex or age of the child. There was no appeal.

In the 1740's German **Moravians-Church of the Brethren** began arriving, working particularly with the Native Americans. In 1756, there was legislation proposed in the Maryland Assembly Lower House, as reported in the "Maryland Gazette" published in Annapolis, that any tract of land belonging to **priests**, which they used to provide funds for charity, education, and **missionary work**, should be taken and sold on October 1, 1756. **Priests** were required to take test oaths and if they refused they were banished as "**Romish recusants**."

The bill, introduced by the Governor's Council, 1756, was titled "To prevent the growth of **Popery** within this province." Not only could **priests** not hold property, they had to register their names and put up a bond for their good conduct. They were prohibited from converting **Protestants** under the penalty of high treason and any person educated at a foreign **Catholic seminary** could not inherit or hold lands in the province.

Charles Carroll, the father of the signer of the Declaration of Independence, wrote to his son that Maryland was no longer fit for a **Catholic** to live in. He planned to sell of his great estate and leave, as many **Catholics** were moving to Pennsylvania, but his son dissuaded him. In 1752, the elder Carroll sailed to France to obtain from Louis XV land in the Louisiana territory for Maryland **Catholics** to move to. When this plan failed, many **Catholics** emigrated from Maryland to Kentucky in 1774.

Maryland's **Protestant** Revolution reduced the **Catholic** population so that in 1708, with 33,000 citizens, only 3,000 were **Catholic**. In 1754, with a population of 153,000, only 8,000 were **Catholic**.

The Revolutionary War changed everything. Maryland at first did not join in the cause of Independence, as almost every member of the **Anglican clergy** supported King George III. It was not until **Catholic** Charles Carroll, the son, who was the wealthiest landowner in the province, took a stand for the patriot movement that Maryland was persuaded to take part.

Charles Carroll was the only **Catholic** to sign the Declaration of Independence and he outlived all the other signers. Considered at his death the wealthiest citizen in America, he was elected a U.S. Senator. Maryland chose his statue to represent their State in the U.S. Capitol's Statuary Hall.

Charles Carroll wrote to **Rev.** John Stanford on October, 9, 1827: "To obtain **religious** as well as civil liberty I entered jealously into the Revolution, and observing the **Christian religion** divided into many **sects**, I founded the hope that no one would be so predominant as to become the **religion** of the State. That hope was thus early entertained because all of them joined in the same cause, with few exceptions of individuals."

Charles Carroll wrote on November 4, 1800, to James McHenry, the signer of the Constitution for whom Fort McHenry was named: "Without **morals** a republic cannot subsist any length of time; they therefore who are decrying the **Christian religion**, whose **morality** is so sublime and pure and which insures to the good **eternal happiness**, are undermining the solid foundation of **morals**, the best security for the duration of free governments."

Charles had a cousin John Carroll, who grew up in Maryland, went to Europe to become a **priest**, and upon his return, since there was not one **Catholic Church** in the entire State, he started one on his families farm. **Protestants** at the time did not think **Catholics** could be both loyal to the **Pope** and loyal to the American cause, but John Carroll was such a strong patriot that the Continental Congress in 1776 sent him to Canada with Ben Franklin in an attempt to persuade that French **Catholic** country to join in the Revolution. **Rev.** Carroll's reputation led several States to give **Catholics** equality.

On June 9, 1784, the **Catholic Church** in the United States was organized and **Rev.** John Carroll was appointed superior of the **missions** in all thirteen of the United States.

In 1789, the nation's first **Catholic diocese** was founded in Baltimore and **Rev.** John Carroll was appointed the first **Catholic Bishop** in the United States.

On January 23, 1789, he founded Georgetown University and the nation's first **Catholic seminary**. He began the **parochial school** system and persuaded Elizabeth Seton to start a girls' school in Baltimore.

Bishop John Carroll wrote: "Freedom and independence, acquired by...the mingled blood of **Protestant** and **Catholic** fellow-citizens, should be equally enjoyed by all."

President Washington wrote to Carroll, March 1790: "Your fellow-citizens will not forget the patriotic part which you took in the accomplishment of their Revolution...May the members of your **society** in America, animated alone by the pure spirit of **Christianity**...enjoy every temporal and **spiritual** felicity."

Another cousin, Daniel Carroll of Duddington, was one of two **Catholics** to sign the U.S. Constitution. He provided much of the land where the U.S. Capitol is built and was elected a U.S. Congressman. Carroll's nephew, Robert Brent, was Washington, D.C.'s first mayor, being reappointed by Jefferson and Madison.

In 1817, a Scotch **Presbyterian** immigrant named Thomas Kennedy was elected to the Maryland Legislature and placed on a committee to consider the political disability of the **Jews**, which numbered about 150 in the State. Believing **religion** was "a question which rests, or ought to rest, between man and his **Creator** alone," Kennedy titled his 1819 committee report: "An Act to extend to the **sect** of people professing the **Jewish religion** the same rights and privileges that are enjoyed by **Christians**."

Kennedy's bill was defeated. He introduced it again, and not only was it defeated, it caused Kennedy to lose reelection. Kennedy ran again in 1825 and was reelected. With the help of H.M. Brackenridge, William Worthington, and **Jews** Jacob I. Cohen and Solomon Etting, public opinion turned. Kennedy's eight year effort saw the bill's approval in 1826. A few months later, two **Jews** were elected to Baltimore's City Council.

In 1851, Maryland's Constitution reflected the change to allow **Jews** to hold office, and in 1867, the Constitution was changed again requiring only **belief** in **God** to hold office.

1632
CHARTER OF MARYLAND

ARTICLE 2. Whereas our...right trusty Subject Caecilius Calvert, Baron of Baltimore, in our Kingdom of Ireland...being animated with a laudable and pious Zeal for extending the **Christian Religion**, and also the Territories of our Empire, hath humbly besought Leave of us, that he may transport, by his own Industry, and Expense, a numerous Colony of the English Nation, to a certain Region...in a Country hitherto uncultivated, in the Parts of America, and partly occupied by Savages, having no knowledge of the **Divine Being**, and that all that Region...be given...unto him, and his Heirs...

ARTICLE 4: All **Churches** which (with the increasing **Worship** and **Religion** of **Christ**) within the said Region...the same to be dedicated and consecrated according to the **Ecclesiastical Laws of our Kingdom of England**...

ARTICLE 5. ...Two Indian Arrows of these parts, to be delivered at the said Castle of Winsdor, every year...

ARTICLE 12. But because, that in so remote a Region, placed among so many barbarous Nations, the Incursions as well of the Barbarians themselves, as of other Enemies, Pirates and Ravagers, probably will be feared...We have Given...full and unrestrained Power...unto the aforesaid now Baron of Baltimore...to wage War, and to pursue, even beyond the Limits of their Province, the Enemies and Ravagers aforesaid, infesting those Parts by Land and by Sea, and (**if God shall grant it**) to vanquish and captivate them, and the Captives to put to Death, or, according to their Discretion...

ARTICLE 22: "And if...any Doubts...should arise concerning the true Sense and Meaning of any Word...in this our present Charter...no Interpretation thereof be made whereby **God's Holy and true Christian Religion**...may in any wise suffer by Change.

1632
DECLARATION OF LORD BALTIMORE'S PLANTATION

It pleased his most Excellent Majesty in June last, 1632, to give under the Great Seale of England, a Province near unto the English Plantation in Virginia, to my Lord Baltimore and his heirs for ever: calling it MARYLAND, in honor of our most gracious Queen. My Lord therefore, meaning to plant and people it, first with this express and chief intention to bring to **CHRIST** that and the Countries adjacent, which from the beginning of the World to this day never knew **GOD**; and then with this end, to enlarge his Majesty's Empire and Dominions."

1634
VOYAGE INSTRUCTIONS FROM CECILIUS CALVERT TO HIS BROTHER, GOVERNOR LEONARD CALVERT

To preserve peace and unity amongst all the passengers and to suffer no scandal or offense, whereby just complaint may be made by them in Virginia or in England...and to treat the **Protestants** with as much mildness and favor as justice will require."

MARCH 25, 1634
NARRATIVE OF THE VOYAGE OF THE ARK & DOVE-RELATIO ITINERIS IN MARYLANDIAM

Jesuit Father Andrew White wrote: We celebrated **Mass** for the first time in the island (St. Clement's). This had never been done before in this part of the world. After we had completed, we took on our shoulders a great cross, which we had hewn out of a tree, and advancing in order to the appointed place, with the assistance of the Governor and his associates...we erected a trophy to **Christ the Savior**.

1649
MARYLAND TOLERATION ACT

Forasmuch as in a well governed and **Christian** Commonwealth matters concerning **Religion** and the honor of **God** ought in the first place to be taken into serious consideration and endeavored to be settled, Be it therefore ordered and enacted by the Right Honorable Cecilius Lord Baron of Baltimore absolute Lord and Proprietary of this Province with the advise and consent of this General Assembly:

That whatsoever person or persons within this Province and the Islands thereunto belonging shall from henceforth blaspheme **God**, that is Curse him, or deny **our Savior Jesus Christ** to be the **Son of God**, or shall deny the **Holy Trinity the Father Son** and **Holy Ghost**, or the **Godhead** of any of the said **Three Persons** of the **Trinity** or the **Unity of the Godhead**, or shall use or utter any reproachful Speeches, words or language concerning the said **Holy Trinity**, or any of the said **Three Persons** thereof, shall be punished with death and confiscation or forfeiture of all his or her lands and goods to the Lord Proprietary and his heirs.

And be it also Enacted by the Authority and with the advise and assent aforesaid, That whatsoever person or persons shall from henceforth use or utter any reproachful words or Speeches concerning the **blessed virgin Mary the Mother of our Savior** or the **Holy Apostles or Evangelists** or any of them shall in such case for the first offense forfeit to the said Lord Proprietary and his heirs Lords and Proprietaries of this Province the sum of five pound Sterling or the value thereof to be Levied on the goods and chattels of every such person so offending, but in case such Offender or Offenders, shall not then have goods and chattels sufficient for the satisfying of such forfeiture, or that the same be not otherwise speedily satisfied that then such Offender or Offenders shall be

publicly whipped and be imprisoned during the pleasure of the Lord Proprietary or the Lieutenant or chief Governor of this Province for the time being.

And that every such Offender or Offenders for every second offense shall forfeit ten pound sterling or the value thereof to be levied as aforesaid, or in case such offender or Offenders shall not then have goods and chattels within this Province sufficient for that purpose then to be **publicly** and severely whipped and imprisoned as before is expressed.

And that every person or persons before mentioned offending herein the third time, shall for such third Offense forfeit all his lands and Goods and be for ever banished and expelled out of this Province.

And be it also further Enacted by the same authority advise and assent that whatsoever person or persons shall from henceforth upon any occasion of Offense or otherwise in a reproachful manner or Way declare call or denominate any person or persons whatsoever inhabiting, residing, trafficking, trading or commercing within this Province or within any the Ports, Harbors, Creeks or Havens to the same belonging an **heretic, Schismatic, Idolater, Puritan, Independent, Presbyterian popish priest, Jesuit, Jesuit Papist, Lutheran, Calvinist, AnaBaptist, Brownist, Antinomian, Barrowist, Roundhead, Separatist,** or any other name or term in a reproachful manner relating to **matter of Religion** shall for every such Offense forfeit and loose the sum of ten shillings sterling or the value thereof to be levied on the goods and chattels of every such Offender and Offenders, the one half thereof to be forfeited and paid unto the person and persons of whom such reproachful words are or shall be spoken or uttered, and the other half thereof to the Lord Proprietary and his heirs Lords and Proprietaries of this Province.

But if such person or persons who shall at any time utter or speak any such reproachful words or Language shall not have Goods or Chattels sufficient and overt within this Province to be taken to satisfy the penalty aforesaid or that the same be not otherwise speedily satisfied, that then the person or persons so offending shall be **publicly** whipped, and shall suffer imprisonment without bail or maineprise until he, she or they respectively shall satisfy the party so offended or grieved by such reproachful Language by asking him or her respectively forgiveness **publicly** for such his Offense before the Magistrate of chief Officer or Officers of the Town or place where such Offense shall be given.

And be it further likewise Enacted by the Authority and consent aforesaid That every person and persons within this Province that shall at any time hereafter profane the **Sabbath** or **Lord's Day** called **Sunday** by frequent swearing, drunkenness or by any uncivil or disorderly recreation, or by working on that day when absolute necessity doth not require it shall for every such first offense forfeit 2s 6d sterling or the value thereof, and for the second offense 5s sterling or the value thereof, and for the third offense and so for every time he shall offend in like manner afterwards 10s sterling or the value thereof.

And in case such offender and offenders shall not have sufficient goods or chattels within this Province to satisfy any of the said Penalties respectively hereby imposed for profaning the **Sabbath** or **Lord's day** called **Sunday** as aforesaid,

That in Every such case the party so offending shall for the first and second offense in that kind be imprisoned till he or she shall **publicly** in open Court before the chief Commander Judge or Magistrate, of that County Town or precinct where such offense shall be committed acknowledge the Scandal and offense he hath in that respect given against **God** and the good and civil Government of this Province, And for the third offense and for every time after shall also be **publicly** whipped.

And whereas the enforcing of the **conscience** in **matters of Religion** hath frequently fallen out to be of dangerous Consequence in those commonwealths where it hath been practiced, And for the more quiet and peaceable government of this Province, and the better to preserve mutual Love and amity amongst the Inhabitants thereof,

Be it Therefore also by the Lord Proprietary with the advise and consent of this Assembly Ordained and enacted (except as in this present Act is before Declared and set forth) that **no person or persons whatsoever within this Province,** or the Islands, Ports, Harbors, Creeks, or havens thereunto belonging **professing to believe in Jesus Christ, shall from henceforth be any ways troubled, Molested or discountenanced for or in respect of his or her religion** nor in the free exercise thereof within this Province or the Islands thereunto belonging nor any way compelled to the **belief** or exercise of any other **Religion** against his or her consent, so as they be not unfaithful to the Lord Proprietary, or molest or conspire against the civil Government **established** or to be **established** in this Province under him or his heirs.

And that all and every person and persons that shall presume Contrary to this Act and the true intent and meaning thereof directly or indirectly either in person or estate willfully to wrong disturb trouble or molest any person whatsoever within this Province **professing to believe in Jesus Christ** for or in respect of his or her **religion** or the free exercise thereof within this Province other than is provided for in this Act that such person or persons so offending, shall be compelled to pay trebble damages to the party so wronged or molested, and for every such offense shall also forfeit 20s sterling in money or the value thereof, half thereof for the use of the Lord Proprietary, and his heirs Lords and Proprietaries of this Province, and the other half for the use of the party so wronged or molested as aforesaid, Or if the party so offending as aforesaid shall refuse or be unable to recompense the party so wronged, or to satisfy such fine or forfeiture, then such Offender shall be severely punished by public whipping and imprisonment during the pleasure of the Lord Proprietary, or his Lieutenant or chief Governor of this Province for the time being without bail or maineprise.

And be it further also Enacted by the authority and consent aforesaid That the Sheriff or other Officer or Officers from time to time to be appointed and authorized for that purpose, of the County Towne or precinct where every particular offense in this present Act contained shall happen at any time to be committed and whereupon there is hereby a forfeiture fine or penalty imposed shall from time to time detain and seize the goods and estate of every such person so offending as aforesaid against this present Act or any part thereof, and sell the same or any part thereof for the full satisfaction of such forfeiture, fine, or penalty as aforesaid, Restoring unto the party so offending the Remainder or overplus of the said goods or estate after such satisfaction so made as aforesaid. The freemen have assented.

1648
OATH OF OFFICE PRESCRIBED BY CECIL CALVERT FOR GOVERNOR WILLIAM STONE:

I do further swear that I will not myself, nor any other person, directly or indirectly, trouble, molest, or discountenance any person whatever, in the said province, professing to believe in **Jesus Christ**.

1650
ASSEMBLY OF MARYLAND, PASSED A EULOGY PROCLAMATION HONORING LEONARD CALVERT THREE YEARS AFTER HIS DEATH:

Great and manifold are the benefits wherewith **Almighty God** hath blessed this colony, first brought and landed within the province of Maryland, at your lordship's charge, and continued by your care and industry, in the happy restitution of a blessed peace unto us, being lately wasted by a miserable dissension and unhappy war. But more estimable are the **blessings** poured on this province, in planting **Christianity** among a people that knew not **God**, nor had heard of **Christ**. All which, we recognize and acknowledge to be done and performed, next under **God**, by your lordship's pious intention towards the advancement and **propagation** of the **Christian religion**, and the peace and happiness of this colony and province.

OCTOBER 20, 1654
ACT CONCERNING RELIGION

That such as profess Faith in **GOD by JESUS CHRIST,** though differing in Judgment from from the Doctrine, Worship or Discipline...should not be restrained but protected in the Profession of the Faith and Exercise of their Religion...**Provided such Liberty was not extended to Popery...nor to...Licentiousness.**

SEPTEMBER 30, 1704
ACT TO PREVENT THE GROWTH OF POPERY

That whatsoever **Popish Bishop, Priest or Jesuit,** shall baptize any child...other than such who have Popish Parents or shall say Mass...shall forfeit...fifty pounds Sterling...and shall also suffer six months imprisonment...

And be it further enacted...if any **Papist**...shall keep school or take upon themselves the education...or boarding of youth...such persons...shall upon conviction be transported out of this Province.

NOVEMBER 11, 1776
CONSTITUTION OF MARYLAND

ARTICLE 33: That, as it is the duty of every man to **worship God** in such manner as he thinks most acceptable to him; all persons, professing the **Christian religion**, are equally entitled to protection in their **religious liberty**; wherefore no person ought by any law to be molested in his person or estate on account of his **religious persuasion** or **profession**, or for his **religious practice**; unless, under **color of religion**, any man shall disturb the good order, peace or safety of the State, or shall infringe the laws of **morality**, or injure others, in their natural, civil, or **religious rights**; nor ought any person to be compelled to frequent or maintain, or contribute, unless on contract, to maintain any particular **place of worship**, or any particular **Ministry**; yet the Legislature may, in their discretion, lay a general and equal tax for the support of the **Christian religion**; leaving to each individual the power of appointing the payment over of the money, collected from him, to the support of any particular **place of worship** or **minister**, or for the benefit of the poor of his own **denomination**, or the poor in general of any particular county: but the **Churches**, **chapels**, **glebes**, and all other property now belonging to the **Church of England**, ought to remain to the **Church of England** forever.

And all acts of Assembly, lately passed, for collecting monies for building or repairing particular **Churches** or **chapels** of ease, shall continue in force, and be executed, unless the Legislature shall, by act, supersede or repeal the same: but no county court shall assess any quantity of tobacco, or sum of money, hereafter, on the application of any vestrymen or **Church-wardens**; and every incumbent of the **Church of England**, who hath remained in his **parish**, and performed his duty, shall be entitled to receive the provision and support **established** by the act, entitled "An act for the support of the **clergy** of the **Church of England**, in this Province," till the November court of this present year to be held for the county in which his **parish** shall lie, or partly lie, or for such time as he hate remained in his **parish**, and performed his duty.

ARTICLE 34. That every gift, sale, or devise of lands to any **minister**, public **teacher** or **Preacher** of the **Gospel**, as such, or to any **religious sect,** order or **denomination**, or to or for the support, use or benefit of, or in trust for, any **minister**, public **teacher** or **Preacher** of the **Gospel**, as such, or any **religious sect,** order or **denomination**; and every gifts of sale of goods or chattels to go in succession, or to take place after the death of the seller or donor, or to or for such support, use or benefit; and also every devise of goods or chattels to, or to or for the support, use or benefit of any **minister**, public **teacher** or **Preacher** of the **Gospel**, as such, or any **religious sect,** order or **denomination**, without the leave of the legislature, shall be void; except always any sale, gift, lease or devise of any quantity of land not exceeding two acres, for a **Church**, meeting, or other house of **worship**, and for a burying ground, which shall be improved, enjoyed or used only for such purpose or such sale, gift, lease or devise shall be void.

ARTICLE 35. That no other test or qualification ought to be required, on admission to any office of trust or profit, than such oath of support and fidelity to this State, and such oath of office, as shall be directed by this Convention or the Legislature of this State, and **a declaration of a belief in the Christian religion.**

ARTICLE 36. ...The manner of administering an oath to any person, ought to be...by the attestation of the **Divine Being**. And that the people called **Quakers**, those called **Dunkers**, and those called **Menonists**, holding it unlawful to take an oath on any occasion, ought to be allowed to make their solemn affirmation, in the manner that **Quakers** have been heretofore allowed to affirm...

ARTICLE 55. That every person, appointed to any office of profit or trust, shall, before he enters on the execution thereof, take the following oath; to wit :

"I, A. B., do swear, that I do not hold myself bound in allegiance to the King of Great Britain, and that I will be faithful, and bear true allegiance to the State of Maryland;" and shall also subscribe **a declaration of his belief in the Christian religion.**

SECTION 61. That every judge...shall take the following oath, or affirmation, to wit,

"I A. B. do swear, or affirm, that I...will in all things execute the office of judge of the said elections according the best of my knowledge, without favor or partiality. **So Help Me God**."

That every clerk, before he enters any vote on the polls, shall take the following oath, to wit, "I A. B. do declare, that I will well and faithfully, without favor, affection, or partiality, execute the office of clerk of the elections for.....county, the city of Annapolis, or Baltimore-town, according to the best of my knowledge. **So Help Me God**."

MARCH 1, 1781
ARTICLES OF CONFEDERATION TOOK EFFECT AS MARYLAND BECAME 13TH STATE TO RATIFY THEM:

Preamble. Whereas the delegates of the United States of America in Congress assembled did on the fifteenth day of November in **the Year of Our Lord** one thousand seven hundred and seventy seven, and in the second year of the independence of America agree on certain Articles of Confederation and perpetual union between the States...

ARTICLE 1. The style of this confederation shall be "The United States of America."

ARTICLE 2. Each state retains its sovereignty, freedom, and independence, and every power, jurisdiction and right, which is not by this confederation expressly delegated to the united States, in Congress assembled.

ARTICLE 3. The said states hereby severally enter into a firm league of friendship with each other, for their common defense, the security of their liberties, and their mutual and general welfare, binding themselves to assist each other, against all force offered to, or attacks made upon them, or any of them, on account of **religion**, sovereignty, trade, or any other pretense...

And whereas it has pleased the Great Governor of the World to incline the hearts of the Legislatures we respectively represent in Congress, to approve of, and to authorize us to ratify the said Articles of Confederation and perpetual union.

In witness whereof we have hereunto set our hands in Congress. Done at Philadelphia in the State of Pennsylvania the ninth day of July in **the Year of Our Lord**, 1778, and in the third year of the independence of America.

DECEMBER 23, 1783
GENERAL GEORGE WASHINGTON WROTE FROM MARYLAND'S CAPITOL AT ANNAPOLIS TO INFORM CONGRESS OF HIS RESIGNATION:

Happy in the confirmation of our independence and sovereignty, and pleased with the opportunity offered the United States of becoming a respectable nation, I resign with satisfaction the appointment I accepted with diffidence, a diffidence in my abilities to accomplish so arduous a task, which however, was superseded by a confidence in the rectitude of our cause, the support of the supreme power of the Union, and the patronage of **Heaven**.

The successful termination of the war has verified the most sanguine expectations; and my gratitude for the Interposition of **Providence**, and the assistance I have received from my countrymen, increases with every review of the momentous contest... I consider it an indispensable duty to close this last solemn act of my Official life by commending the Interest of our dearest Country to the protection of **Almighty God**, and those who have the superintendence of them, to his **Holy** keeping.

APRIL 28, 1788
MARYLAND'S STATE SEAL

Approved, picturing a farmer and a fisherman, which reflected the occupations of the early settlers; a shield with the coat of arms of the Calverts and the Crosslands (Alicia Crossland was the mother of the first Baron of Baltimore, George Calvert); and beneath the shield is the Latin motto: Scuto Bonae Voluntatis Tuae Coronasti Nos (Thou hast crowned us with the shield of Thy good will. Ps. 5:12)

1790
BISHOP JOHN CARROLL WROTE TO ROME:

In 1776, American Independence was declared, and a revolution effected, not only in political affairs, but also in those relating to Religion. For a while the thirteen provinces of North America rejected the yoke of England, they proclaimed, at the same time, freedom of conscience and the right of worshipping the Almighty, according to the spirit of the religion to which each one should belong. Before this great event, the Catholic faith had penetrated two provinces only, **Maryland** and **Pennsylvania**.

In all the others the laws against Catholics were in force. Any priest coming from foreign parts, was subject to the penalty of death; all who professed the Catholic faith, were not merely excluded from offices of government, but hardly could be tolerated in a private capacity...

By the Declaration of Independence, every difficulty was removed: the Catholics were placed on a level with their fellow-Christians, and every political disqualification was done away.

MARCH 15, 1790
GEORGE WASHINGTON TO CATHOLIC BISHOP JOHN CARROLL IN MARYLAND:

I feel that my conduct, in war and in peace, has met with more general approbation than could reasonably have been expected and I find myself disposed to consider that fortunate circumstance, in a great degree, resulting from the able support and extraordinary candor of my fellow-citizens of all **denominations**...

America, under the smiles of a **Divine Providence**, the protection of a good government, and the cultivation of manners, **morals**, and **piety**, cannot fail of attaining an uncommon degree of eminence, in literature, commerce, agriculture, improvements at home and respectability abroad... I presume that your fellow-citizens will not forget the patriotic part which you took in the accomplishment of their Revolution, and the **establishment** of their government; or the important assistance which they received from a nation in which the **Roman Catholic faith** is professed...

May the members of your **society** in America, animated alone by the pure spirit of **Christianity**, and still conducting themselves as the faithful subjects of our free government, enjoy every temporal and **spiritual** felicity.

JANUARY 27, 1793
GEORGE WASHINGTON TO CONGREGATION OF THE NEW CHURCH IN BALTIMORE:

We have abundant reason to rejoice that in this Land the light of truth and reason has triumphed over the power of bigotry and superstition, and that every person may here **worship God** according to the **dictates of his own heart**. In this enlightened Age and in this land of equal liberty it is our boast that a man's **religious tenets** will not forfeit the protection of the laws nor deprive him of the right of attaining and holding the highest offices that are known in the United States.

1795
AMENDMENT TO MARYLAND CONSTITUTION

ARTICLE 3. That every person being a member of either of the **religious sects** or **societies** called **Quakers, Menonists, Tunkers**, or **Nicolites**, or **New Quakers**, and who shall be conscientiously scrupulous of taking an oath on any occasion...on making affirmation instead of taking the several oaths appointed by the constitution and form of government, and the several acts of Assembly of this State now in force...such persons may hold and exercise any office of profit or trust to which he may be appointed or elected.

1795
CONSTITUTION OF MARYLAND, AMENDMENT, PROPOSED BY ACT OF 1794.

CHAPTER 49. Every person being a member of either of the **Religious sects** or **societies** called **Quakers, Menonists, Dunkers** or **Nicolites** or **New Quakers** and who shall be conscientiously scrupulous of taking an oath on any occasion being otherwise qualified and duly Elected a Senator, Delegate, or Elector of the Senate, or being otherwise qualified and duly appointed or elected to any office of Profit or Trust, on making affirmation instead of taking the several Oaths appointed by the Constitution and Form of Government, and the several Acts of Assembly of this State now in force, or that hereafter may be made, such person may hold and exercise any office of Profit or Trust to which he may be appointed or elected, and may by such affirmation qualify himself to take a seat in the Legislature and to act therein as a Member of the same in all cases whatever, or to be an Elector of the Senate in as full and ample a manner to all intents and purposes whatever, as persons are now competent and qualified to act who are not conscientiously Scrupulous of taking such Oaths.

1798
AMENDMENT TO MARYLAND CONSTITUTION

ARTICLE 5, SECTION 1. That the people called **Quakers**, those called **Nicolites**, or **New Quakers**, those called **Tunkers**, and those called **Menonists**, holding it unlawful to take an oath on any occasion, shall be allowed to make their solemn affirmation as witnesses, in the manner that **Quakers** have been heretofore allowed to affirm, which affirmation shall be of the same avail as an oath, to all intents and purposes whatever.

1798
CONSTITUTION OF MARYLAND, AMENDMENT, PROPOSED BY ACT OF 1797,

CHAPTER 118. SECTION 1. The people called **Quakers**, those called **Nicolites**, or new **Quakers**, those called **Dunkers**, and those called **Menonists**, holding it unlawful to take an oath on any occasion, shall be allowed to make their solemn affirmation as witnesses in the manner that **Quakers** have been heretofore allowed to affirm, which affirmation shall be of the same avail as an oath, to all intents and purposes whatever.

SECTION 2. Before any of the person's aforesaid shall be admitted as a Witness in any Court of Justice in this State, the court shall be satisfied by such Testimony as they may require, that such person is one of those who profess to be conscientiously scrupulous of taking an oath.

1799
MARYLAND SUPREME COURT, RUNKEL V. WINEMILLER

Chief Justice Samuel Chase rendered the decision:

Religion is of general and public concern, and on its support depend, in great measure, the peace and good order of government, the safety and happiness of the people. By our form of government, the **Christian religion** is the **established religion**; and all **sects** and **denominations** of **Christians** are placed upon the same equal footing, and are equally entitled to protection in their **religious liberty**.

1799
MARYLAND SUPREME COURT, M'CREERY'S LESSEE V. ALLENDER

Regarding a dispute over whether Irish emigrant Thomas M'Creery had become a naturalized American citizen and thereby able to leave an estate to a relative living in Ireland. The Court decided in M'Creery's favor, based on an executed certificate, which stated:

Thomas M'Creery, in order to become... naturalized according to the Act of **Assembly**...on the 30th of September, 1795, took the oath...before the Honorable Samuel Chase, Esquire, then being the Chief Judge of the State of Maryland...and did then and there receive from the said Chief Judge, a certificate thereof...:

Maryland; I, Samuel Chase, Chief Judge of the State of Maryland, do hereby certify all whom it may concern, that...personally appeared before me Thomas M'Creery, and did repeat and subscribe a declaration of his **belief** in the **Christian Religion**, and take the oath required by the Act of **Assembly** of this State, entitled, "An Act for Naturalization."

1810
CONSTITUTION OF MARYLAND, AMENDMENT, PROPOSED BY ACT OF 1809.

CHAPTER 167. It shall not be lawful for the General **Assembly** of this State to lay an equal and general Tax, or any other Tax, on the people of this State, for the support of any **religion**.

1812
JAMES MCHENRY OF MARYLAND SIGNER OF U.S. CONSTITUTION

The namesake of Fort McHenry, he wasa physician who served under General Washington during the Revolution and the U.S. Secretary of War who supervised the **establishment** of West Point Military Academy. As president of the first **Bible society** in Baltimore, Maryland, James McHenry wrote:

Neither, in considering this subject, let it be overlooked, that public utility pleads most forcibly for the general distribution of the **Holy Scriptures**. The **doctrine** they **preach**, the obligations they impose, the punishment they threaten, the rewards they promise, the stamp and image of divinity they bear, which produces a conviction of their truths, can alone secure to society, order and peace, and to our courts of justice and constitutions of government, **purity**, stability and usefulness.

In vain, without the **Bible**, we increase penal laws and draw intrenchments around our institutions. **Bibles** are strong intrenchments. Where they abound, men cannot pursue wicked courses, and at the same time enjoy quiet **conscience**. Consider also, the rich do not possess aught more precious than their **Bible**, and that the poor cannot be presented by the rich with anything of greater value.

Withhold it not from the poor. It is a book of councils and directions, fitted to every situation in which man can be placed. It is an oracle which reveals to mortals the secrets of **heaven** and the hidden **Will of the Almighty**...

It is an estate, whose title is guaranteed by **Christ**, whose delicious fruits ripen every season, survive the worm, and keep through eternity. It is for the purpose of distributing this **Divine** book more effectually and extensively among the multitudes, whose circumstances render such a donation necessary, that your cooperation is most earnestly requested.

1818
CONSTITUTION OF MARYLAND, AMENDMENT, PROPOSED BY ACT OF 1817.

CHAPTER 61. SECTION 1. All persons professing the **Christian Religion**, who hold it unlawful to take an oath on any occasion shall be allowed to make their solemn affirmation, in the same manner that **Quakers** have heretofore been allowed to affirm, which affirmation shall be of same avail as an oath to all intents and purposes whatever.

SECTION 2. Before any such person shall be admitted as a witness or Juror in any Court of Justice in this State, the Court shall be satisfied by competent testimony that such person is conscientiously scrupulous of taking an oath.

1825
CONSTITUTION OF MARYLAND, AMENDMENT, PROPOSED BY THOMAS KENNEDY, ACT OF 1824, CHAPTER 205.

Every Citizen of this State professing the **Jewish Religion**, and who shall hereafter be appointed to any office or public trust under the State of Maryland, shall in addition to the oaths required to be taken by the Constitution and Laws of the State, or of the United States, make and subscribe a declaration of his **belief in a future state of Rewards and Punishments**, in the stead of the declaration now required by the constitution and form of Government of this State.

OCTOBER 9, 1827
CHARLES CARROLL OF MARYLAND, THE ONLY CATHOLIC SIGNER OF THE DECLARATION, WRITING TO REV. JOHN STANFORD:

To obtain **religious** as well as civil liberty I entered jealously into the Revolution, and observing the **Christian religion** divided into many **sects**, I founded the hope that no one would be so predominant as to become the **religion** of the State. That hope was thus early entertained because all of them joined in the same cause, with few exceptions of individuals.

1851
CONSTITUTION OF MARYLAND

PREAMBLE. We, the People of the State of Maryland, grateful to **Almighty God** for our civil and

religious liberty, and taking into our serious consideration the best means of **establishing** a good Constitution in this State, for the sure foundation and more permanent security thereof, declare...

ARTICLE 33. That as it is the duty of every man to **worship God** in such manner -as he thinks most acceptable to Him, all persons are equally entitled to protection in their **religious liberty**, wherefore, no person ought, by any law, to be molested in his person or estate, on account of his **religious persuasion** or **profession**, or for his **religious practice**, unless under **color of religion** any man shall disturb the good order, peace, or safety of the State, or shall infringe the **laws of morality**, or injure others in their natural, civil, or **religious rights**; nor ought any person to be compelled to frequent or maintain or contribute, unless on contract, to maintain any **place of worship** or any **Ministry**; nor shall any person be deemed incompetent as a witness or juror who believes in the **existence of** a **God**, and that under his dispensation such person will be held **morally accountable** for his acts, and be rewarded or punished therefore, either in this world or the world to come.

ARTICLE 34. That no other test or qualification ought to be required, on admission to any office of trust or profit, than such oath of office as may be prescribed by this Constitution, or by the laws of the State, and **a declaration of belief in the Christian religion;** and if the party shall profess to be a **Jew**, the declaration shall be of his **belief** in a **future state of rewards and punishments.**

ARTICLE 35. That every gift, sale or devise of land, to any **minister, public teacher** or **Preacher** of the **Gospel**, as such, or to any **religious sect, order** or **denomination**, or to or for the support, use or benefit of, or in trust for any **minister, public teacher** or **Preacher** of the **Gospel**, as such, or any **religious sect, order** or **denomination**, and every gift or sale of goods or chattels to go in succession, or to take place after the death of the seller or donor, to or for such support, use or benefit; and, also, every devise of goods or chattels, to or for the support, use or benefit of any **minister**, **public teacher** or **Preacher** of the **Gospel**, as such; or any **religious sect, order** or **denomination**, without the leave of the Legislature, shall be void; except always, any sale, gift, lease or devise of any quantity of land, not exceeding five acres, for a **Church**, **meeting house** or other **house of worship**, or **parsonage**, or for a **burying ground**, which shall be improved, enjoyed or used only for such purpose; or such sale, gift, lease or devise shall be void.

ARTICLE 36. That the manner of administering an oath or affirmation to any person ought to be such as those of the **religious persuasion**, **profession** or **denomination** of which he is a member, generally esteem the most effectual confirmation by the attestation of the **Divine Being**.

1864
CONSTITUTION OF MARYLAND

PREAMBLE: We, the People of the State of Maryland, grateful to **Almighty God** for our civil and **religious liberty**, and taking into our serious consideration the best means of **establishing** a good Constitution in this State for the sure foundation and more permanent security thereof, declare...

ARTICLE 24. That hereafter, in this State, there shall be neither slavery nor involuntary servitude, except in punishment of crime, whereof the party shall have been duly convicted; and all persons held to service or labor as slaves, are hereby declared free...

ARTICLE 36. That as it is the duty of every man to **worship God** in such manner as he thinks most acceptable to **Him**, all persons are equally entitled to protection in their **religious liberty**, wherefore, no person ought, by any law, to be molested in his person or estate, on account of his **religious persuasion** or **profession**, or for his **religious practice**, unless under the **color of religion** any man shall disturb the good order, peace, or safety of the State, or shall infringe the **laws of morality**, or injure others in their natural, civil, or **religious rights**; nor ought any person to be compelled to frequent or maintain or contribute, unless on contract, to maintain any **place of worship** or any **Ministry**; nor shall any person be deemed incompetent as a witness or juror who believes in the **existence of God**, and that under his dispensation such person will be held **morally accountable** for his acts, and be rewarded or punished therefore, either in this world or the world to come.

ARTICLE 37. That no other test or qualification ought to be required on admission to any office of trust or profit, than such oath of allegiance and fidelity to this State and the United States, as may be prescribed by this Constitution, and such oath of office and qualification as may be prescribed by this Constitution, or by the laws of the State, and a **declaration of belief in the Christian religion;** or in the **existence of God,** and in a **future state of rewards and punishments.**

ARTICLE 38. That every gift, sale or devise of land, to any **minister**, public **teacher** or **Preacher** of the **Gospel**, as such, or to any **religious sect, order** or **denomination**, or to or for the support, use or benefit of, or in trust for any **minister**, public **teacher** or **Preacher** of the **Gospel** as such, or any **religious sect, order** or **denomination**, and every gift or sale of goods or chattels to go in succession, or to take place after the death of the seller or donor, to or for such support, use or benefit; and, also, every devise of goods or chattels, to or for the support, use or benefit of any **minister**, public **teacher** or **Preacher** of the **Gospel**, as such; or any **religious sect,** order or **denomination**, without the prior or subsequent sanction of the Legislature, shall be void; except always, any sale, gift, lease or devise of any quantity of land, not exceeding five acres, for a **Church**, **meeting house** or other **house of worship**, or **parsonage**, or for a

burying ground, which shall be improved, enjoyed, or used only for such purpose; or such sale, gift, lease or devise shall be void.

ARTICLE 39. That the manner of administering an oath or affirmation to any person, ought to be such as those of the **religious persuasion, profession** or **denomination**, of which he is a member, generally esteem the most effectual confirmation by the attestation of the **Divine Being**.

1867
CONSTITUTION OF MARYLAND:

PREAMBLE. We, the People of the State of Maryland, grateful to **Almighty God** for our civil and **religious liberty**, and taking into our serious consideration the best means of **establishing** a good Constitution in this State for the sure foundation and more permanent security thereof, declare...

ARTICLE 24. That Slavery shall not be re-**established** in this State; but having been abolished, under the policy and authority of the United States, compensation, in consideration thereof, is due from the United States...

ARTICLE 36. That as it is the duty of every man to **worship God** in such manner as he thinks most acceptable to **Him**, all persons are equally entitled to protection in their **religious liberty**; wherefore, no person ought, by any Law to be molested in his person or estate, on account of his **religious persuasion**, or **profession**, or for his **religious practice**, unless, under the **color of religion**, he shall disturb the good order, peace or safety of the State, or shall infringe the **laws of morality**, or injure others in their natural, civil or **religious rights**; nor ought any person to be compelled to frequent, or maintain, or contribute, unless on contract, to maintain, any **place of worship**, or any **Ministry**; nor shall any person, otherwise competent, be deemed incompetent as a witness, or juror, on account of his **religious belief**; provided, he believes in the **existence of**

God, and that under **His dispensation** such person will be held **morally accountable** for his acts, and be rewarded or punished therefore either in this world or the world to come.

ARTICLE 37. That no **religious test** ought ever to be required as a qualification for any office of profit or trust in this State, other than **a declaration of belief in the existence of God;** nor shall the Legislature prescribe any other oath of office than the oath prescribed by this Constitution.

ARTICLE 38. That every gift, sale or devise of land, to any **Minister**, Public **Teacher** or **Preacher** of the **Gospel**, as such, or to any **Religious sect, Order** or **Denomination**, or to, or for the support, use or benefit of, or in trust for, any **Minister**, Public **Teacher** or **Preacher** of the **Gospel**, as such, or any **Religious sect,** Order or **Denomination**; and every gift or sale of goods, or chattels, to go in succession, or to take place after the death of the Seller or Donor, to or for such support, use or benefit; and also every devise of goods or chattels to or for the support, use or benefit of any **Minister**, Public **Teacher** or **Preacher** of the **Gospel**, as such, or any **Religious sect, Order** or **Denomination**, without the prior, or subsequent, sanction of the Legislature, shall be void; except always, any sale, gift, lease or devise of any quantity of land, not exceeding five acres, for a **Church**, **meeting house**, or other **house of worship**, or **parsonage**, or for a **burying ground**, which shall be improved, enjoyed, or used only for such purpose; or such sale, gift, lease, or devise shall be void.

ARTICLE 39. That the manner of administering an oath or affirmation to any person, ought to be such as those of the **religious persuasion**, **profession**, or **denomination**, of which he is a member, generally esteem the most effectual confirmation by the attestation of the **Divine Being**.

NOVEMBER 5, 2002
CONSTITUTION OF MARYLAND

PREAMBLE. We, the People of the State of Maryland, grateful to **Almighty God** for our civil and **religious liberty**, and taking into our serious consideration the best means of **establishing** a good Constitution of this State for the sure foundation and more permanent security thereof, declare...

ARTICLE 24. That Slavery shall not be re-**established** in this State; but having been abolished under the policy and authority of the United States, compensation, in consideration thereof, is due from the United States...

ARTICLE 36. That as it is the duty of every man to **worship God** in such manner as he thinks most acceptable to **Him**, all persons are equally entitled to protection in their **religious liberty**; wherefore, no person ought by any Law to be molested in his person or estate, on account of his **religious persuasion**, or **profession**, or for his **religious practice**, unless, under the **color of religion**, he shall disturb the good order, peace or safety of the State, or shall infringe the **laws of morality**, or injure others in their natural, civil or **religious rights**; nor ought any person to be compelled to frequent, or maintain, or contribute, unless on contract, to maintain, any **place of worship**, or any **Ministry**; nor shall any person, otherwise competent, be deemed incompetent as a witness, or juror, on account of his **religious belief**; provided, he believes in the **existence of God**, and that under His dispensation such person will beheld **morally accountable** for his acts, and be rewarded or punished therefore either in this world or in the world to come.

ARTICLE 37. That no **religious test** ought ever to be required as a qualification for any office of profit or trust in this State, other than **a declaration of belief in the existence of God;** nor shall the Legislature prescribe any other oath of office than the oath prescribed by this Constitution.

ARTICLE 38. That every gift, sale or devise of land to any **Minister**, Public **Teacher** or **Preacher** of the **Gospel**, as such, or to any **Religious sect, Order** or **Denomination**, or to, or for the support, use or benefit of, or in trust for, any **Minister**, Public **Teacher** or **Preacher** of the **Gospel**, as such, or any **Religious sect, Order** or **Denomination** ; and every gift or sale of goods, or chattels, to go in succession, or to take place after the death of the Seller or Donor, to or for such support, use or benefit; and also every devise of goods or chattels to or for the support, use or benefit of any **Minister**, Public **Teacher** or **Preacher** of the **Gospel**, as such, or any **Religious sect, Order** or **Denomination**, without the prior or subsequent sanction of the Legislature, shall be void; except always, any sale, gift, lease or devise of any quantity of land, not exceeding five acres, for a **Church, meeting-house**, or other **house of worship**, or **parsonage**, or for a **burying ground**, which shall be improved, enjoyed, or used only for such purpose; or such sale, gift, lease, or devise shall be void. Provided, however, that except in so far as the General Assembly shall hereafter by law otherwise enact, the consent of the Legislature shall not be required to any gift, grant, deed, or conveyance executed after the 2nd day of November, 1 948, or to any devise or bequest contained in the will of any person dying after said 2nd day of November, 1948 for any of the purposes hereinabove in this Article mentioned.

ARTICLE 39. That the manner of administering an oath or affirmation to any person, ought to be such as those of the **religious persuasion, profession,** or **denomination**, of which he is a member, generally esteem the most effectual confirmation by the **attestation of the Divine Being.**

ELECTIVE FRANCHISE, ARTICLE 1, SECTION 2. No person above the age of twenty-one years, convicted of larceny, or other infamous crime, unless pardoned by the

Governor, shall ever thereafter be entitled to vote at any election in this State; and no person under guardianship, as a lunatic, or, as a person non composmentis, shall be entitled to vote.

MARYLAND RELIGIOUS AFFILIATION

The Encyclopedia Britannica, 11th edition, published in 1911, stated:

There are about 59 **religious sects**, of which the members of the **Roman Catholic Church**, which was prominent in the early history of Maryland, are far the most numerous, having in 1906 166,941 members out of 473,257 **communicants** of all **denominations**; in the same year there were 137,156 **Methodists**, 34,965 **Protestant Episcopalians**, 32,246 **Lutherans**, 30,928 **Baptists**, 17,895 **Presbyterians** and 13,442 members of the **Reformed Church** in the United States.

http://www.1911encyclopedia.org/Maryland

The Catholic Encyclopedia, Volume XV, Copyright 1912 by Robert Appleton Company, stated as of 1906, a census listed **Maryland** as:

Total population - 1,275,434; of this total 37.1 per cent was reported in the census as claiming to be regular **Church**-members

Protestant - 23.7 percent
Catholic - 13.1 percent
Other - 0.3 percent
Not regular attenders - 62.9 percent

The state census of 1908 shows 401 **Church** organizations with a membership (**communicants**) of 473,257. In this enumeration the **Catholics** are set down at

166,941, which is, owing to the government method of computation, 15 per cent less than the actual claim of the **Church** authorities.

Other totals are:
Baptists - 30,928
Disciples, or **Christians** - 2,984
Dunkers - 4450
Friends - 2,079
German Evangelicals - 8,343
Lutheran bodies - 32,246
Methodists - 137,156
Presbyterians - 17,895
Reformed Presbyterians - 13,461
United Brethren - 6,541

The total number of **Church** edifices reported was 2814, with a seating capacity of 810,701 and a valuation of $23,765,172.

http://www.newadvent.org/cathen/09755b.htm

The Wikipedia Online Encyclopedia, as of 2006, listed **Maryland** as:

Christian - 82 percent, consisting of:
- **Baptist** - 18 percent
- **Methodist** - 11 percent
- **Lutheran** - 5 percent
- **Episcopal** - 3 percent
- **Other Protestant** - 19 percent
- **Catholic** - 23 percent
- **Other Christian** - 3 percent

Jewish - 3 percent
Other Religions - 1 percent
Non-Religious/Non-Reporting - 14 percent

http://en.wikipedia.org/wiki/Maryland#Religion

The U.S. Religious Landscape Survey, conducted by The Pew Forum on Religion & Public Life, 2007, published in the USA Today, listed **Maryland** as:

Christian - 72.5 percent, consisting of:
- **Evangelical Protestant** - 15 percent
- **Mainline Protestant** - 20 percent
- **Black Protestant** - 18 percent
- **Catholic** - 18 percent
- **Orthodox** - 1 percent
- **Other Christian** - <0.5 percent

Mormon - <0.5 percent
Jehovah's Witnesses - 1 percent
Jewish - 5 percent
Muslim - <0.5 percent
Buddhist - 1 percent
Hindu - 1 percent
Other World Religions - <0.5 percent
Other Faiths - 1 percent
Unaffiliated - 17 percent
Did not answer - 1 percent

www.pewforum.org
www.usatoday.com/news/graphics/pew-religion-08/flash.htm

THE GREAT SEAL OF THE STATE OF THE NEW YORK
EXCELSIOR

NEW YORK

New York was founded as New Netherlands by the Dutch in 1613 with trading posts on the Hudson River. The early population was about half **Dutch Reformed**, a significant portion English, and a growing number of Germans, Swedes and Finns, who began immigrating after 1639, numbering about 500 out of the colony's total population of 3,500 in 1655.

A controversy arose regarding the German and Scandinavian **Lutheran** immigrants in Middleburg, Long Island, as they were holding **Church** services without an approved **Preacher**. The **Dutch Reformed pastors** of New Amsterdam protested of this to the Director General Peter Stuyvesant, insisting these services be stopped, as **Dutch Reformed** was the **established religion**. The dispute went on for years until the West India Company directors in Amsterdam decided to permit the **Lutherans** the right to **worship** by adjusting the **catechism**.

The **Presbyterians** erected their first meeting house on Eastern Long Island in 1640. **Quakers**, though, were prohibited in New Netherlands in the 1650's.

In 1664, the British navy, led by Admiral William Penn, father of Pennsylvania's founder, defeated the Dutch navy in the first Anglo-Dutch War. England took control of New Netherlands, renaming it New York. The property **rights of the Dutch Reformed Church** were preserved and other **Protestant denominations were tolerated**, though they attempted to **establish** the **Church of England** with varying levels of intensity.

In 1682, the General **Assembly** of the province under the Governor Thomas Dongan, an Irish **Catholic** nobleman, adopted the Charter of Liberties, which proclaimed **religious liberty** to all **Christians**. Although this charter did not receive formal royal sanction, it reflected the growing attitude of **religious toleration**.

In 1688, the Stuart Revolution in England reversed this policy of liberality, and the Province of New York discouraged **denominations** other than **Church of England**. A royal charter founded the **Anglican Trinity Church** in New York City in 1697 and gave it grants of land and civil privileges.

The **Dutch Reformed Churches** continued to grow so that by the time of the Revolution, Dutch were a large percentage of New York's population, including the ancestors of Theodore Roosevelt and Franklin D. Roosevelt.

French **Protestant Huguenots** began arriving in 1680. **Presbyterian minister, Rev.** Francis Makemie founded the first **Presbyterian Church** in the colonies in Maryland in 1684, then founded **Presbyterian Churches** in New York. He was prosecuted by Edward Hyde, Viscount Cornbury, the notorious Governor of New York known for corruption, bribes, and scandalously cross-dressing at public functions to look like his cousin Queen Anne. Viscount Cornbury arrested Francis Makemie for **preaching** without a license, seized a **Presbyterian parsonage** and a **Presbyterian Church** in Jamaica, New York.

New York's provincial legislature passed laws ordering **Catholic priests** and **teachers** to stay away from the province and if there, to depart at once. Penalties included imprisonment or death.

Though directed primarily against French **Catholic missionaries** working among the Iroquois Indians, these laws resulted in the execution of schoolmaster John Ury, accused of being a "**Popish priest**" during the so-called

Negro Plot of 1741. After the Revolutionary War, these laws were repealed in the first session of New York's legislature.

Catholics in New York in 1755 consisted of seafaring people, emigrants, Spanish Blacks from the West Indies, and thousands of French Acadians living along the Atlantic seaboard who were driven from Nova Scotia by the British. From 1752 to 1786, a German **priest** from Philadelphia, **Father** Ferdinand Farmer, occasionally visited them, but they had no **Catholic Church** or organization of any kind. **Archbishop** James Roosevelt Bayley, a relative of both Theodore and Franklin Roosevelt, later wrote that "a **chapel**, if they had had means to erect one, would have been torn down."

The first mention of **Catholic public worship** in New York City was in 1781, after the American victory over the British at Yorktown. **Mass** was held in a carpenter shop, then later at Vauxhall Garden, near the Hudson River by Warren Street. **Father** Farmer listed their number at about two hundred.

The first **Methodist** meeting in the American Colonies was in New York City in 1766.

In 1654, twenty-three **Sephardic Jewish** refugees, mostly of Spanish and Portuguese origin, arrived in the city of New Amsterdam from Recife, Brazil. Though Governor Peter Stuyvesant attempted to expel them, they were allowed to stay. They began the **Shearith Israel Congregation**, but were not allowed to **worship** outside of their homes, hold office, vote, or even volunteer for the militia. Only reluctantly were they granted a **burial ground**.

Only after the city of New Amsterdam became New York were **Jews** permitted to buy land and build the small **"Mill Street Synagogue"** in 1730. This was the first **Jewish house of worship** in North America.

In 1700, there were an estimated 250 **Jews** in the American colonies and by the time of the Revolutionary

War, the remnant was between 1,500 to 2,000 **Jews** out of a total American population of 3 million.

Persecution of **Ashkenazic Jews** in Bavaria, Germany, in the 1830's led to an estimated 250,000 **Jews** immigrating to the United States. It was during this time that the **Jewish** population divided into **Conservative Judaism** and **Reform Judaism.**

The violent pogroms of Russia's Czar in the 1880's forced millions of **Jews** to flee. **Jewish** population in the United States grew from 280,000 in 1880 to 4,500,000 in 1925. In 2006, New York City's **Jewish** population was 1,750,000.

For a period of time New York claimed Vermont and parts of western Massachusetts and Connecticut. After the Revolution of 1776, the British system, which financially supported the **Anglican Church** and set the salaries of **clergymen**, was ended by New York's State Constitution of 1777: "that all such parts of the said Common Law...as may be construed to **establish** or maintain **any particular denomination** of **Christians** or their **ministers**, are repugnant to this constitution and hereby are abrogated and rejected."

The Constitution continued:

"Nothing herein contained shall be construed, adjudged, or taken to abridge or affect the **rights of conscience** or private judgment or in the least to alter or change the **religious** constitutions or governments of either of the said **Churches, congregations** or **societies**, so far as respects or in any wise concerns the **doctrine, discipline** or **worship** thereof."

New York was the first State to write a Constitution after the Revolution began, thus it influenced other States. In 1784, New York legislation was passed "that an universal equality between every **religious denomination**, according to the true spirit of the Constitution, toward each other shall forever prevail."

Immigrants came from the British Islands and Germany in large numbers, and the population of New York City increased from 33,131 in 1790 to 202,589 in 1830, and statewide from 340,120 in 1790 to 1,918,608 in 1830. From 1820 to the late 20th century, New York was the most populous state, now exceeded by California and Texas.

New York's constitutional conventions, courts and legislatures recognized the **Christian religion**. In 1811, Chancellor James Kent, Chief Justice of New York's Supreme Court and the first professor of law at Columbia University, wrote in the case of People vs. Ruggles (8 Johnson 294): "We are a **Christian** people and the **morality** of the country is deeply ingrafted upon **Christianity**."

Some who objected to the Ruggles decision proposed an amendment during New York's 1821 Constitutional Convention that the judiciary should not declare any particular **religion** to be the law of the land. This amendment was defeated, as was stated in the floor debate "that the **Christian religion** was engrafted upon the law and entitled to protection as the basis of **morals** and the strength of Government."

European immigration to New York brought a large proportion of **Catholics**. In 1808, the **Catholic Diocese of New York** was created. **Father** Anthony Kohlmann rebuilt **St. Peter's Church** on Barclay Street and built the old **St. Patrick's Cathedral** on Mott Street. In 1809, he purchased land at 5th Avenue and 50th Street to build the present **St. Patrick's Cathedral**. He **established** a boys' school named the New York Literary Institution.

In 1813, Judge DeWitt Clinton, presiding judge of the New York City Mayor's Court, ruled that **priests** could not be compelled to testify regarding statements made to them during **confession**. This was the first time since the **Reformation** that an English-speaking country protected the confidentiality of **confessions** made to **priests**.

In 1815, **Bishop** John Connolly arrived from Europe as New York's first resident **Bishop** and, together with four **priests**, they **minister**ed to New York's 17,000 mostly Irish **Catholics**. By 1822, New York State had six **Catholic Churches** served one **bishop** and eight **priests**.

Bishop Connolly died in 1825, and was buried in under the **altar** of **St. Patrick's Cathedral**. He was succeeded in 1826 by a French **Bishop**, John Dubois, who had been a classmate of Robespierre and was one of the **priests** who fled France in 1791 during the French Revolution. With a letter of introduction from Marquis de Lafayette, he moved to Richmond, Virginia, where he tutored Patrick Henry's children while learning English. In 1794, he moved to Emmitsburg, Maryland, where he founded Mount **St. Mary's University**.

In 1826, John Dubois was named New York's third **Bishop**. In 1830, he estimated there were 35,000 **Catholics** in New York City and 150,000 across the State, comprised largely of poor Irish immigrants. **Bishop** Dubois served in New York City during the 1832 cholera epidemic, where 3,000 people died in 4 months.

In 1836, he ordained John Neuman at **St. Patrick's Cathedral**, one of New York State's 36 **priests** serving 200,000 **Catholics**. John Neuman became **Bishop** of Philadelphia in 1852. In 1838, the fourth **Bishop** of New York was a native of Ireland, John Hughes. In 1850, he was made the first **Archbishop** of New York.

The 1846 potato famine in Ireland caused millions of Irish **Catholics** to immigrate to New York. By 1890, **Catholics** comprised 55 percent of New York's attending **Church** population.

This influx of **Catholic** immigrants gave rise to an **anti-Catholic** movement called Knownothingism, which pressured New York's legislature to pass a statute in 1855 preventing **Catholic bishops** from holding title to property in trust for **Churches** or **congregations**.

In the 1853 case of Williams v. Williams (8 New York Court of Appeals Reports, p. 525), property could not be given to incorporated **Catholic Churches** in exchange for **Masses**, as this was against the laws that "came to us by inheritance from our British ancestors and as part of our common law" (108 ibid., p. 336). This was reversed in the 1888 case of Holland vs. Alcock.

In the early 1800's, each **Protestant denomination** had schools for their own children, but for the inner-city poor, they had begun common public schools, where would be taught only what all **Protestant denominations** held in common, such as the **King James Bible**, considered a **"non-sectarian"** book.

With the arrival of large numbers of **Catholic** immigrants in the 1850's, **Bishop** John Hughes tried to remove the **King James Bible** from the public schools, considering it a **Protestant** book. When this effort failed, he pulled **Catholic** children out of the public schools and founded an independent **Catholic parochial school system**, which included St. John's College, now Fordham University.

Since Irish **Catholics** had become tax paying citizens, **Bishop** Hughes tried to get the portion of their taxes that went for education redirected to the new **Catholic** schools. He was not successful in this and a heated backlash resulted in the **Archbishop's** residence being stoned. Senator James Blaine of Maine even introduced an Amendment in the U.S. Congress to prohibit any tax revenue from going to **Catholic** schools.

Though Blaine's Amendment did not pass on a Federal level, many States passed "Blaine Amendments," prohibiting State tax money from going to **Catholic** "**sectarian**" schools. Over the years, progressive courts have changed the 1875 use of the word "**sectarian**" from its implied "**anti-Catholic**" meaning to a broader "**anti-Christian**" meaning, thereby prohibiting tax funds from supporting any **Christian** influence in schools.

Early records of **Jews** on Long Island mention Aaron Isaacs, a merchant in the 1700's who was a part owner of Sag Harbor wharf. When the British occupied New York during the Revolutionary War, he fled to Connecticut. Beginning in 1867, **Jewish** settlers in Glen Cove, New York, held services in private homes and, in 1897, founded **Tifereth Israel**, Long Island's oldest continually operating, year-round **congregation**. In 1882, a **Christian** named Joseph Fahys relocated his watch case factory to Sag Harbor, New York, bringing 50 **Jewish** immigrants who had just arrived from Ellis Island. By 1900, the factory employed 100 **Jewish** men, mostly of Polish, Russian and Hungarian descent.

New York's 1905 State Census listed population of 8 million, of which 4,821 were Indians on reservations. The 1910 Federal Census listed New York's population at 9 million, of which 99,232 African Americans. In 2006, New York's population was 19 million.

Through much of American history tensions existed between **Protestants** and **Catholics**. Recent efforts, though, of secularists and atheists to remove public references to **Judeo-Christian faith**, in addition to the growth of Islamic jihadism, has resulted in a growing accomodation of **Protestants** and **Catholics** toward each other, as well as with **orthodox Jews**, as many traditional views sre held in common.

MARCH 27, 1614
CHARTER FOR THOSE WHO DISCOVER ANY NEW PASSAGES, HAVENS, COUNTRIES OR PLACES

The States-General of the United Netherlands... Greeting...Whereas...it would be honorable...that the good inhabitants should...occupy themselves in seeking out and discovering passages, havens, countries, and places that have not before now been discovered...and being informed by some traders that they intend, with **God's merciful help**, by diligence, labor, danger, and expense, to employ themselves thereat...Therefore...wishing that the experiment be free and open to all and every of the inhabitants of this country, have invited and do hereby invite all and every of the inhabitants of the United Netherlands to the aforesaid search.

1624
CHAMBER OF AMSTERDAM ARTICLES FOR THE NEW NETHERLANDS COLONY

They shall within their territory practice no other form of divine worship than that of the **Reformed religion**...and thus **by their Christian life and conduct seek to draw the Indians and other blind people to the knowledge of God and His word**, without, however, persecuting any on account of his faith, but leaving each one the use of his conscience.

NOVEMBER 5, 1626
NOTIFICATION OF THE PURCHASE OF MANHATTAN BY THE DUTCH

High and Mighty Lords: Yesterday arrived here the ship the Arms of Amsterdam, which sailed from New Netherlands, out of the river Mauritius, on the 23rd September. They report that our people are in good heart and live in peace there; the women also have borne some children there. They have purchased the island Manhattes from the Indians for the value of 60 guilders; tis 11,000 morgens in size. They had all their grain sowed by the middle of May and reaped by the middle of August. They send thence samples of summer grain such as wheat, rye, barley, oats, buckwheat, canary seed, beans, and flax. The cargo of the aforesaid ship is: 7246 beaver skins, 17886 otter skins, 675 otter skins, 48 mink skins, 36 wildcat skins, 33 minks, 34 rat skins, considerable oak, timber and hickory.

Herewith, high and mighty Lords, be commended to the **mercy of the Almighty.**

AUGUST, 11, 1628
LETTER TO REV. ADRIANUS SMOUTIUS, MEMBER OF THE CONSISTORY OF THE DUTCH REFORMED CHURCH, AMSTERDAM

At the first administration of **the Lord's Supper** which was observed, not without great joy and comfort to many, we had fully **fifty communicants-Walloons and Dutch;** of whom, a portion made their first **confession of faith** before us, and others exhibted their church certificates. Others had forgotten to bring their certificates with them not thinking that a **church** would be formed and established here; and some who brought them, had lost them unfortunately in a general conflagration, but they were admitted upon the satisfactory testimony of others to whom they were known, and also upon their daily good deportment, since we can not observe strictly all the usual formalities in making a beginning under such circumstances...

We administered the **Holy Sacrament of the Lord** once in four months, provisionally, until a larger number of people shall otherwise require. The Walloons and French have no service on Sundays, otherwise than in the Dutch language, for those who understand no Dutch are very few.

A portion of the Walloons are going back to the Fatherland...Some of them live far away and could not well come in time of heavy rain and storm, so that it is not advisable to appoint any special service in French for so small a number, and that upon an uncertainty. Nevertheless, the **Lord's Supper** was administered to them in the French language, and according to the **French mode**, with a discourse preceding, which I had before me in writing, as I could not trust myself extemporaneously.

JUNE 7, 1629
CHARTER OF FREEDOMS AND EXEMPTIONS TO PATROONS, NEW NETHERLANDS

ARTICLE 27: The Patroons and colonists shall in particular, and in the speediest manner, endeavor to find out ways and means whereby they may support a **Minister** and Schoolmaster, that thus the **service of God** and zeal for **religion** may not grow cool and be neglected among them, and they shall, for the first, procure a Comforter of the sick there.

1655
PETITION TO NEW AMSTERDAM COUNCIL & GOVERNOR GENERAL PETER STUYVESANT

We, Jacob Barsimson and Asser Levy, members of the **Jewish community** wish to be included, not exempted or excluded, from Military Service in the common defense of New Amsterdam.

DECEMBER 27, 1657
REMONSTRANCE OF THE INHABITANTS OF FLUSHING TO NEW NETHERLANDS GOVERNOR PETER STUYVESANT:

Right Honorable, You have been pleased to send up unto us a certain prohibition or command that we should not receive or entertain any of those people called **Quakers** because they are supposed to be by some, seducers of the people. For our part we cannot condemn them in this case, neither can we stretch out our hands against them, to punish, banish or persecute them for out of **Christ God** is a consuming fire, and it is a fearful thing to fall into the hands of the living **God**.

We desire therefore in this case not to judge least we be judged, neither to condemn least we be condemned, but rather let every man stand and fall to his own Master. We are bound by the Law to Do good unto all men, especially to those of the household of **faith**. And though for the present we seem to be unsensible of the law and the Law giver, yet when death and the Law assault us, if we have our advocate to seek, who shall plead for us in this case of **conscience** betwixt **God** and our own **souls**; the powers of this world can neither attack us, neither excuse us, for if **God** justify who can condemn and if **God** condemn there is none can justify.

And for those jealousies and suspicions which some have of them, that they are destructive unto Magistracy and **Ministry**, that can not be, for the magistrate hath the sword in his hand and the **minister** hath the sword in his hand, as witness those two great examples which all magistrates and **ministers** are to follow, **Moses** and **Christ**, whom **God** raised up maintained and defended against all the enemies both of flesh and spirit; and therefore that which is of **God** will stand, and that which is of man will come to nothing.

And as the **Lord** hath taught **Moses** or the civil power to give an outward liberty in the state by the law written in his heart designed for the good of all, and can truly judge who is good, who is civil, who is true and who is false, and can pass definite sentence of life or death against that man which rises up against the fundamental law of the States General; so he hath made his **ministers** a savor of life unto life, and a savor of death unto death.

The law of love, peace and liberty in the states extending to **Jews**, **Turks**, and **Egyptians**, as they are considered the **sons of Adam**, which is the glory of the outward state of Holland, so love, peace and liberty, extending to all in **Christ Jesus**, condemns hatred, war and bondage. And because **our Savior** saith it is impossible but that offenses will come, but woe unto him by whom they cometh, our desire is not to offend one of his little ones, in whatsoever form, name or title he appears in, whether **Presbyterian**, Independent, **Baptist** or **Quaker**, but shall be glad to see anything of **God** in any of them, desiring to doe unto all men as we desire all men should do unto us, which is the true law both of **Church** and State; for **our Savior** saith this is **the law and the prophets.**

Therefore, if any of these said persons come in love unto us, we cannot in **conscience** lay violent hands upon them, but give them free egress and regress unto our Town, and houses, as **God** shall persuade our **consciences**. And in this we are true subjects both of **Church** and State, for we are bound by the **law of God** and man to do good unto all men and evil to no man. And this is according to the patent and charter of our Town, given unto us in the name of the States General, which we are not willing to infringe, and violate, but shall hold to our patent and shall remain, your humble subjects, the inhabitants of Flushing.

Written this 27th day of December, in the year 1657, by me, Edward Heart, Clericus.

OCTOBER 30, 1683
CHARTER OF LIBERTIES AND PRIVILEGES

PARAGRAPH 27 RELIGIOUS TOLERATION:

That no person or persons which **profess faith in God by Jesus Christ** shall at any time be any ways molested punished disquieted or called in question for any difference in **opinion** or matter of religious concernment, who does not actually disturb the civil peace of the province, But that all and every such person or persons may from time to time and at all times freely have and fully enjoy his or their judgments or **consciencies in matters of religion** throughout all the province, they behaving themselves peaceably and quietly and **not using this Liberty to Licentiousness** nor to the civil injury or outward disturbance of others...

AND WHEREAS All the respective **Christian Churches** now in practice within the City of New York and the other places of this province do appear to be priviledged **Churches** and have been so established and confirmed by the former authority of this Government BE it hereby enacted by this General Assembly and by the authority thereof that all the said respective **Christian Churches** be hereby confirmed therein And that they and every of them shall from henceforth forever be held and reputed as priviledged **Churches** and enjoy all their former freedoms; of their **Religion** in **Divine Worship** and **Church discipline** And that all former contracts made and agreed upon for the maintenances of the severall **ministers** of the said **Churches** shall stand and continue in full force and virtue And...all **Christian Churches** that shall hereafter come and settle with in this province shall have the same priviledges.

[Part of paragraph 27 is included in paragraph 38 of New York's 1777 Constitution.]

APRIL 20, 1777
CONSTITUTION OF NEW YORK

Whereas the Delegates of the United American States, in general (Congress convened, did, on the fourth day of July now last past, solemnly publish and declare, in the words following; viz:

"When, in the course of human events, it becomes necessary for one people to dissolve the political bands which have connected them with another, and to assume among the powers of the earth the separate and equal station to which the laws of nature and of **nature's God** entitle them...

"We hold these truths to be self-evident, that all men are created equal; that they are endowed by their **Creator** with certain unalienable rights; that among these are, life, liberty, and the pursuit of happiness; that to secure these rights, governments are instituted among men, deriving their just powers from the consent of the governed; that whenever any form of government becomes destructive of these ends, it is the right of the people to alter or to abolish it, and to institute new government...

"We therefore, the Representatives of the United States of America, in general Congress assembled, appealing to the **Supreme Judge of the world** for the rectitude of our intentions...And for the support of this declaration, with a firm reliance on the protection of **Divine Providence**, we mutually pledge to each other our lives, our fortunes, and our sacred honor."...

7...Every person who now is a freeman of the city of Albany, or...of the city of New York on or before the fourteenth day of October, in **the Year of Our Lord** one thousand seven hundred and seventy-five, and shall be actually and usually resident in the said cities, respectively, shall be entitled to vote...

8. That every elector, before he is admitted to vote, shall...take an oath, or, if of the people called **Quakers**, an affirmation, of allegiance to the State...

35. And this convention doth further, in the name and by the authority of the good people of this State, ordain...that such parts of the common law of England, and of the statute law of England and Great Britain, and of the acts of the legislature of the colony of New York, as together did form the law of the said colony on the 19th day of April, in **the Year of Our Lord** one thousand seven hundred and seventy-five, shall...continue the law of this State...

That all such parts of the said common law, and all such of the said statutes and acts aforesaid, or parts thereof, as may be construed to **establish** or maintain any particular **denomination** of **Christians** or their **ministers**, or concern the allegiance heretofore yielded to, and the supremacy, sovereignty, government, or prerogatives claimed or exercised by, the King of Great Britain and his predecessors, over the colony of New York and its inhabitants, or are repugnant to this constitution, be, and they hereby are, abrogated and rejected...

37. And whereas it is of great importance to the safety of this State that peace and amity with the Indians within the same be at all times...maintained; and whereas the frauds too often practiced towards the said Indians, in contracts made for their lands, have, in divers instances, been productive of dangerous discontents and animosities: Be it ordained, that no purchases or contracts for the sale of lands, made since the fourteenth day of October, in **the Year of Our Lord** one thousand seven hundred and seventy-five, or which may hereafter be made with or of the said Indians, within the limits of this State, shall be binding on the said Indians...unless made...with the consent of the legislature of this State.

38. And whereas we are required, by the benevolent principles of rational liberty, not only to expel civil tyranny, but also to guard against that **spiritual** oppression and intolerance wherewith the bigotry and ambition of weak and wicked **priests** and princes have scourged mankind, this convention doth further, in the name and by the authority of the good people of this State, ordain, determine, and declare, that the free exercise and enjoyment of **religious profession** and **worship**, without discrimination or preference, shall forever hereafter be allowed, within this State, to all mankind: Provided, **That the liberty of conscience, hereby granted, shall not be so construed as to excuse acts of licentiousness,** or justify practices inconsistent with the peace or safety of this State.

39. And whereas the **ministers** of the **Gospel** are, by their **profession**, dedicated to the **service of God** and the **care of souls**, and ought not to be diverted from the great duties of their function; therefore, no **minister** of the **Gospel**, or **priest** of any **denomination** whatsoever, shall, at any time hereafter, under any presence or description...be eligible to, or capable of holding, any civil or military office or place within this State.

40...Every man who enjoys the protection of society to be prepared...to defend it...the militia of this State, at all times...shall be armed...and in readiness for service. That all such of the inhabitants of this State being of the people called **Quakers** as, from scruples of **conscience**, may be averse to the bearing of arms, be there from excused...and do pay to the State such sums of money, in lieu of their personal service.

JULY 6, 1777
JEWISH MARRIAGE CERTIFICATE

Haym Salomon's Ketubah with Rachel Franks was published in New York. President Calvin Coolidge paid tribute to Haym Solomon, May 3, 1925, laying the cornerstone of the **Jewish Community Center**, Washington, D.C.:

There is a romance in the story of Haym Solomon, Polish **Jew** financier of the Revolution. Born in Poland, he was made prisoner by the British forces in New York, and when he escaped set up in business in Philadelphia. He negotiated for Robert Morris all the loans raised in France and Holland, pledged his personal faith and fortune for enormous amounts, and personally advanced large sums to such men as James Madison, Thomas Jefferson, Baron Steuben, General St. Clair, and many other patriot leaders who testified that without his aid they could not have carried on in the cause.

OCTOBER 23, 1779
OATH TO HOLD OFFICE IN NEW YORK:

I do hereby solemnly without any mental reservations and equivocation whatsoever, swear and declare, and call God to witness (or if of the People called Quaker affirm) that I renounce and abjure all allegiance to the King of Great Britain; and that I will bear true faith and allegiance to the State of New York as a free and independent State; and that I will in all things to the best of my knowledge and ability do my duty as a good and faithful subject of the State ought to do. So help me God.

MAY 29, 1789
GEORGE WASHINGTON TO METHODIST EPISCOPAL BISHOP OF NEW YORK:

It shall still be...the sincerity of my desires to contribute whatever may be in my power towards the preservation of the civil and **religious** liberties of the American people. I trust the people of every **denomination**, who demean themselves as good citizens, will have every occasion to be convinced that I shall always strive to prove a **faithful** and impartial patron of genuine, vital **religion**, I must assure you in particular, that I take in the kindest part the promise you make of presenting your **prayers** at the **throne of grace** for me, and that I likewise implore the **Divine benediction** on yourselves and your **religious community**.

OCTOBER 9, 1789
PRESIDENT GEORGE WASHINGTON TO NORTH AMERICA'S SYNOD OF DUTCH REFORMED CHURCHES

While just government protects all in their **religious rights**, **true religion** affords to government its surest support.

1811
NEW YORK SUPREME COURT
PEOPLE V. RUGGLES, 8 JOHNS 545-547

The defendant was indicted...in December, 1810, for that he did, on the 2nd day of September, 1810...wickedly, maliciously, and blasphemously, utter, and with a loud voice publish, in the presence and hearing of divers good and **Christian** people, of and concerning the **Christian religion**, and of and concerning **Jesus Christ**, the false, scandalous, malicious, wicked and blasphemous words following:

"**Jesus Christ** was a bastard, and his mother must be a whore," in contempt of the **Christian religion**...the defendant was tried and found guilty, and was sentenced by the court to be imprisoned for three months, and to pay a fine of $500.

The prosecuting attorney presented to the court:

While the constitution of the State has saved the **rights of conscience**, and allowed a free and fair discussion of all points of controversy among **religious sects**, it has left the principal engrafted on the body of our common law, that **Christianity** is part of the laws of the State, untouched and unimpaired.

Chief Justice Chancellor Kent delivered the decision:

Such words uttered with such a disposition were an offense at common law. In Taylor's case the defendant was convicted upon information of speaking similar words, and the Court...said that **Christianity** was parcel of the law, and to cast contumelious reproaches upon it, tended to weaken the foundation of **moral** obligation, and the efficacy of oaths.

And in the case of Rex v. Woolston, on a like conviction, the Court said...that whatever strikes at the root of **Christianity** tends manifestly to the dissolution of civil government...the authorities show that **blasphemy** against **God** and...profane ridicule of **Christ** or the **Holy Scriptures** (which are equally treated as **blasphemy**), are offenses punishable at common law, whether uttered by words or writings...because it tends to corrupt the **morals** of the people, and to destroy good order.

Such offenses have always been considered independent of any **religious establishment** or the **rights of the Church**. They are treated as affecting the essential interests of civil society...We stand equally in need, now as formerly, of all the **moral discipline**, and of those **principles** of virtue, which help to bind society together.

The people of this State, in common with the people of this country, profess the general **doctrines** of **Christianity**, as the rule of their **faith** and **practice**; and to scandalize the author of these **doctrines** is not only, in a **religious** point of view, extremely impious, but, even in respect to the obligations due to society, is a gross violation of decency and good order. Nothing could be more injurious to the tender **morals** of the young, than to declare such profanity lawful...

The free, equal, and undisturbed enjoyment of **religious** opinion, whatever it may be, and free and decent discussions on any **religious** subject, is granted and secured; but to revile....the **religion** professed by almost the whole community, is an abuse of that right...

We are a **Christian** people, and the **morality** of the country is deeply engrafted upon **Christianity**, and not upon the **doctrines** or **worship** of those impostors. [We are] people whose manners are refined and whose **morals** have been elevated and inspired with a more enlarged benevolence, by means of the **Christian religion**.

Though the constitution has discarded **religious establishments**, it does not forbid judicial cognizance of those offenses against **religion** and **morality** which have no reference to any such **establishment**...[offenses which] strike at the root of **moral obligation**, and weaken the security of the social ties...

This declaration (noble and magnanimous as it is, when duly understood) never meant to withdraw **religion** in general, and with it the best sanctions of **moral** and social obligation from all consideration and notice of the law...

To construe it as breaking down the common law barriers against licentious, wanton, and impious attacks upon **Christianity** itself, would be an enormous perversion of its meaning...**Christianity**, in its enlarged sense, as a **religion revealed** and taught in the **Bible**, is not unknown to our law...The Court are accordingly of opinion that the judgment...must be affirmed.

1821
NEW YORK CONSTITUTION

PREAMBLE: We, the people of the state of New York, acknowledging with gratitude the grace and beneficence of God, in permitting us to make choice of our form of government, do establish this constitution.

ARTICLE 7, SECTION 3. The free exercise and enjoyment of **religious profession** and **worship**, without discrimination or preference, shall be forever hereafter be allowed, within this state, to all mankind: but the **liberty of conscience**, hereby secured, shall not be so construed as to excuse acts of licentiousness, or justify practices inconsistent with the peace or safety of this state.

ARTICLE 7, SECTION 4. And whereas the **ministers** of the **Gospel** are, by their **profession**, dedicated to the **service of God** and the **care of souls**, and ought not to be diverted from the great duties of their function, therefore, no **minister** of the **Gospel**, or **priest** of any **denomination** whatsoever, shall, at any time hereafter, under and preference or description whatever, be eligible to, or capable of holding, any civil or military office or place within this state. (The restriction on **ministers** and **priests** from holding office was removed in the 1846.)

AUGUST 31, 1831
ALEXIS DE TOCQUEVILLE WROTE IN HIS WORK "DEMOCRACY IN AMERICA", 1835:

While I was in America, a witness, who happened to be called at the assizes of the county of Chester (State of New York), declared that he did not believe in the **existence of God** or in the immortality of the soul. The judge refused to admit his evidence, on the ground that the witness had destroyed beforehand all confidence of the court in what he was about to say. The newspapers related the fact without any further comment.

The New York Spectator of August 23d, 1831, relates the fact in the following terms: "The court of common pleas of Chester county (New York), a few days since rejected a witness who declared his **disbelief in the existence of God**. The presiding judge remarked, that he had not before been aware that there was a man living who did not believe in the **existence of God**; that this belief constituted the sanction of all testimony in a court of justice: and that he knew of no case in a **Christian country**, where a witness had been permitted to testify without such **belief**."

1838
NEW YORK STATE LEGISLATURE

In all countries, some kind of **religion** or other has existed in all ages. No people on the face of the globe are without a prevailing national **religion**....

With us it is wisely ordered that no one **religion** shall be **established** by law, but that all persons shall be left free in their choice and in their **mode of worship**. Still, this is a **Christian nation**. Ninety-nine hundredths, if not a larger proportion, of our whole population, believe in the general **doctrines** of the **Christian religion**. Our Government depends for its being on the virtue of the people, - on that virtue that has its foundation in the **morality** of the **Christian religion**; and that **religion** is the common and prevailing **faith** of the people.

There are, it is true, exceptions to this **belief**; but general laws are not made for excepted cases. There are to be found, here and there, the world over, individuals who entertain opinions hostile to the common sense of mankind on subjects of honesty, humanity, and decency; but it would be a kind of republicanism with which we are not acquainted in this country, which would require the great mass of mankind to yield to and be governed by this few.

It is quite unnecessary to enter into a detailed review of all the evidences that **Christianity** is the **common creed** of this nation. We know it, and we feel it, as we know and feel any other unquestioned and admitted truth; the evidence is all around us, and before us, and with us. We know, too, that the exceptions to this general **belief** are rare, - so very rare that they are sufficient only, like other exceptions, to prove a general rule.

1846
NEW YORK CONSTITUTION

PREAMBLE: We, the People of the State of New York, grateful to **Almighty God** for our freedom, in order to secure its blessings, do establish this Constitution.

1861
NEW YORK SUPREME COURT
LINDENMULLER V. THE PEOPLE, 33 BARBOUR REPORTS, 548, 561

The decision of the New York Supreme Court, written by Justice William F. Allen, was adopted by the U.S. Court of Appeals in 1877 and cited by Supreme Court Justice David Josiah Brewer in his 1905 lecture, **"The United States a Christian Nation"**.)

The plaintiff wanted to restrain New York City police from interfering with theatrical performances on **Sunday**, claiming that "the **Bible**, and **religion** with all its ordinances, including the **Sabbath**, are as effectually abolished by the Constitution as they were in France during the Revolution, and so effectually abolished that duties may not be enforced as duties to the State because they have been heretofore associated with acts of **religious worship** or connected with **religious duties**."

New York's Supreme Court wrote:

"It would be strange that a people, **Christian** in **doctrine** and **worship**, many of whom or whose forefathers had sought these shores for the privilege of **worshipping God** in simplicity and **purity** of **faith**, and who regarded **religion** as the basis of their civil liberty and the foundation of their rights, should, in their zeal to secure to all the **freedom of conscience** which they valued so highly, solemnly repudiate and put beyond the pale of the law the **religion** which was as dear to them as life and dethrone the **God**, who, they openly and avowedly profess to believe, had been their protector and guide as a people. **Christianity**...is in fact, and ever has been, the **religion** of the people. This fact is everywhere prominent in all our civil and political history, and has been, from the first, recognized and acted upon by the people, as well as by constitutional conventions, by legislatures and by courts of justice."

The Court decided that every act done maliciously tending to bring **religion** into contempt, may be punished at common law, and the **Christian Sabbath**, as one of the institutions of **religion**, may be protected from desecration by such laws as the Legislature in their wisdom may deem necessary to secure. The Court decision firmly **established** the proposition that, as a civil and political institution, the **establishment** and regulation of a **Sabbath** are within the just powers of civil government.

1894, 1938
NEW YORK CONSTITUTION

PREAMBLE: We, the People of the State of New York, grateful to **Almighty God** for our freedom, in order to secure its blessings, do establish this Constitution.

1958
NEW YORK SUPREME COURT
BAER V. KOLMORGEN 181 N.Y S. 2D. 230, 237

Judge Gallagher rendered the court's decision:

Much has been written in recent years concerning Thomas Jefferson's reference in 1802 to "**a wall of separation between Church and State**."...Jefferson's figure of speech has received so much attention that one would almost think at times that it is to be found somewhere in our Constitution.

NEW YORK RELIGIOUS AFFILIATION

The Encyclopedia Britannica, 11th edition, published in 1911, stated:

Of 3,591,974 members of all **religious denominations** in 1906, 2,285,768 were **Roman Catholics**, 313,689 **Methodist Episcopalians**, 199,923 **Presbyterians**, 193,890 **Protestant Episcopalians**, 176,981 **Baptists**, 124,644 **Lutherans**, 57,351 **Congregationalists**, 35,34 2 **Jews** (heads of families only), 26,183 members of the **German Evangelical Synod**, 19,302 members of **Eastern Orthodox Churches** and 10,761 **Universalists**.

http://www.1911encyclopedia.org/New_York

The Catholic Encyclopedia, Volume XV, Copyright 1912 by Robert Appleton Company, stated:

As of 1890, the Federal Census Bureau listed **Catholics** as 55 percent of **New York's** total **Church** members. As of 1905, New York's population was 8,067,308, of which 43.7 percent were regular **Church** members. In 1906, the Federal Census Bureau listed the number of **Churches** and halls for **worship** in New York at 9,193, with a seating capacity of 3,191,267. **Catholics** were 63.6 percent of New York's total **Church** members and **Protestant Episcopalian** were 2.4 percent.

In 1908, the Department of Education of New York listed the **Catholic Church** of New York as having 451 **parochial schools** with 210,000 students, plus numerous **Catholic** academies and colleges. In 1910, The **Catholic** Annual showed New York's **Catholic** population at 2,722,547 in 1,280 **Churches** with 2,350 **priests**, and 269,420 students in 469 **parochial schools**.

http://www.newadvent.org/cathen/11029a.htm

The Wikipedia Online Encyclopedia, as of 2006, listed **New York** as:

Christian 71.5 percent, consisting of:
- **Baptist** 7.4 percent
- **Methodist** 6 percent
- **Lutheran** 3 percent
- **Charismatic** 2.8 percent
- **Non-Denominational Christian** 7.7 percent
- **Other Protestant** 1.6 percent
- **Catholic** 38.4 percent
- **Greek Orthodox/ Other Christian** 4.4 percent
- **Mormon** 0.2 percent

Jewish 5 percent
Islam 1.9 percent
Other Religious.Non-Reporting 11.6 percent

http://en.wikipedia.org/wiki/New_york#Religion

The U.S. Religious Landscape Survey, conducted by The Pew Forum on Religion & Public Life, 2007, published in the USA Today, listed **New York** as:

Christian - 72.5 percent, consisting of:
- **Evangelical Protestant** - 11 percent
- **Mainline Protestant** - 16 percent
- **Black Protestant** - 5 percent
- **Catholic** - 39 percent
- **Orthodox** - 1 percent
- **Other Christian** - <0.5 percent

Mormon - <0.5 percent
Jehovah's Witnesses - 1 percent
Jewish - 6 percent
Muslim - 1 percent
Buddhist - 1 percent
Hindu - 1 percent
Other World Religions - <0.5 percent

Other Faiths - 1 percent
Unaffiliated - 17 percent
Did not answer - 1 percent

www.pewforum.org
www.usatoday.com/news/graphics/pew-religion-08/flash.htm

THE GREAT SEAL OF THE STATE OF NEW JERSEY
LIBERTY AND PROSPERITY
1776

NEW JERSEY

Italian explorer John Cabot first saw the coast of New Jersey in 1497, as did explorer Giovanni da Verrazano in 1524, but it was explorer Henry Hudson sailing for the Dutch East India Company who dropped anchor in Cape May on September 4, 1609, and went ashore with 20 men to explore. In 1610, English Captain Samuel Argall named the river and the land southwest of it "Delaware," after the Governor of Virginia Thomas West, 3rd Baron De la Warr.

In 1620, Dutch Captain Cornelius Jacobsen Mey first sailed up the Delaware River, and in 1623 built Fort Nassau to trade fur with the Indians. This is considered the first permanent settlement in the State of New Jersey.

In 1637, **Lutherans** intending to settle "New Sweden" in America set sail from the Kingdom of Sweden, which in the 17th century included parts of Finland, Norway, Russia, Poland, Germany, Estonia, and Latvia. The expedition was organized by Finnish Admiral Klaus Fleming, fitted out by Dutch Samuel Blommaert, and led by German Walloon, Peter Minuit.

In March of 1638, the ships Fogel Grip and Kalmar Nyckel arrived in Delaware Bay, an area claimed by the Dutch. They sailed past Cape May and Cape Henlopen and anchored at a rocky point on the Minquas Kill, known today as Swedes' Landing. They built Fort Christina, named after Sweden's Queen Christina, at the present-day site of Wilmington, Delaware.

Within a short time, 600 Swedes and Finns settled there with their **Protestant** Governor, Peter Minuit, who had previously been Director of the Dutch West India Company.

The area was occupied by the Lenni-Lenape tribe, part of the larger Algonquian-speaking Indians. Each with its own chief, the Lenni-Lenape were divided into three groups: Minsi of the stony north country; Unilachitgo near the ocean in the south; and Unami on the river in the center. The chief of the Unami had a reputation for keeping peace and was the leader in settling inter-tribal conflicts. The Lenni-Lenape made a treaty with Peter Minuit in his cabin on the Kalmar Nyckel and arranged the purchase of areas of Pennsylvania, Delaware, and Maryland.

The **Dutch Reformed** settlers protested the landing of the Swedish **Lutherans**, but Minuit ignored the Dutch as their military was weak at the time. After finishing Fort Christina in 1638, Minuit sailed back to Stockholm for more settlers, but died on the way, caught in a hurricane while sailing through the Caribbean to get a load of tobacco.

Finnish **Lutheran** Captain Mauno Kling became the second governor of New Sweden and the colony expanded on the north bank of the Delaware River, **establishing** the trading Fort Nya Elfsborg in 1643, near present-day Salem, New Jersey.

In May 1654, the New Sweden colony, led by Governor Johan Rising, captured without force the Dutch Fort Casimir, present-day New Castle, Delaware. It was renamed **Fort Trinity**. In retaliation, Governor Peter Stuyvesant of the Dutch New Netherland colony came the next year and captured Swedish **Fort Trinity** and Fort Christina. The Dutch allowed Swedish and Finnish **Lutherans** to have a fair amount of freedom.

In 1632, England's Charles I had granted to Sir Edmund Plowden the land of New Jersey, Pennsylvania, Delaware, and Maryland, although he had previously granted Maryland to Lord Baltimore. In 1634, Plowden granted 10,000 acres to Sir Thomas Danby on condition he would settle 100 planters there and prevent "any to live thereon not believing or professing the three **Christian creeds** commonly called the **Apostolical, Athanasian,** and **Nicene."**

In 1642, Plowden sailed up the Delaware River and founded Salem City. Disputes arose between the English, Swedes and Dutch as to who had title to the land. These disputes continued until the British defeated the Dutch in the first Anglo-Dutch War in 1654. Admiral William Penn, father of the famous **Quaker** convert, was instrumental in the English victory.

In 1655, **Jewish** fur traders had ventured to southern New Jersey.

In 1662, a small **Dutch Reformed** school in Bergen, now Jersey City, marked the beginning of New Jersey's free public school system.

On March 12, 1664, England's Charles II deeded to his brother James, Duke of York, the land of New York, New Jersey, and much of New England. In the summer of 1664 armed British vessels appeared in Dutch New Netherlands and after negotiations, the Dutch surrendered.

The British attempted to **establish** the **Church of England**, though enforced with varying degrees of intensity. The Duke of York, who later became England's King James II, transferred New Jersey to Lord John Berkeley and Sir George Carteret. George's brother, Philip Cateret, was made Governor and landed at Elizabeth in August, 1665. By granting a liberal form of government, settlers were attracted from England, Scotland, New England, Long Island and Connecticut. These were largely **Calvinists** from **Presbyterian** and **Congregational communities.**

There was no longer a "New Sweden," yet the Swedish settlers moved further up the Delaware river and in 1669 built Fort Wicaco across the river from New Jersey. This land was later granted to Admiral William Penn's son, who founded Philadelphia there in 1681.

The **Old Swedes' Gloria Dei Church** originally was begun in 1646 on Tinicum Island, the capitol of New Sweden from 1643 to 1655. It was founded by **missionary Johannes Campanius**, who was one of the first to spread the **Gospel** among native Americans. His translation of **Martin Luther's Small Catechism** is the first book published in the Algonquin language. In 1677, the **Church** moved to a blockhouse at Fort Wicaco, now in South Philadelphia, and its new building on the same site, dedicated July 2, 1700, is the oldest **Church** in Pennsylvania.

In 1698, **Jews** settlers Aaron Louzada and his family came to Bound Brook, New Jersey.

A few **Catholics** lived in Woodbridge and Elizabethtown, New Jersey, in 1672, being **ministere**d to by visiting **Father** Harvey and **Father** Gage. **Catholics** were viewed with suspicion, as seen in the case of **Catholic** William Douglass, who was elected a representative from Bergen County but was not allowed in the General Assembly of 1668 because of his **faith**.

On March 18, 1673, Lord Berkeley sold his interest in New Jersey to **Quakers** John Fenwick and Edward Byllinge for one thousand pounds. A dispute arose and William Penn was called to arbitrate, resulting in the divisions of East and West Jersey, the East resembling New England civil government and the West resembling Virginia civil government.

New Jersey was recaptured in 1673 by the Dutch, who held the colony until the British captured in again in 1674, and Sir Edmund Andros was made the new Governor.

New York's **Assembly** passed its first anti-**Catholic** bill in 1691, which was mirrored in New Jersey.

In 1702, Queen Anne united East and West Jersey and appointed her cousin, Lord Cornbury, as Governor. His instruction from Queen Anne was to permit **liberty of conscience** to all persons except "**Papists**." One of the most corrupt Governors and notorious for his cross-dressing as a woman, Lord Cornbury attempted increase his personal wealth by requiring all men to join the militia or pay a fine. When **Quakers** refused, as their **faith** prohibited military service, they had to pay high fines and much of their land was confiscated.

In 1738, Lewis Morris was made Governor and in 1763, William Franklin, son of Ben Franklin, served as the last Royal Governor of New Jersey. He performed the marriage of John and Betsy Ross, and signed the charter for Queen's College, which later became Rutgers University. The first **Jewish** graduate from Rutgers University was Samuel Judah in 1816.

In the 1740's, German **Moravians**, called the "**Church of the Brethren**," began arriving, working particularly with the Native Americans.

In 1744, **Father Theodore Schneider** visited the few **Catholics** in New Jersey. Having some skill in medicine, he traveled under the name Dr. Schneider so as not to be discovered. In 1749, **Father Robert Harding** arrived in Philadelphia from England and occasionally crossed the river to **minister** in New Jersey until his death in 1772. **Father Ferdinand Farmer** also visited New Jersey. Patrick Colvin, perhaps the only **Catholic** in Trenton in 1776, helped furnish boats to transport Washington's army across the Delaware on December 25, 1776.

When the Revolution began, New Jersey was mostly **Episcopal**, **Quaker** and Scotch-Irish **Calvinist**. New Jersey was called "The Crossroads of the Revolution" as so many military engagements occurred there: Trenton, Princeton, Monmouth, Red Bank, Salem, Springfield, Elizabeth, Hackensack, and Morristown.

New Jersey's first State Constitution, July 2, 1776, provided: "that no **Protestant** inhabitant of this colony shall be denied the enjoyment of any civil right."

For four months in 1783, Princeton University was the nation's Capital. It was there the Continental Congress learned the Revolutionary War had ended with the signing of the Treaty of Paris. The President of Princeton was **Presbyterian minister** John Witherspoon, who signed the Declaration of Independence and was a leading member in Congress. Originally from Scotland, Witherspoon taught 9 of the writers of the U.S. Constitution, including James Madison.

New Jersey was the 3rd state to ratify the U.S. Constitution in 1789 and the first to ratify the Bill of Rights in 1791. In 1799, **St. John's parish** at Trenton, now the **parish of the Sacred Heart,** was the first **Catholic parish established** in New Jersey.

On February 15, 1804, New Jersey enacted legislation that slowly phased out slavery.

Beginning in 1846, the terrible famine in Ireland brought a great number of Irish **Catholics** to New Jersey. In 1848, **Father** Bernard J. McQuaid began **pastor** at Madison, New Jersey, and had **missions** at Morristown, Dover, Mendham, Basking Ridge, and Springfield.

He opened the first **Catholic** school in New Jersey at Madison. James Roosevelt Bayley was appointed the first **Bishop** of Newark.

The second Constitution of New Jersey, adopted in 1844, provided: "no **religious test** shall be required as a qualification for any office or public trust; and no person shall be denied the enjoyment of any civil right merely on account of his **religious principles**."

No Civil War battles took place in the state, though over 80,000 enlisted in the Union army.

During the years 1870 to 1910, over a million Swedish **Lutheran** immigrants came to the United States, though most eventually went west, settling in large numbers in Minnesota. With the exception of Ireland and Norway, no other European country has had a higher percentage of its population leave for the United States.

As of 1910, State statutes prohibited worldly business on **Sunday**, except works of necessity or charity.

Oaths were administered to witnesses in courts by the uplifted hand or on the **Bible**, except where one declared himself, for conscientious reasons, to be scrupulous concerning the taking of an oath, in which case his solemn affirmation was accepted.

Blasphemy and profanity were punishable by fine. Legislative sessions were opened by **prayer**.

Catholic clergymen frequently officiated in both houses on such occasions.

Statutes in 1910 stated that marriages could be officiated by state officers and every "**ordained minister of the Gospel**" and that "a man shall not marry any of his ancestors or descendants, or his sister, or the daughter of his brother or sister, or the sister of his father or mother, whether such collateral kindred be of the whole or half blood.

A woman shall not marry any of her ancestors or descendants, or her brother, or the son of her brother or sister, or the brother of her father or mother, whether such collateral kindred be of the whole or half blood."

In 1910, the **Catholic** population of the state was 500,000. According to a 2000 census, New Jersey was 46 percent **Catholic** and 35 percent **Protestant**. Since 2000, **Pentacostal**s have had a 22 percent growth and **Baptists** have had a 10 growth.

The small percent of **Hindus** and **Sikhs** have also grown. New Jersey is 6 percent **Jewish**, making it the State with the largest **Jewish** population by percent. New Jersey also has the second largest **Muslim** population by percent, after Michigan. Immigrants include: Italian, Irish, Black, German, Polish, Slavic, Puerto Rican, Hispanic, Arab and Asian.

Though a small **Jewish** population existed in New Jersey since the late 1600's, the majority of **Jews** arrived between 1892 and 1954, when two thirds of the 12 million **Jewish** immigrants who passed through Ellis Island took the ferry to New Jersey.

They founded Newark's **Beth Israel Hospital**, worked in the silk looms in Paterson, baked challahs in Trento, worked as chicken farmers in Monmouth County, worked in garment factories in Roosevelt and storekeepers in New Brunswick.

Among the **Jews** who came to New Jersey was Albert Einstein, serving as a professor at Princeton.

MARCH 27, 1614
CHARTER FOR THOSE WHO DISCOVER ANY NEW PASSAGES, HAVENS, COUNTRIES OR PLACES

The States-General of the United Netherlands... Greeting...Whereas...it would be honorable...that the good inhabitants should...occupy themselves in seeking out and discovering passages, havens, countries, and places that have not before now been discovered...and being informed by some traders that they intend, with **God's merciful help**, by diligence, labor, danger, and expense, to employ themselves thereat...

Therefore...wishing that the experiment be free and open to all and every of the inhabitants of this country, have invited and do hereby invite all and every of the inhabitants of the United Netherlands to the aforesaid search.

1634
SIR EDMUND PLOWDEN'S GRANT OF TEN THOUSAND ACRES TO SIR THOMAS DANBY

The Grant prevented: "any to live thereon not believing or professing the three **Christian creeds** commonly called the **Apostolical, Athanasian,** and **Nicene.**"

FEBRUARY 10, 1664
CONCESSION & AGREEMENT OF LORDS PROPRIETORS OF PROVINCE OF NEW CAESAREA, OR NEW JERSEY, WITH EVERY ADVENTURER & ALL SUCH AS SHALL SETTLE OR PLANT THERE

ITEM. That no person qualified as aforesaid within the said Province, at any time shall be any ways molested, punished, disquieted or called in question for any difference in opinion or practice in **matter of religious concernments**, who do not actually disturb the civil peace of the said Province;

But that all and every such person and persons may from time to time, and at all times, freely and fully have and enjoy his and their judgments and **consciences** in **matters of religion** throughout the said Province they behaving themselves peaceably ant quietly, and not using this liberty to licentiousness, nor to the civil injury or outward disturbance of others;

Any law, statute or clause contained, or to be contained, usage or custom of this Realm of England, to the contrary thereof in any wise notwithstanding...

AND THAT THE PLANTING OF THE SAID PROVINCE MAY BE THE MORE SPEEDILY PROMOTED

1. We do hereby grant unto all persons who have already adventured to the said Province of New Caesarea or New Jersey, or shall transport themselves, or servants, before the first day of January, which shall be in **the Year of Our Lord** one thousand six-hundred sixty-five, these following proportions, viz: To every freeman that shall go with the first Governor, from the port where he embarks...for the settlement of a plantation there, armed with a good musket, bore twelve bullets to the pound, with ten pounds of powder, and twenty pounds of bullets...and with six months provision for his own person arriving there, one hundred and fifty acres of land English measure...

And for every **Christian servant**, exceeding the age aforesaid, after the expiration of their time of service, seventy-five acres of land for their own use.

2. ITEM. To every master or mistress that shall go...one hundred and twenty acres of land...And for every weaker servant or slave, male or female, exceeding the age of fourteen years, arriving there, sixty acres of land: And to every **Christian servant** to their own use and benefit sixty acres of land...

4. ITEM. For every weaker servant or slave, aged as aforesaid, that shall be so carried or sent thither within the second year, as aforesaid, forty-five acres of land of like measure: And to every **Christian servant** that shall arrive the second year, forty-five acres of land of like after the expiration of his or their time of service, for their own use and benefit.

5. ITEM. To every free man and free woman, armed and provided as aforesaid, that shall go and arrive with an intention to plant...threescore acres of land of like measure: And for every able man servant...armed and provided as aforesaid, the like quantity of threescore acres of land. And for every weaker servant or slave, aged as aforesaid, that he or she shall carry or send within the third year, thirty acres of land: And to every **Christian servant** so carried or sent in the third year, thirty acres of land of like measure, after the expiration of their time of service.

AND THAT THE LANDS MAY BE THE MORE REGULARLY LAID OUT AND ALL PERSONS THE BETTER ASCERTAINED OF THEIR TITLE AND POSSESSION

The Lords proprietors of the Province of New Caesarea or New Jersey, do hereby grant unto A. B. of the in the Province aforesaid, a plantation containing acres

English measure, bounded (as in the certificate) to hold to him or her, his or her heirs or assigns for ever, yielding and paying yearly...the first payment of which rent to begin the five and twentieth day of March, which shall be in **the Year of Our Lord** one thousand six hundred and seventy, according to the English account...

3. ITEM. We do also grant convenient proportions of land for highways and for streets, not exceeding one hundred foot in breadth in cities, towns and villages, &c. and for **Churches**, forts, wharfs, keys, harbors and for public houses; and to each **parish** for the use of their **ministers** two hundred acres, in such places as the General Assembly shall appoint...

Given under our seal of our said Province the tenth day of February in **the Year of Our Lord** one thousand six hundred sixty and four.

DECEMBER 6, 1672
DECLARATION OF THE TRUE INTENT OF LORDS PROPRIETORS & EXPLANATION OF CONCESSIONS TO ADVENTURERS AND PLANTERS OF NEW CAESAREA-NEW JERSEY

2. As to the 8th article, it shall be in the power of the Governor and Council, to constitute and appoint such **ministers** and **Preachers** as shall be nominated and chosen by the several corporations, without the General Assembly and to **establish** their maintenance, giving liberty besides any person or persons to keep and maintain what **Preachers** or **ministers** they please.

JULY 29, 1674
HIS ROYAL HIGHNESS'S GRANT TO THE LORDS PROPRIETORS, SIR GEORGE CARTERET

Charles the Second, by the **Grace of God** of England, Scotland, France and Ireland, King, **Defender of**

the Faith, &c. Anno Domini, one thousand six hundred seventy-four...Whereas his Majesty...grant unto his said Royal Highness James Duke of York...all that part of the main land of New England...

Now...his Royal Highness James Duke of York...hath granted...all that tract of land adjacent to New England, and lying and being to the westward of Long Island and Manhattan Island, and bounded on the east part by the main sea, and part by Hudson's river...unto the said Sir George Carteret...paying...to the said James Duke of York...yearly the sum of twenty nobles of lawful money of England...in the Inner Temple Hall, London, at the feast of **St. Michael** the Arch Angel.

1676
FUNDAMENTAL LAWS OF WEST NEW JERSEY

CHAPTER 16: That no men, nor number of men upon earth, hath power or authority to rule over men's **consciences in religious** matters, therefore it is consented, agreed and ordained, that no person or persons whatsoever within the said Province, at any time...shall be any ways...called in question, or in the least punished or hurt, either in person, estate, or privilege, for the sake of his opinion, judgment, **faith** or **worship** towards **God** in **matters of religion**. But that all and every such person, and persons may from time to time, and at all times, freely and fully have, and enjoy his and their judgments, and the exercises of their **consciences** in **matters of religious worship** throughout all the said Province.

CHAPTER 23: That in all public courts of justice...any person...may freely...attend the said courts, and hear and be present...that justice may not be done in a corner nor in any covert manner, being intended and resolved, by the help **of the Lord**, and by these...Fundamentals...every person...inhabiting the said Province, shall, as far as in us lies, be free from oppression and slavery.

NOVEMBER 25, 1681
PROVINCE OF WEST NEW JERSEY

Forasmuch as it hath pleased **God**, to bring us into this Province of West New Jersey, and settle us here in safety, that we may be a people to the praise and honor of His name, who hath so dealt with us, and for the good and welfare of our posterity to come, we the Governor and Proprietors, freeholders and inhabitants of West New Jersey...do make and constitute these our agreements to be as fundamentals...

10. That **liberty of conscience** in **matters of faith** and **worship** towards **God** shall be granted to all people within the Province aforesaid; who shall live peaceably and quietly therein; and that none of the free people of the said Province, shall be rendered incapable of office in respect of their **faith** and **worship**.

1683
FUNDAMENTAL CONSTITUTIONS OF EAST NEW JERSEY

3...the election shall be after this manner, the names of all the persons qualified in each county...shall be put in a box, and fifty shall be taken out by a boy under ten years of age...These nominators first solemnly declaring before the sheriff, that they shall not name any known to them to be guilty for the time, or to have been guilty for a year before, of adultery, whoredom, drunkeness, or any such **immorality**, or who is insolvent or a fool...

16. All persons living in the Province who confess and acknowledge the one **Almighty** and **Eternal God**, and holds themselves obliged in **conscience** to live peaceably and quietly in a civil society, shall in no way be molested or prejudged for their **religious persuasions** and exercise in **matters of faith** and **worship**; nor shall they be compelled to frequent and maintain any **religious worship, place** or **Ministry** whatsoever:

Yet it is also hereby provided, that no man shall be admitted a member of the great or common Council, or any other place of public trust, who shall not **profaith** in **Christ Jesus**, and solemnly declare that he doth no ways hold himself obliged in **conscience** to endeavor alteration in the government, or seeks the turning out of any in it or their ruin or prejudice, either in person or estate, because they are in his opinion heretics, or differ in their judgment from him: Nor by this article is it intended, that any under the notion of this liberty shall allow themselves to avow **atheism, irreligiousness,** or to practice cursing, swearing, drunkenness, profaness, whoring, adultery, murdering or any kind of violence...

20. That all marriages not forbidden in the **law of God**, shall be esteemed lawful, where the parents or guardians being first acquainted, the marriage is publicly intimated in such places and manner as is agreeable to men's different **persuasions in religion**, being afterwards still solemnized before creditable witnesses, by taking one another as husband and wife...

APRIL, 17, 1709
QUEEN'S ACCEPTANCE OF SURRENDER

This day the several Proprietors of East and West New Jersey in America, did in person present a deed of surrender by them executed under their hands and seals, to her Majesty in Council...

Be it remembered, that on the tenth day of September 1748, John Waddell of the city of New York, merchant, appeared before Robert Hunter Morris, Esq; Chief Justice of the Province of flew Jersey, and **being duly sworn on the Holy Evangelists**, on his oath declared, that the name of John Waddell, signed to the preceding certificate of the 7th of October, 1747, is the proper hand writing of the declarant, and that the matter contained in the said certificate is true.

1776
CONSTITUTION OF NEW JERSEY

ARTICLE 18: That no person shall ever, within this Colony, be deprived of the inestimable privilege of **worshipping Almighty God** in a manner agreeable to the **dictates of his own conscience**; nor, under any pretense whatever, be compelled to attend any **place of worship**, contrary to his own **faith** and judgment; nor shall any person, within this Colony, ever be obliged to pay **tithes**, taxes, or any other rates, for the purpose of building or repairing any other **Church** or **Churches**, place or places of **worship**, or for the maintenance of any **minister** or **Ministry**, contrary to what he believes to be right, or has deliberately or voluntarily engaged himself to perform.

ARTICLE 19: That there shall be no **establishment** of any one **religious sect** in this Province, in preference to another; and that no **Protestant** inhabitant of this Colony shall be denied the enjoyment of any civil right, merely on account of his **religious principles**; but that all persons, professing a **belief** in the **faith** of any **Protestant sect,** who shall demean themselves peaceably under the government, as hereby **established**, shall be capable of being elected into any office of profit or trust, or being a member of either branch of the Legislature, and shall fully and freely enjoy every privilege and immunity, enjoyed by others their fellow subjects.

1844
CONSTITUTION OF NEW JERSEY

PREAMBLE. We, the people of the State of New Jersey, grateful to **Almighty God** for the civil and **religious liberty** which He hath so permitted us to enjoy, and looking to Him for a **blessing** upon our endeavors to secure and transmit the same unimpaired to succeeding generations, do ordain and **establish** this constitution.

ARTICLE 1, SECTION 3. No person shall be deprived of the inestimable privilege of **worshipping Almighty God** in a manner agreeable to the **dictates of his own conscience**; nor under any pretense whatever be compelled to attend any **place of worship** contrary to his **faith** and judgment; nor shall any person be obliged to pay **tithes**, taxes, or other rates for building or repairing any **Church** or **Churches**, place or places of **worship**, or for the maintenance of any **minister** or **Ministry**, contrary to what he believes to be right, or has deliberately and voluntarily engaged to perform.

ARTICLE 1, SECTION 4. There shall be no **establishment** of one **religious sect** in preference to another; no **religious test** shall be required as a qualification for any office or public trust; and no person shall be denied the enjoyment of any civil right merely on account of his **religious principles**.

1947
CONSTITUTION OF NEW JERSEY

PREAMBLE. We, the people of the State of New Jersey, grateful to **Almighty God** for the civil and **religious liberty** which He hath so long permitted us to enjoy, and looking to Him for a **blessing** upon our endeavors to secure and transmit the same unimpaired to succeeding generations, do ordain and **establish** this Constitution.

ARTICLE 1, SECTION 3. No person shall be deprived of the inestimable privilege of **worshipping Almighty God** in a manner agreeable to the **dictates of his own conscience**; nor under any pretense whatever be compelled to attend any **place of worship** contrary to his **faith** and judgment; nor shall any person be obliged to pay **tithes**, taxes, or other rates for building or repairing any **Church** or **Churches**, place or places of **worship**, or for the maintenance of any **minister** or **Ministry**, contrary to what he believes to be right or has deliberately and voluntarily engaged to perform.

ARTICLE 1, SECTION 4. There shall be no **establishment** of one **religious sect** in preference to another; no **religious** or racial test shall be required as a qualification for any office or public trust.

ARTICLE 1, SECTION 5. No person shall be denied the enjoyment of any civil or military right, nor be discriminated against in the exercise of any civil or military right, nor be segregated in the militia or in the public schools, because of **religious principles**, race, color, ancestry or national origin.

NEW JERSEY RELIGIOUS AFFILIATION

The Encyclopedia Britannica, 11th edition, published in 1911, stated:

> As regards **Church** affiliation, in 1906 **Roman Catholics** were the most numerous, with 442,432 members out of a total of 857,548 **communicants** of all **denominations**; there were 122,511 **Methodists**, 79,912 **Presbyterians**, 65,248 **Baptists**, 53,921 **Protestant Episcopalians**, 32,290 members of the **Reformed (Dutch) Church** in America, and 24,147 **Lutherans**.

http://www.1911encyclopedia.org/New_Jersey

The Catholic Encyclopedia, Volume XV, Copyright 1912 by Robert Appleton Company, stated:

> In 1765, **New Jersey** listed the number of **Churches** as:
>
> **Presbyterian** - 55 **Churches**
> **Quaker** - 39 **Churches**
> **Church of England** - 21 **Churches**
> **Dutch Reformed** - 21 **Churches**
> **Baptist** - 19 **Churches**

Dutch Lutheran - 4 Churches
Seventh Day Baptist - 2 Churches
German Reformed - 2 Churches

In 1910, New Jersey's population was 2,537,167, of which 20 percent were **Catholic**.

http://www.newadvent.org/cathen/10790a.htm

According to the 1990 census, **Roman Catholics** formed the largest single **religious** group, constituting 45.9 percent of the population. Other leading **religious** groups in the state included **Baptists** 10.2 percent, **Methodists** 6.7 percent, and **Jews** 4.3 percent.

http://www.worldalmanacforkids.com/explore/states/newjersey.html

The Wikipedia Online Encyclopedia, as of 2006, listed **New Jersey** as:

Christian - 77 percent, consisting of:
- **Baptist** - 9 percent
- **Methodist** - 6 percent
- **Presbyterian** - 4 percent
- **Other Protestant** - 17 percent
- **Catholic** - 39 percent
- **Other Christian** - 2 percent

Jewish - 6 percent
Muslim - 1 percent
Other Religions, e.g. **Hindu, Sikh** - 1 percent
Non-Religious/Non-Reporting - 15 percent

http://en.wikipedia.org/wiki/New_jersey#Religion

The U.S. Religious Landscape Survey, conducted by The Pew Forum on Religion & Public Life, 2007, published in the USA Today, listed **New Jersey** as:

Christian - 73.5 percent, consisting of:
- **Evangelical Protestant** - 12 percent
- **Mainline Protestant** - 13 percent
- **Black Protestant** - 5 percent
- **Catholic** - 42 percent
- **Orthodox** - 1 percent
- **Other Christian** - <0.5 percent

Mormon - <0.5 percent
Jehovah's Witnesses - 1 percent
Jewish - 6 percent
Muslim - 1 percent
Buddhist - 1 percent
Hindu - 2 percent
Other World Religions - <0.5 percent
Other Faiths - 1 percent
Unaffiliated - 12 percent
Did not answer - 2 percent

www.pewforum.org
www.usatoday.com/news/graphics/pew-religion-08/flash.htm

SEAL OF THE STATE OF PENNSYLVANIA

PENNSYLVANIA

As much of the early history of Pennsylvania was included in the history of New Jersey, it will not be repeated here, other than the first settlement in present Pennsylvania was by Swedish settlers in 1642. In 1669 Swedish settlers came up the Delaware River built Fort Wicaco, at a place later granted William Penn. **Old Swedes' Church, "Gloria Dei,"** met in a blockhouse at Fort Wicaco in 1677, being served by German **pastor** Jacobus Fabritius and Swedish schoolmaster Jacob Jongh. Its new building, dedicated July 2, 1700, is the oldest **Church** in Pennsylvania.

Charles II granted the land to William Penn as his personal estate, in repayment of a debt owed to his deceased father, Admiral William Penn. Admiral William Penn fought in the First and Second Anglo-Dutch Wars, 1652-1654 and 1665-1667, and captured Jamaica from Spain in 1655. The son, William Penn, had been persecuted with imprisonment in the Tower for his **conversion** to the **Society of Friends** or **Quakers**. This influenced him to invite all the persecuted **Christians** of Europe to join his colony as a "**Holy experiment.**"

In 1682, twenty-three ships arrived with Welsh **Quaker** settlers. This was the beginning a **Quaker** migration which lasted until 1696, overwhelming the Swedish and Finnish population. In 1693, letters were sent to Sweden's King Charles XI requesting Swedish **Lutheran ministers**, **Bibles** and **Hymnals,** which he send in 1696, under the direction of Jesper Svedberg.

In 1706, **Rev. Francis Makemi**e organized the first meeting of **Presbyterian** leaders in America in Philadelphia.

By 1716 there were a total of four **Presbyteries** in America: Snow Hill; New Castle, Delaware; New York; and Philadelphia. In 1717 those four **Presbyteries** united to form a **Synod - the Synod of Philadelphia.**

A 1718 census listed white population at 40,000, of which half were **Quakers**. Between 1720 and 1729, German settlers known as **New Baptists**, or **Dunkers**, began arriving in Pennsylvania, as well as settlers of the older **denominations** of Swiss and German **AnaBaptists** or **Mennonites** and **Amish.**

They were followed by the **Schwenkfelders**, from the Rhine Valley, Alsatia, Suabia, Saxony, and the Palatinate. Members of the **Lutheran Reformed Congregations** came between 1730 and 1740. **German Moravians**, or **Church of the Brethren**, settled Bethlehem in 1739, having previously been in Georgia. They worked particularly with the Native Americans.

British laws against **dissenters** drove 200,000 Scotch-Irish **Presbyterians** from Scotland and Northern Ireland between 1700 and 1750, most of whom came to Western Pennsylvania, settling in Lehigh, Bucks, and Lancaster Counties, and in the Cumberland Valley.

The first **Jew** in Pennsylvania was Indian trader Isaac Miranda, who settled near Lancaster in the early 1710's. In 1735, the first **Jew** to live in Philadelphia was merchant and shipper Nathan Levy, who purchased land for the first **Jewish cemetery** in Pennsylvania. During the revolutionary war the British continued the European custom of executing deserters at the gates of **Jewish cemeteries** and the gate of the Walnut Street cemetery still has the marks of British bullets.

Several **Jewish** families organized the first **congregation**, Mikveh Israel, in 1740, building the first **Sephardic synagogue** in 1782. The first **Ashkenazic Synagogue, Rodeph Shalom**, was built in 1795. In 1848, Isaac Leeser formed the **Hebrew Education Society of**

Philadelphia and in 1856, banker Hyman Gratz joined him in **establishing** a trust for a **teacher's** college. Beginning in 1895, **Gratz College** is the first **transdenominational Jewish** college in the United States, and the oldest **Hebrew** college in the Western Hemisphere. In 2006, Philadelphia had a population of 285,000 **Jews**.

The Pennsylvania Supreme Court, in Updegraph vs. Commonwealth, 1824, declared the law of 1700 still in force which imposed a penalty upon any who "willfully, premeditatedly and despitefully blaspheme, or speak lightly or profanely of **Almighty God**, **Christ Jesus**, the **Holy Spirit**, or the **Scriptures of Truth**."

1681
CHARTER OF PENNSYLVANIA

Whereas Our Trusty and well beloved Subject William Penn, Esquire, Son and heir of Sir William Penn deceased, out of a commendable Desire to enlarge our English Empire, and promote such useful commodities as may be of Benefit to us and Our Dominions, as also to reduce the savage Natives by gentle and just manners to the Love of Civil Society and **Christian Religion**, hath humbly besought Leave of Us to transport an ample Colony unto a certain Country hereinafter described, in the Parts of America not yet cultivated and planted...

And, because in so remote a Country, and situated near many Barbarous Nations, the incursions as well of the Savages themselves, as of other enemies, pirates and robbers, may probably be feared; Therefore We have given...power by these presents unto the said William Penn...to levy, muster and train all sorts of men...to pursue the enemies and Robbers aforesaid, as well by Sea as by Land, even without the Limits of the said Province, and by **God's assistance** to vanquish and take them, and being taken to put them to death by the Law of War or to save them, at their pleasure...

And...We...require, that if any of the inhabitants of the said Province...shall at any time...signify such their desire to the **Bishop of London** for the time being that any **Preacher** or **Preachers** to be approved of by the said **Bishop**, may be sent unto them for their instruction, that then such **Preacher** or **Preachers** shall and may be and reside within the said Province, without any denial or molestation whatsoever.

JULY 11, 1681
CONCESSIONS TO PROVINCE OF PENNSYLVANIA

That so soon as it pleaseth **God** that the above said persons arrive there, a certain quantity of land, or ground plat, shall be laid out, for a large town or city...

12. And forasmuch, as it is usual with the planters to over-reach the poor natives of the country, in trade, by goods not being good of the kind, or debased with mixtures, with which they are sensibly aggrieved, it is agreed, whatever is sold to the Indians, in consideration of their furs, shall be sold in the market place, and there suffer the test, whether good or bad; if good, to pass; if not good, not to be sold for good, that the natives may not be abused, nor provoked.

13. That no man shall, by any ways or means, in word, or deed, affront, or wrong any Indian, but he shall incur the same penalty of the law, as if he had committed it against his fellow planter, and if any Indian shall abuse, in word, or deed, any planter of this province, that he shall not be his own judge upon the Indian, but he shall make his complaint to the governor of the province, or his lieutenant, or deputy...who shall, to the utmost of his power, take care with the king of the said Indian, that all reasonable satisfaction be made to the said injured planter.

14. That all differences, between the planters and the natives, shall also be ended by twelve men, that is, by six planters and six natives; that so we may live friendly together as much as in us lieth, preventing all occasions of heart-burnings and mischief.

15. That the Indians shall have liberty to do all things relating to improvement of their ground, and providing sustenance for their families, that any of the planters shall enjoy.

16. That the laws, as to slanders, drunkenness, swearing, cursing, pride in apparel, trespasses, distresses, replevins, weights, and measures, shall be the same as in England.

APRIL 25, 1682
FRAME OF GOVERNMENT

Whereas, king Charles the Second, by his letters patents, under the great seal of England, bearing date the fourth day of March in the Thirty and Third Year of the King, for divers considerations therein mentioned, hath been graciously pleased to give and grant unto me William Penn, by the name of William Penn, Esquire, son and heir of Sir William Penn, deceased, and to my heirs and assigns forever, all that tract of land, or Province, called Pennsylvania, in America, with divers great powers, pre-eminences, royalties, jurisdictions, and authorities, necessary for the well-being and government thereof:

Now know ye, that...I, the said William Penn, have...granted...these liberties, franchises, and properties, to be held, enjoyed and kept by the freemen, planters, and inhabitants of the said province of Pennsylvania for ever...

12. That the Governor and provincial Council, shall erect and order all public schools, and encourage and reward the authors of useful sciences and laudable inventions in the said province...

22. That, as often as any day of the month, mentioned in any article of this charter, shall fall upon the first day of the week, commonly called the **Lord's Day**, the business appointed for that day shall be deferred till the next day, unless in case of emergency...

LAWS AGREED UPON IN ENGLAND, &c...

10. That all prisons shall be work-houses, for felons, vagrants, and loose and idle persons; whereof one shall be in every county...

13. That all prisons shall be free, as to fees, food and lodging...

19. That all marriages (not forbidden by the **law of God**, as to nearness of blood and affinity by marriage) shall be encouraged; but the parents, or guardians, shall be first consulted, and the marriage shall be published before it be solemnized; and it shall be solemnized by taking one another as husband and wife, before credible witnesses...

30. That all scandalous and malicious reporters, backbiters, defamers and spreaders of false news, whether against Magistrates, or private persons, shall be accordingly severely punished, as enemies to the peace and concord of this province...

34. That all Treasurers, Judges, Masters of the Rolls, Sheriffs, Justices of the Peace, and other officers and persons whatsoever, relating to courts, or trials of causes or any other service in the government; and all Members elected to serve in provincial Council and General Assembly and all that have right to elect such Members, shall be such as possess **faith in Jesus Christ**, and that are not convicted of ill fame, or unsober and dishonest conversation, and that are of one and twenty years of age, at least; and that all such so qualified, shall be capable of the said several employments and privileges, as aforesaid.

35. That all persons living in this province, who confess and acknowledge the **one Almighty and Eternal God, to be the Creator, Upholder and Ruler of the world;**

and that hold themselves obliged in **conscience** to live peaceably and justly in civil society, shall, in no ways, be molested or prejudiced for their **religious persuasion**, or **practice, in matters of faith and worship**, nor shall they be compelled, at any time, to frequent or maintain any **religious worship, place** or **Ministry** whatever.

36. That, according to the good example of the **primitive Christians**, and the case of the **creation**, every first day of the week, called the **Lord's Day**, people shall abstain from their common daily labor, that they may the better dispose themselves to **worship God** according to their understandings.

37. That as a careless and corrupt administration of justice draws the **wrath of God** upon magistrates, so the wildness and looseness of the people provoke the **indignation of God** against a country: therefore, that all such offenses against **God**, as swearing, cursing, lying, profane talking, drunkenness, drinking of healths, obscene words, incest, sodomy, rapes, whoredom, fornication, and other uncleanness (not to be repeated) all treasons, misprisions, murders, duels, felony, seditions, maims, forcible entries, and other violences, to the persons and estates of the inhabitants within this province; all prizes, stage-plays, cards, dice, May-games, gamesters, masques, revels, bull-battings, cock-fightings, bear-battings, and the like, which excite the people to rudeness, cruelty, looseness, and **irreligion,** shall be respectively discouraged, and severely punished, according to the appointment of the Governor and freemen in provincial Council and General **Assembly**; as also all proceedings contrary to these laws, that are not here made expressly penal.

MAY 5, 1682
PREFACE TO PENNSYLVANIA FRAME OF GOVERNMENT

When the great and wise **God** had made the world, of all his creatures, it pleased him to choose man his Deputy to rule it: and to fit him for so great a charge and trust, he did not only qualify him with skill and power, but with integrity to use them justly.

This native goodness was equally his honor and his happiness, and whilst he stood here, all went well; there was no need of coercive or compulsive means; the precept of **Divine** love and truth, in his bosom, was the guide and keeper of his innocency.

But lust prevailing against duty, made a lamentable breach upon it; and the law, that before had no power over him, took place upon him, and his disobedient posterity, that such as would not live conformable to the **Holy** law within, should fall under the reproof and correction of the just law without, in a Judicial administration.

This the Apostle teaches in divers of his epistles: "The law (says he) was added because of transgression." In another place, "Knowing that the law was not made for the righteous man; but for the disobedient and **unGodly**, for **sinners**, for **unHoly** and profane, for murderers, for whoremongers, for them that defile themselves with mankind, and for man-stealers, for liers, for perjured persons," &c., but this is not all, he opens and carries the matter of government a little further: "Let every soul be subject to the higher powers; for there is no power but of **God**.

The powers that be are ordained of **God**: whosoever therefore resisteth the power, resisteth the **ordinance of God**. For rulers are not a terror to good works, but to evil: wilt thou then not be afraid of the power? Do that which is good, and thou shalt have praise of the same." "He is the

minister of God to thee for good." "Wherefore ye must needs be subject, not only for wrath, but for **conscience sake**."

This settles the **Divine right of government** beyond exception, and that for two ends: first, to terrify evil doers: secondly, to cherish those that do well; which gives government a life beyond corruption, and makes it as durable in the world, as good men shall be.

So that government seems to me a part of **religion** itself, a filing **sacred** in its institution and end.

For, if it does not directly remove the cause, it crushes the effects of evil, and is as such, (though a lower, yet) an emanation of the same **Divine Power**, that is both **author and object of pure religion**; the difference lying here, that the one is more free and mental, the other more corporal and compulsive in its operations: but that is only to evil doers; government itself being otherwise as capable of kindness, goodness and charity, as a more private society.

They weakly err, that think there is no other use of government, than correction, which is the coarsest part of it: daily experience tells us, that the care and regulation of many other affairs, more soft, and daily necessary, make up much of the greatest part of government; and which must have followed the peopling of the world, had Adam never fell, and will continue among men, on earth, under the highest attainments they may arrive at, by **the coming of the blessed Second Adam, the Lord from Heaven**. Thus much of government in general, as to its rise and end.

For particular frames and models, it will become me to say little; and comparatively I will say nothing. My reasons are:

FIRST. That the age is too nice and difficult for it; there being nothing the wits of men are more busy and divided upon. It is true, they seem to agree to the end, to wit, happiness; but, in the means, they differ, as to **Divine**, so to this human felicity; and the cause is much the same, not always want of light and knowledge, but want of using them rightly. Men side with their passions against their reason, and their sinister interests have so strong a bias upon their minds, that they lean to them against the good of the things they know.

SECONDLY. I do not find a model in the world, that time, place, and some singular emergencies have not necessarily altered; nor is it easy to frame a civil government, that shall serve all places alike.

THIRDLY. I know what is said by the several admirers of monarchy, aristocracy and democracy, which are the rule of one, a few, and many, and are the three common ideas of government, when men discourse on the subject. But I choose to solve the controversy with this small distinction, and it belongs to all three: Any government is free to the people under it (whatever be the frame) where the laws rule, and the people are a party to those laws, and more than this is tyranny, oligarchy, or confusion.

But, LASTLY, when all is said, there is hardly one frame of government in the world so ill designed by its first founders, that, in good hands, would not do well enough; and story tells us, the best, in ill ones, can do nothing that is great or good; witness the **Jewish** and Roman states.

Governments, like clocks, go from the motion men give them; and as governments are made and moved by men, so by them they are ruined too. Wherefore governments rather depend upon men, than men upon governments.

Let men be good, and the government cannot be bad; if it be ill, they will cure it. But, if men be bad, let the government be never so good, they will endeavor to warp and spoil it to their turn.

I know some say, let us have good laws, and no matter for the men that execute them: but let them consider, that though good laws do well, good men do better: for good laws may want good men, and be abolished or evaded by ill mend but good men will never want good laws, nor suffer ill ones.

It is true, good laws have some awe upon-ill ministers, but that is where they have not power to escape or abolish them, and the people are generally wise and good: but a loose and depraved people (which is the question) love laws and an administration like themselves.

That, therefore, which makes a good constitution, must keep it, vie: men of wisdom and virtue, qualities, that because they descend not with worldly inheritances, must be carefully **propagated** by a **virtuous education of youth**; for which after ages will owe more to the care and prudence of founders, and the successive magistracy, than to their parents, for their private patrimonies.

These considerations of the weight of government, and the nice and various opinions about it, made it uneasy to me to think of publishing the ensuing frame and conditional laws, foreseeing both the censures, they will meet with, from melt of differing humors and engagements, and the occasion they may give of discourse beyond my design.

But, next to the power of necessity, (which is a solicitor, that will take no denial) this induced me to a compliance, that we have (with **reverence to God**, and **good conscience to men**) to the best of our skill, contrived and composed the frame and laws of this government, to the great end of all government, viz:

To support power in reverence with the people, and to secure the people from the almost of power; that they may be free by their just obedience, and the magistrates honorable, for their just administration: for liberty without obedience is confusion, and obedience without liberty is slavery.

To carry this evenness is partly owing to the constitution, and partly to the magistracy: where either of these fail, government will be subject to convulsions; but where both are wanting, it must be totally subverted; then where both meet, the government is like to endure. Which I humbly **pray** and hope **God** will please to make the lot of this of Pennsylvania. **Amen**. WILLIAM PENN.

FEBRUARY 2, 1683
FRAME OF GOVERNMENT OF PENNSYLVANIA

20. That as often as any days of the month mentioned in any article of this charter, shall fall upon the first day of the week, commonly called the **Lord's Day**, the business appointed for that day, shall be deferred until the next day, unless in cases of emergency...

22. And that the inhabitants of this province and territories thereof may be accommodated with such food and sustenance, as **God, in His Providence**, hath freely afforded, I do also further grant to the inhabitants of this province and territories thereof, liberty to fowl and hunt upon the lands they hold, and all other lands therein not enclosed; and to fish, in all waters in the said lands, and in all rivers and rivulets in, and belonging to, this province and territories thereof, with liberty to draw his or their fish on shore on any man's lands, so as it be not to the detriment, or annoyance of the owner thereof, except such lands as do lie upon inland rivulets that are not bootable, or which are, or may be hereafter erected into manors.

NOVEMBER 1, 1696
FRAME OF GOVERNMENT OF PENNSYLVANIA

Whereas divers persons within this government, cannot, for **conscience sake**, take an oath, upon any account whatsoever, Be it therefore enacted by the authority aforesaid, That all and every such person and persons, being, at any time hereafter, required, upon any lawful occasion, to give evidence, or take an oath, in any case whatsoever, shall, instead of swearing, be permitted to make his, or their solemn affirmation, attest, or declarations...

And be it further enacted by the authority aforesaid, That all persons who shall be hereafter either elected to serve in Council and Assembly, or commissioned or appointed to be Judges, Justices, Masters of the Rolls, Sheriffs, Coroners, and all other offices of State and trust, within this government, who shall conscientiously scruple to take an oath, but when lawfully required, will make and subscribe the declaration and **profession** of their **Christian belief,** according to the late act of parliament, made in the first year of king William, and the late queen Mary, entitled,

An act for exempting their Majesties' **Protestant** subjects, **dissenting** from the **Church of England**, from the penalty of certain laws, shall be adjudged, and are hereby declared to be qualified to act in their said respective offices and places...

Be it further enacted by the authority aforesaid, That as oft as any days of the month, mentioned in any article of this act, shall fall upon the first day of the week, commonly called the **Lord's Day**, the business appointed for that day, shall be deferred till the next day, unless in cases of emergency...

And that the people may be accommodated with such food and sustenance as **God**, in his **Providence**, hath freely afforded, Be it enacted by the authority aforesaid, That the inhabitants of this province and territories thereof, shall have liberty to fish and hunt, upon the lands they hold.

OCTOBER 28, 1701
CHARTER OF PRIVILEGES GRANTED BY WM. PENN TO INHABITANTS OF PENNSYLVANIA

FIRST. Because no People can be truly happy, though under the greatest Enjoyment of Civil Liberties, if abridged of the **Freedom of their Consciences**, as to their

Religious Profession and **Worship**: And **Almighty God** being the **only Lord of Conscience, Father of Lights and Spirits; and the Author as well as Object of all Divine Knowledge, Faith and Worship**, who only doth enlighten the Minds, and persuade and convince the Understandings of People,

I do hereby grant and declare, That no Person or Persons, inhabiting in this Province or Territories, who shall confess and acknowledge **One Almighty God, the Creator, Upholder and Ruler of the World**; and profess him or themselves obliged to live quietly under the Civil Government, shall be in any Case molested or prejudiced, in his or their Person or Estate, because of his or their conscientious **Persuasion** or **Practice**, nor be compelled to frequent or maintain any **religious Worship, Place** or **Ministry**, contrary to his or their Mind, or to do or super any other Act or Thing, contrary to their **religious Persuasion**.

And that all Persons who also profess to believe in **Jesus Christ, the Savior of the World**, shall be capable (notwithstanding their other **Persuasions** and **Practices** in **Point of Conscience** and **Religion**) to serve this Government in any Capacity, both legislatively and executively, he or they solemnly promising, when lawfully required, Allegiance to the King as Sovereign, and Fidelity to the Proprietary and Governor, and taking the Attests as now **established** by the Law made at New-Castle, in the Year One Thousand and Seven Hundred, entitled, An Act directing the Attests of several Officers and Ministers, as now amended and confirmed this present Assembly...

But because the Happiness of Mankind depends so much upon the Enjoying of **Liberty of their Consciences** as aforesaid, I do hereby solemnly declare, promise and grant, for me, my Heirs and Assigns, That the First Article of this Charter relating to Liberty of **Conscience**, and every Part and Clause therein, according to the true Intent and

Meaning thereof, shall be kept and remain, without any Alteration, inviolably for ever.

SEPTEMBER 28, 1776
CONSTITUTION OF PENNSYLVANIA

Whereas all government ought to be instituted and supported for the security and protection of the community as such, and to enable the individuals who compose it to enjoy their natural rights, and the other **blessings** which the **Author of Existence** has bestowed upon man; and whenever these great ends of government are not obtained, the people have a right, by common consent to change it, and take such measures as to them may appear necessary to promote their safety and happiness...

A DECLARATION OF THE RIGHTS OF THE INHABITANTS OF PENNSYLVANIA

1. That all men are born equally free and independent, and have certain natural, inherent and inalienable rights, amongst which are, the enjoying and defending life and liberty, acquiring, possessing and protecting property, and pursuing and obtaining happiness and safety.

2. That all men have a natural and unalienable right to **worship Almighty God** according to the **dictates of their own consciences** and understanding: And that no man ought or of right can be compelled to attend any **religious worship**, or erect or support any **place of worship**, or maintain any **Ministry**, contrary to, or against, his own free will and consent: Nor can any man, who acknowledges the **being of a God**, be justly deprived or abridged of any civil right as a citizen, on account of his **religious sentiments** or peculiar **mode of religious worship**: And that no authority can or ought to be vested in, or assumed by any power whatever, that shall in any case interfere with, or in any manner control, the right of **conscience** in the **free exercise of religious worship**...

FRAME OF GOVERNMENT, SECTION 10.

And each member, before he takes his seat, shall make and subscribe the following declaration, viz:

I do believe in one **God**, the **Creator and Governor of the Universe, the Rewarder of the good and the Punisher of the wicked**. And I do acknowledge the **Scriptures** of the **Old and New Testament** to be given by **Divine Inspiration**. And no further or other **religious test** shall ever hereafter be required of any civil officer or magistrate in this State...

SECTION 45. Laws for the **encouragement of virtue**, and **prevention of vice and immorality**, shall be made and constantly kept in force, and provision shall be made for their due execution: And all **religious societies** or bodies of men heretofore united or incorporated for the advancement of **religion** or learning, or for other pious and charitable purposes, shall be encouraged and protected in the enjoyment of the privileges, immunities and estates which they were accustomed to enjoy, or could of right have enjoyed, under the laws and former constitution of this state...

Passed...the 28th day of September, 1776, and signed by their order. BENJ. FRANKLIN, President.

JULY 1789
GEORGE WASHINGTON TO SOCIETY OF THE UNITED BRETHREN FOR PROPOGATING THE GOSPEL AMONG THE HEATHEN:

It will be a desirable thing, for the protection of the Union, to cooperate, as far as the circumstances may conveniently admit, with the disinterested endeavors of your **Society** to civilize and **Christianize** the Savages of the Wilderness.

OCTOBER 1789
GEORGE WASHINGTON TO QUAKERS OF PENNSYLVANIA, NEW JERSEY, DELAWARE, WESTERN VIRGINIA & MARYLAND

The liberty enjoyed by the People of these States of **worshipping Almighty God** agreeable to their **consciences** is not only among the choicest of their **blessings**, but also of their rights. While men perform their social duties faithfully, they do all that society or the state can with propriety demand or expect; and remain responsible only to their Maker for the **religion**, or modes of **faith**, which they may prefer or profess. Your principles and conduct are well known to me; and it is doing the people called **Quakers** no more than justice to say, (except their declining to share with others the burden of the common defense) there is no **denomination** among us, who are more exemplary and useful citizens.

JANUARY 1790
GEORGE WASHINGTON TO HEBREW CONGREGATIONS OF PHILADELPHIA, NEWPORT, CHARLESTOWN & RICHMOND

The liberal sentiment towards each other which marks every political and **religious denomination** of men in this country stands unrivaled in the history of nations....The power and goodness of the **Almighty** were strongly manifested in the events of our late glorious revolution and His kind interpositions in our behalf has been no less visible in the **establishment** on our present equal government. In war He directed the sword and in peace He has ruled in our councils. My agency in both has been guided by the best intentions, and a sense of the duty which I owe my country....May the same temporal and **eternal blessings** which you implore for me, rest upon your **congregations**.

1790
PENNSYLVANIA CONSTITUTION

We, the people of the Commonwealth of Pennsylvania, grateful to **Almighty God** for the **blessings** of civil and **religious liberty**, and humbly invoking His guidance, do ordain and **establish** this Constitution...

ARTICLE 9, SECTION 3. That all men have a natural and indefeasible right to **worship Almighty God** according to the **dictates of their own consciences**; that no man can of right be compelled to attend, erect, or support any **place of worship**, or to maintain any **Ministry**, against his consent; that no human authority can, in any case whatever, control or interfere with the **rights of conscience**; and that no preference shall ever be given, by law, to any **religious establishment** or **modes of worship**.

ARTICLE 9, SECTION 4. That no person, who acknowledges the **being of a God** and a **future state of rewards and punishments**, shall, on account of his **religious sentiments**, be disqualified to hold any office or place of trust or profit under this commonwealth.

AUGUST 29, 1796
GEORGE WASHINGTON, FROM PHILADELPHIA, DICTATED A "TALK" TO THE CHEROKEE NATION:

Beloved Cherokees, The wise men of the United States meet together once a year, to consider what will be for the good of all their people...

I have thought that a meeting of your wise men once or twice a year would be alike useful to you...I now send my best wishes to the Cherokees, and **pray** the Great Spirit to preserve them.

1814
FIRST HEBREW BIBLE PRINTED IN AMERICA

Thomas Dobson of Philadelphia printed the first **Hebrew Bible** in America. Based on the Amsterdam edition. Text was prepared by Jonathan (Jonas) Horwitz.

1815
PENNSYLVANIA SUPREME COURT COMMONWEALTH V. JESSE SHARPLESS & OTHERS, 2 SERG. & R. 91-92, 97, 101-104

Rendered the grand jury indictment as follows:

Jesse Sharpless...John Haines...George Haines... John Steel...Ephriam Martin...and Mayo...designing, contriving, and intending the **morals**, as well of youth as of divers other citizens of this commonwealth, to debauch and corrupt, and to raise and create in their minds inordinate and lustful desires...in a certain house there...scandalously did exhibit and show for money...a certain lewd...obscene painting, representing a man in an obscene...and indecent posture with a woman, to the manifest corruption and subversion of youth, and other citizens of this commonwealth...offending...[the] dignity of the Commonwealth of Pennsylvania.

Judge Duncan rendered the court's decision:

The defendants have been convicted, upon their own **confession**, of conduct indicative of great **moral** depravity....This court is...invested with power to punish not only open violations of decency and **morality**, but also whatever secretly tends to undermine the principles of society....

Whatever tends to the destruction of **morality**, in general, may be punishable criminally. Crimes are public offenses, not because they are perpetrated publicly, but because their effect is to injure the public. Burglary, though done in secret, is a public offense; and secretly destroying fences is indictable.

Hence, it follows, that an offense may be punishable, if in its nature and by its example, it tends to the corruption of **morals**; although it be not committed in public.

The defendants are charged with exhibiting and showing...for money, a lewd...and obscene painting. A picture tends to excite lust, as strongly as writing; and the showing of a picture is as much a publication as the selling of a book....If the privacy of the room was a protection, all the youth of the city might be corrupted, by taking them, one by one, into a chamber, and there inflaming their passions by the exhibition of lascivious pictures. In the eye of the law, this would be a publication, and a most pernicious one.

Demonstrating the Court's strong feelings on the issue, a second Justice, by the name of Judge Yeates, added to the pronouncement of the court's decision:

Although every **immoral** act, such as lying, etc., is not indictable, yet where the offense charged is destructive of **morality** in general....it is punishable at common law. The destruction of **morality** renders the power of the government invalid...

The corruption of the public mind, in general, and debauching the manners of youth, in particular, by lewd and obscene pictures exhibited to view, must necessarily be attended with the most injurious consequences....No man is permitted to corrupt the **morals** of the people; secret poison cannot be thus disseminated.

1817
PENNSYLVANIA SUPREME COURT
COMMONWEALTH V. WOLF, 3 SERG.,R 48, 50

The Court rendered its decision:

Laws cannot be administered in any civilized government unless the people are taught to revere the sanctity of an oath, and look to **a future state of rewards and punishments** for the deeds of this life. It is of the utmost moment, therefore, that they should be reminded of their **religious** duties at stated periods...

A wise policy would naturally lead to the formation of laws calculated to subserve those salutary purposes. The invaluable privilege of the **rights of conscience** secured to us by the constitution of the commonwealth, was never intended to shelter those persons, who, out of mere caprice, would directly oppose those laws for the pleasure of showing their contempt and abhorrence of the **religious opinions** of the great mass of the citizens.

1824
PENNSYLVANIA SUPREME COURT UPDEGRAPH V. COMMONWEALTH, 11 SERG. & R. 393-394, 398-399, 402-407

The Court rendered it decision: Abner Updegraph...on the 12th day of December [1821]...not having the fear of **God** before his eyes...contriving and intending to scandalize, and bring into disrepute, and vilify the **Christian religion** and the **Scriptures** of truth, in the presence and hearing of several persons...did unlawfully, wickedly and premeditatively, despitefully and blasphemously say..."The **Holy Scriptures** were a mere fable: that they were a contradiction, and that although they contained a number of good things, yet they contained a great many lies." To the great dishonor of **Almighty God**, to the great scandal of the **profession** of the **Christian religion**....

The jury...finds a malicious intention in the speaker to vilify the **Christian religion** and the **Scriptures**, and this court cannot look beyond the record, nor take any notice of the allegation, that the words were uttered by the defendant, a member of a debating association, which convened weekly for discussion and mutual information...

That there is an association in which so serious a subject is treated with so much levity, indecency and scurrility...I am sorry to hear, for it would prove a nursery of vice, a school of preparation to qualify young men for the gallows, and young women for the brothel, and there is not a skeptic of decent manners and good **morals**, who would not consider such debating clubs as a common nuisance and disgrace to the city...

It was the out-pouring of an invective, so vulgarly shocking and insulting, that the lowest grade of civil authority ought not to be subject to it, but when spoken in a **Christian land**, and to a **Christian audience**, the highest offense contra bonos mores; and even if **Christianity** was not part of the law of the land, it is the **popular religion** of the country, an insult on which would be indictable...

Assertion is once more made, that **Christianity** never was received as part of the common **law of this Christian land**; and...added, that if it was, it was virtually repealed by the constitution of the United States, and of this state...If the argument be worth anything, all the laws which have **Christianity** for their object - all would be carried away at one fell swoop - the act against cursing and swearing, and breach **of the Lord's Day**; the act forbidding incestuous marriages, perjury by taking a false oath upon **the book**, fornication and adultery...for all these are founded on **Christianity** - for all these are restraints upon civil liberty...

We will first dispose of what is considered the grand objection - the constitutionality of **Christianity** - for, in effect, that is the question. **Christianity**, general **Christianity**, is and always has been a part of the common law...not **Christianity** founded on any particular **religious** tenets; not **Christianity** with an **established Church**...but **Christianity** with **liberty of conscience** to all men...

I would have it taken notice of, that we do not meddle with the difference of opinion, and that we interfere only where the root of **Christianity** is struck at...The **true principles** of **natural religion** are part of the common law; the essential **principles** of **revealed religion** are part of the common law; so that a person vilifying, subverting or ridiculing them may be prosecuted at common law; but temporal punishments ought not to be inflicted for mere opinions;

Thus this wise legislature framed this great body of laws, for a **Christian country** and **Christian people**. This is the **Christianity** of the common law...and thus, it is irrefragably proved, that the laws and institutions of this state are built on the foundation of reverence for **Christianity**...

In this the Constitution of the United States has made no alteration, nor in the great body of the laws which was an incorporation of the common-law **doctrine** of **Christianity**...without which no free government can long exist. To prohibit the open, public and explicit denial of the **popular religion** of a country is a necessary measure to preserve the tranquillity of a government. Of this, no person in a **Christian country** can complain...

In the Supreme Court of New York it was solemnly determined, that **Christianity** was part of the law of the land, and that to revile the **Holy Scriptures** was an indictable offense.

The case assumes, says Chief Justice Kent, that we are a **Christian people**, and the **morality** of the country is deeply engrafted on **Christianity**. The People v. Ruggles. No society can **tolerate** a willful and despiteful attempt to subvert its **religion**, no more than it would to break down its laws - a general, malicious and deliberate intent to overthrow **Christianity**, general **Christianity**.

Religion and **morality**...are the foundations of all governments. Without these restraints no free government could long exist. It is liberty run mad to declaim against the punishment of these offenses, or to assert that the punishment is hostile to the spirit and genius of our government. They are far from being true friends to liberty who support this **doctrine**, and the promulgation of such opinions, and general receipt of them among the people, would be the sure forerunners of anarchy, and finally, of despotism.

No free government now exists in the world unless where **Christianity** is acknowledged, and is the **religion** of the country...Its foundations are broad and strong, and deep...it is **the purest system of morality,** the firmest auxiliary, and only stable support of all human laws...

Christianity is part of the common law; the act against **blasphemy** is neither obsolete nor virtually repealed; nor is **Christianity** inconsistent with our free governments of the genius of the people.

While our own free constitution secures **liberty of conscience** and **freedom of religious worship** to all, it is not necessary to maintain that any man should have the right **publicly** to vilify the **religion** of his neighbors and of the country; these two privileges are directly opposed.

1838
PENNSYLVANIA CONSTITUTION

SECTION 3. That all men have a natural and indefeasible right to **worship Almighty God** according to the **dictates of their own consciences**; that no man can of right be compelled to attend, erect, or support any **place of worship**, or to maintain any **Ministry**, against his consent; that no human authority can, in any such case whatever, control or interfere with the **rights of conscience**; and that no preference shall ever be given, by law, to any **religious establishments** or modes of **worship**.

SECITION 4. That no person who acknowledges the **being of God** and **a future state of rewards and**

punishments, shall, on account of his **religious sentiments**, be disqualified to hold any office or place of trust or profit under this commonwealth.

1874
PENNSYLVANIA CONSTITUTION

We, the people of the Commonwealth of Pennsylvania, grateful to **Almighty God** for the **blessings** of civil and **religious liberty**, and humbly invoking **His guidance**, do ordain and **establish** this Constitution. Natural right of **conscience** and **freedom of worship**...

SECTION 3. All men have a natural and indefeasible right to **worship Almighty God** according to the **dictates of their own consciences**; no man can of right be compelled to attend, erect or support any **place of worship**, or to maintain any **Ministry** against his consent; no human authority can, in any case whatever, control or interfere with the **rights of conscience**, and no preference shall ever be given by law to any **religious establishments** or modes of **worship**. **Religious opinions** not to disqualify for holding office.

SECTION 4. No person who acknowledges the **being of a God** and **a future state of rewards and punishments** shall, on account of his **religious sentiments**, be disqualified to hold any office or place of trust or profit under this Commonwealth.

1968
PENNSYLVANIA CONSTITUTION

We, the people of the Commonwealth of Pennsylvania, grateful to **Almighty God** for the **blessings** of civil and **religious liberty**, and humbly invoking His guidance, do ordain and **establish** this Constitution...

ARTICLE 1, SECTION 3. All men have a natural and indefeasible right to **worship Almighty God** according to the **dictates of their own consciences**; no man can of right be compelled to attend, erect or support any **place of worship** or to maintain any **Ministry** against his consent; no human authority can, in any case whatever, control or interfere with the **rights of conscience**, and no preference shall ever be given by law to any **religious establishments** or modes of **worship**.

ARTICLE 1, SECTION 4. No person who acknowledges the **being of a God** and **a future state of rewards and punishments** shall, on account of his **religious sentiments**, be disqualified to hold any office or place of trust or profit under this Commonwealth.

PENNSYLVANIA RELIGIOUS AFFILIATION

The Encyclopedia Britannica, 11th edition, published in 1911, stated:

In 1906 the members of different **religious denominations** in the state totalrd 2,977,022, of whom 1,717,037 were **Protestants** and 1,214,734 were **Catholics**.

Thought there are many smaller **religious sects** in the state; the main **denominations** in 1906 are: **Methodist**-363,443, **Lutheran**-335,643, **Presbyterian**-322,542, **Reformed Church**-177,270, **Baptist**-141,694, **Protestant Episcopalian**-99,021, **United Brethren**-55,574, **United Evangelical**-45,480, **Disciples of Christ**-26,458, **German Baptist Brethren**-23,176, **Eastern Orthodox**-22,123, **Mennonites**-16,527, **Congregational**-14,811, **Evangelical Association**-13,294, **Friends**-12,457, **Church of God** or **"Winnebrennerians"**-11,157, and **Moravian**-5,322.

http://www.1911encyclopedia.org/Pennsylvania

The Catholic Encyclopedia, Volume XV, Copyright 1912 by Robert Appleton Company, stated as of 1906, a census listed **Pennsylvania** as second most populated State with 6,928,515 citizens of whom 43 percent reported membership in some denomination. Pennsylvania was the first State in Union in the number of **Church organizations** and the second state in the number of **Church members**, consisting of:

Methodists - 363,443
Lutherans - 335,643
Presbyterians - 322,542
Reformed - 181,350
Baptists - 141,694
Episcopalians - 99,021, with their first **Church** built in Philadelphia, **Christ Church,** in 1695.
United Brethren - 55,571
Other Protestant - 217,773
Catholics - 1,214,734, with their first **Church**, **St. Joseph**, founded in Philadelphia in 1731, being the first **Catholic Church** in the entire English speaking world since the **Reformation**. It began with 22 Irish and 15 Germans, and, by 1787 its membership had increased to 3,000. In 1727, there arrived 6,755 Irish **Catholics** in Philadelphia and, in 1729, there arrived 5,655 more. The Irish Potato Famine of 1846-49 brought thousands of **Catholics** to Pennsylvania.

In 1910, the U.S. Census listed **Pennsylvania's** population as 7,665,111, consisting of 1,494,766 **Catholics,** of whom 38,235 were African American. **Catholic** schools had 225,224 pupils, taught by 2896 **religious** and lay **teachers** in 443 schools, orphan asylums and charitable institutions.

http://www.newadvent.org/cathen/11638c.htm

The Wikipedia Online Encyclopedia, as of 2006, listed **Pennsylvania** as:

Christian - 83 percent, consisting of:
- **Methodist** - 10 percent
- **Baptist** - 10 percent
- **Lutheran** - 9 percent
- **Presbyterian** - 5 percent
- **United Church of Christ** - 2 percent
- **Amish/Pietist** - 1 percent
- **Other Protestant** - 18 percent
- **Catholic** - 27 percent
- **Other Christian** - 1 percent

Jewish - 2 percent
Other Religions - 2 percent
Non-Religious/Non-Reporting - 13 percent

http://en.wikipedia.org/wiki/Pennsylvania

The U.S. Religious Landscape Survey, conducted by The Pew Forum on Religion & Public Life, 2007, published in the USA Today, listed **Pennsylvania** as:

Christian - 80.5 percent, consisting of:
- **Evangelical Protestant** - 18 percent
- **Mainline Protestant** - 25 percent
- **Black Protestant** - 7 percent
- **Catholic** - 29 percent
- **Orthodox** - 1 percent
- **Other Christian** - <0.5 percent

Mormon - <0.5 percent
Jehovah's Witnesses - 1 percent
Jewish - 2 percent
Muslim - <0.5 percent
Buddhist - <0.5 percent
Hindu - <0.5 percent
Other World Religions - <0.5 percent

Other Faiths - 1 percent
Unaffiliated - 13 percent
Did not answer - 1 percent

www.pewforum.org
www.usatoday.com/news/graphics/pew-religion-08/flash.htm

GREAT SEAL OF THE STATE OF DELAWARE
•1704•1776•1787•
LIBERTY AND INDEPENDENCE

DELAWARE

As much of the early Swedish and Dutch history of Delaware was covered in the history of New Jersey, it is not necessary to repeat it here.

In 1629, under the authority of the Dutch West India Company, a tract of land from Cape Henlopen to the mouth of the Delaware River was purchased from the natives, and a company was formed in Holland to colonize it. In the spring of 1631, a ship of immigrants reached Delaware to build a settlement, but an Indian attack destroyed it with its settlers.

In 1638, Peter Minuit brought two ship with 50 settlers into Delaware Bay to found New Sweden. They founded Fort Christina, named for Sweden's Queen Christina, at the present site of Wilmington, Delaware.

After two years, sickness almost caused the colony's abandonment, but ships with new settlers revived it. In 1655, the Dutch fleet arrived and New Sweden surrendered. In 1664, the British fleet arrived and they surrendered again, being annexed by New York.

The controversy over the location of the borders between Delaware, Pennsylvania and Maryland led to bloodshed and was not resolved until 1750.

The **Society of Friends** erected their first meeting house in Delaware about 1687 and for the greater part of the State's history they were the most influential.

The first school in the State was opened before 1700, by the **pastor** of **Old Swedes' Church.**

In 1703, immigrants from South Wales settled the "Welsh Tract" and erected a **Baptist Church**. This was the third **Baptist** meeting house in America.

The first **Presbyterian Church** in the State was **established** around 1705.

Methodists had their first recorded meeting in Delaware, at Wilmington in 1766. In 1780, **Methodists** built **"Barratt's Chapel"** in Kent County, and the area became a cradle of **Methodism** for America, having the first General Conference of American **Methodism**.

In 1730 Cornelius Hallahan, an Irish **Catholic**, settled in New Castle and the first **Catholic** services in the State were most likely at his house. Sometime before 1750, **Jesuits established Apoquiniminck Mission** in New Castle Country.

In 1748, a report from the **Episcopal Mission** at Dover, Kent County, to **clergymen** of the Pennsylvania province stated that the "**Quakers** and **Roman Catholics** were long accustomed to bury their dead at their own plantations." A 1751 report by the **Episcopal Mission** in Dover stated: "There are about five or six families of **Papists**, who are attended once a month from Maryland with a **priest**."

In 1765, Wilmington Academy was founded, aided by **Presbyterian** Gunning Bedford, who signed the U.S. Constitution.

Prior to 1772, there are no records regarding any regularly **established Catholic Church** in Delaware. In January of 1772, **Father Matthew Sittensperger**, going under the name Manners, purchased a farm in Mill Creek Hundred and erected a log **chapel** called **St. Mary's.** He was succeeded by the French **Rev. Stephen Faure**, who was driven from **St. Domingo** during slave uprisings. He was assisted by **Rev. John Rosseter**, who had been an officer in Rochambeau's army that aided General

Washington at the Battle of Yorktown during the Revolutionary War.

During the Revolutionary War Delaware enlisted 3,763 men. In 1776, the Constitution of the State of Delaware stated in Article XXII: "Every person who shall be chosen a member of either house, or appointed to any office or place of trust...shall...make and subscribe the following declaration, to wit: 'I, _____, do profess **faith** in **God the Father**, and in **Jesus Christ His only Son**, and in the **Holy Ghost**, **one God**, **blessed** for evermore; and I do acknowledge the **Holy Scriptures** of the **Old and New Testaments** to be given by **Divine inspiration**.'"

Richard Bassett, Governor of Delaware and signer of the U.S. Constitution, became friends with circuit-riding **Preacher** Francis Asbury and converted to **Methodism**. Bassett gave half the cost to build the First **Methodist Church** in Dover. He freed his slaves and paid them as hired labor, riding with them to revival camp meetings. In 1787, Major William Pierce, Georgia delegate to the Constitutional Convention, described Bassett as: A **religious enthusiast**, lately turned **Methodist**, who serves his country because it is the will of the people that he should do so. He is a man of plain sense, and has modesty enough to hold his tongue. He is a gentlemanly man and is in high estimation among **Methodists**."

In 1785, Delaware was one of the four states, the others being Pennsylvania, Maryland, and Virginia, where **Catholics** were not under civil disabilities.

On December 7, 1787, Delaware was the first State to ratify the Federal Constitution. In 1790, the population of the State was 59,094, of whom 8,887 were slaves. About 1791 the Swedish **Lutheran Church** merged into the **Protestant Episcopal**.

In 1816, St. Peter's was the second **Catholic Church** in the State. In 1839 the first **parochial school** in the State was built adjoining **St. Peter's.** From 1825 to 1860, there was a large **Catholic** immigration, primarily from Ireland. In 1900, there were 153,977 whites, 30,697 African Americans and 61 persons of other races. In 1906, Delaware's population was 194,479.

The first **Jewish congregation** in Delaware began in 1879 and the **Adas Kodesch Shel Emeth Congregation** began in 1885, which is the oldest existing **Jewish congregation** in the State. In 1898, the **B'Nai B'rith Wilmington Lodge** was formed, the oldest **Jewish** organization in the State. In 1898, Louis Finger formed a branch of the **B'nai Zion**, the first **Zionist Organization** in Delaware. In 1901, the Chesed Shel Emeth **Congregation** was founded in Wilmington. The **Ladies Bichor Cholem Society** was formally organized in 1902. In Wilmington, the **Beth Emeth Congregation** was formed in 1906, and the **Beth Shalom Congregation** was formed 1922. In 1936, the **Beth Sholom Congregation** was founded in Dover. **Hebrew** schools began in Wilmington in 1943.

DECEMBER 21, 1624
WARRANT FOR WILLIAM USSLING TO ESTABLISH A GENERAL COMPANY FOR TRADE TO ASIA, AFRICA, AMERICA & MAGELLANICA.

Gustavus Adolphus, by the **Grace of God**, King of Sweden...Know you, that...William Ussling has humbly...proved to us how a general trading company here from our kingdom of Sweden to Asia, Africa, America, and Magellanica could be **established** for the considerable improvement of our and the Crown's revenues and...has...promised to...organize this company using the utmost of his diligence and power, while he cherishes the certain hope that, with **God's gracious blessing and help**, it shall have a good beginning and progress as well as a favorable result and end.

Such being the proposition which he made, we have taken it into consideration and find it to be founded and based upon so good reasons that we cannot disapprove of it nor do we see but what it is sure that if **God** will give success it shall tend to the honor of his **Holy Name**, to our and the state's welfare, and the advancement and advantage of our subjects."

JUNE 14, 1626
CHARTER GRANTED BY GUSTAVUS ADOLPHUS TO SWEDISH SOUTH COMPANY

Whereas...we have received reliable and certain intelligence that there are in...America...many rich countries and islands, of which some are inhabited by quiet and rather effeminate people, some by **heathens** and savages, some uninhabited, and some as yet only imperfectly explored.

With which said countries it will not only be possible to carry on an extraordinary large commerce from our kingdom, but it is also most likely that the said people may likewise be made more civilized and taught **morality** and the **Christian religion** by the mutual intercourse and trade.

Therefore, we have maturely considered and as far as in our power concluded that the advantages, profits, and welfare of our kingdom and faithful subjects, besides the **further propagation of the Holy Gospel,** will be much improved and increased by the discovery of new commercial relations and navigation...The association shall commence on the first of May of next year, the 1627th after **the birth of Christ...**

Every six years all the general accounts shall be closed and new ones opened. If, which **God** may prevent, it then should happen that the profits are not so large or the results such as to justify the shareholders to resolve by a majority of votes not to let the company continue, it shall be dissolved and the funds divided.

OCTOBER 28, 1701
DELAWARE CHARTER FROM WILLIAM PENN

ARTICLE 1. Because no People can be truly happy, though under the greatest Enjoyment of Civil Liberties, if abridged of the **Freedom of their Consciences**, as to their **Religious Profession** and **Worship**:

And **Almighty God** being the only **Lord of Conscience, Father of Lights and Spirits;** and the **Author** as well as **Object of all Divine Knowledge, Faith and Worship,** who only doth enlighten the Minds, and persuade and convince the Understandings of People,

I do hereby grant and declare, That no Person or Persons, inhabiting In this Province or Territories, who shall confess and acknowledge **One Almighty God**, the **Creator, Upholder and Ruler of the World**; and professes him or themselves obliged to live quietly under the Civil Government, shall be in any Case molested or prejudiced, in his or their Person or Estate, because of his or their conscientious **Persuasion** or **Practice**, nor be compelled to frequent or maintain any **religious Worship**, **Place** or **Ministry**, contrary to his or their Mind, or to do or suffer any other Act or Thing, contrary to their **religious Persuasion.**

And that all Persons who also profess to believe in **Jesus Christ, the Savior of the World**, shall be capable (notwithstanding their other **Persuasions** and **Practices** in **Point of Conscience** and **Religion**) to serve this Government in any Capacity, both legislatively and executively, he or they solemnly promising, when lawfully required, Allegiance to the King as Sovereign, and Fidelity to the Proprietary and Governor, and taking the Attests as now **established** by the Law made at Newcastle, in the Year One Thousand and Seven Hundred, entitled, An Act directing the Attests of several Officers and **Ministers**, as now amended and confirmed this present **Assembly**.

But, because the Happiness of mankind depends so much upon the Enjoying of **Liberty of their Consciences,** as foresaid, I do hereby solemnly declare...That the FIRST Article of this Charter relating to **Liberty of Conscience**, and every Part and Clause therein, according to the true Intent and Meaning thereof, shall be kept and remain, without any alteration, inviolably for ever.

1776
CONSTITUTION OF DELAWARE

ARTICLE 22. Every person who shall be chosen a member of either house, or appointed to any office or place of trust, before taking his seat, or entering upon the execution of his office, shall...make and subscribe the following declaration, to wit:

"I, A B. do profess **faith in God the Father**, and in **Jesus Christ His only Son**, and in the **Holy Ghost**, **one God**, **blessed for evermore**; and I do acknowledge the **Holy Scriptures** of the **Old and New Testament** to be given by **Divine inspiration**."

ARTICLE 29. There shall be no **establishment** of any **religious sect** in this State in preference to another; and no **clergyman** or **Preacher** of the **Gospel**, of any **denomination**, shall be capable of holding any civil office in this state, or of being a member of either of the branches of the legislature, while they continue in the exercise of the **pastoral function**.

1776
DECLARATION OF RIGHTS OF DELAWARE

ARTICLE 2. That all Men have a natural and unalienable Right to **worship Almighty God** according to the **Dictates of their own Consciences** and Understandings; that no Man ought or of Right can be compelled to attend any **religious Worship** or maintain any **Ministry** contrary to or against his own free Will and Consent, and that no Authority can or ought to be vested in, or assumed by any Power whatever that shall in any Case interfere with, or in any Manner control the **Right of Conscience** in the **Free Exercise of Religious Worship**.

ARTICLE 3. That all Persons professing the **Christian Religion** ought forever to enjoy equal Rights and Privileges in this State, unless, under **Color of Religion**, any Man disturb the Peace, the Happiness or Safety of Society.

1779
DELAWARE APPROVED THE ARTICLES OF CONFEDERATION WRITTEN MARCH 1, 1781:

Preamble. Whereas the delegates of the United States of America in Congress assembled did on the fifteenth day of November in **the Year of Our Lord** one thousand seven hundred and seventy seven, and in the second year of the independence of America agree on certain Articles of Confederation and perpetual union between the States...

ARTICLE 1. The style of this confederation shall be "The United States of America."

ARTICLE 2. Each state retains its sovereignty, freedom, and independence, and every power, jurisdiction and right, which is not by this confederation expressly delegated to the united states, in Congress assembled.

ARTICLE 3. The said states hereby severally enter into a firm league of friendship with each other, for their common defense, the security of their liberties, and their mutual and general welfare, binding themselves to assist each other, against all force offered to, or attacks made upon them, or any of them, on account of **religion**, sovereignty, trade, or any other pretense....

And whereas it has pleased the Great Governor of the World to incline the hearts of the Legislatures we respectively represent in Congress, to approve of, and to authorize us to ratify the said Articles of Confederation and perpetual union...

Done at Philadelphia in the State of Pennsylvania the ninth day of July in **the Year of Our Lord**, 1778, and in the third year of the independence of America.

1792
CONSTITUTION OF DELAWARE

PREAMBLE. Through **Divine goodness** all men have, by nature, the **rights of worshipping** and serving their **Creator** according to the **dictates of their consciences**, of enjoying and defending life and liberty, of acquiring and protecting reputation and property, and, in general, of attaining objects suitable to their condition, without injury by one to another; and as these rights are essential to their welfare, for the due exercise thereof, power is inherent in them; and, therefore, all just authority in the institutions of political society is derived from the people, and **established** with their consent, to advance their happiness; and they may, for this end, as circumstances require, from time to time, alter their constitution of government.

ARTICLE 1, SECTION 1. Although it is the duty of all men frequently to assemble together for the **public worship** of the **Author of the universe**, and **piety** and **morality**, on which the prosperity of communities depends, are thereby promoted; yet no man shall or ought to be compelled to attend any **religious worship**, to contribute to the erection or support of any **place of worship**, or to the maintenance of any **Ministry**, against his own free will and consent; and no power shall or ought to be vested in or assumed by any magistrate that shall in any case interfere with, or in any manner control, the **rights of conscience**, in the **free exercise of religious worship**, nor a preference be given by law to any **religious societies, denominations**, or **modes of worship.**

SECTION 2. No **religious test** shall be required as a qualification to any office, or public trust, under this State.

SECTION 9. The Rights, privileges, immunities, and estates of **religious societies** and corporate bodies shall remain as if the constitution of this state had not been altered. No **clergyman** or **Preacher** of the **Gospel** of **any denomination**, shall be capable of holding any civil office in this state, or of being a member of either branch of the legislature, while he continues in the exercise of the **pastoral** or **clerical** functions.

1831
CONSTITUTION OF DELAWARE

BILL OF RIGHTS, ARTICLE I, SECTION 1.

Although it is the duty of all men frequently to assemble together for the **public worship** of **Almighty God**; and **piety** and **morality**, on which the prosperity of communities depends, are hereby promoted; yet no man shall or ought to be compelled to attend any **religious worship**, to contribute to the erection or support of any **place of worship**, or to the maintenance of any **Ministry**, against his own free will and consent; and no power shall or ought to be vested in or assumed by any magistrate that shall in any case interfere with, or in any manner control the **rights of conscience**, in the **free exercise of religious worship**, nor a preference given by law to any **religious societies, denominations**, or modes of **worship**.

ARTICLE 1, SECTION 2. No **religious test** shall be required as a qualification to any office, or public trust, under this State...

1897
CONSTITUTION OF DELAWARE (CURRENT)

PREAMBLE. Through **Divine goodness**, all men have by nature the **rights of worshipping** and serving their **Creator** according to the **dictates of their consciences**, of enjoying and defending life and liberty, of acquiring and protecting reputation and property, and in general of obtaining objects suitable to their condition, without injury by one to another; and as these rights are essential to their welfare, for due exercise thereof, power is inherent in them; and therefore all just authority in the institutions of political society is derived from the people, and **established** with their consent, to advance their happiness; and they may for this end, as circumstances require, from time to time, alter their Constitution of government.

BILL OF RIGHTS, ARTICLE I, SECTION 1. Although it is the duty of all men frequently to assemble together for the **public worship of Almighty God**; and **piety** and **morality**, on which the prosperity of communities depends, are hereby promoted; yet no man shall or ought to be compelled to attend any **religious worship**, to contribute to the erection or support of any **place of worship**, or to the maintenance of any **Ministry**, against his own free will and consent; and no power shall or ought to be vested in or assumed by any magistrate that shall in any case interfere with, or in any manner control the **rights of conscience**, in the **free exercise of religious worship**, nor a preference given by law to any **religious societies, denominations**, or **modes of worship.**

ARTICLE 1, SECTION 2. No **religious test** shall be required as a qualification to any office, or public trust, under this State...

ARTICLE 14, SECTION 1. Members of the General Assembly and all public officers executive and judicial...shall...subscribe the following oath or affirmation: "I, ____do proudly swear (or affirm) to carry out the responsibilities of the office of____ to the best of my ability, freely acknowledging that the powers of this office flow from the people I am privileged to represent. I further swear (or affirm) always to place the public interest above any special or personal interests, and to respect the right of future generations to share the rich historic and natural heritage of Delaware. In doing so I will always uphold and defend the Constitutions of my Country and my State, **So Help Me God.**" No other oath, declaration or test shall be required as a qualification for any office of public trust.

1912
DELAWARE STATUTES

Blasphemy is punishable as a misdemeanor. By statute any worldly employment, labor or business (works of necessity or charity excepted), peddling goods, droving, fishing, fowling, gaming, horseracing, cock fighting or hunting game, and playing and dancing, on the **Sabbath day,** are all prohibited and made punishable as misdemeanors.

The usual form of oath is swearing upon the **Holy Evangels of Almighty God**. A person believing in any other than the **Christian religion** may be sworn according to the peculiar ceremonies of his **religion**, if there be any such. A person conscientiously scrupulous of taking an oath may be permitted to affirm to the truth of the matters to be testified.

A **chaplain** is appointed by either branch of the legislature, and the daily sessions (by force of custom only) are opened with **prayer**.

Christmas and **Sunday** are the only **religious** holidays recognized as legal holidays. There is neither statute nor court decision in the State, regarding the seal of **confession**. **Ordained ministers of the Gospel** are not liable to serve as jurors.

By the constitution, no divorce may be granted except by the judgment of a court. Annulment of marriage for certain causes, existing at the time of marriage, is provided for. For divorce, the reasons are adultery, bigamy, imprisonment, cruelty, desertion, habitual drunkenness, and hopeless insanity. Hearings and trials in divorce matters must in all cases be had before the court and in public.

2006
DELAWARE CODE ANNOTATED

TITLE 10, CHAPTER 53. OATHS, Subchapter II. Procedure and Form of Oaths, SECTION 5321. Method of administering. The usual oath in this State shall be by swearing upon the **Holy Evangels of Almighty God.** The person to whom an oath is administered shall lay his or her right hand upon the book. (Code 1852, § 2359; Code 1915, § 4245; Code 1935, § 4715; 10 Del. C. 1953, § 5321; 70 Del. Laws, c. 186, § 1.)

SECTION 5322. Uplifted hand. A person may be permitted to swear with the uplifted hand; that is to say, a person shall lift up his or her right hand and swear by the **ever living God, the searcher of all hearts,** that etc., and at the end of the oath shall say, "**as I shall answer to God at the Great Day.**" (Code 1852, § 2360; Code 1915, § 4247; Code 1935, § 4717; 10 Del. C. 1953, § 5322; 70 Del. Laws, c. 186, § 1.)

SECTION 5324. **Non-Christians**. A person believing in any other than the **Christian religion**, may be sworn according to the peculiar ceremonies of such person's **religion**, if there be any such. (Code 1852, § 2362; Code 1915, § 4249; Code 1935, § 4719; 10 Del. C. 1953, § 5324; 70 Del. Laws, c. 186, § 1.)

TITLE 27, **Religion**, CHAPTER 1. **RELIGIOUS** SOCIETIES AND CORPORATIONS, SECTION 114. Formation of **Protestant Episcopal Church** corporations. The rector, wardens and vestrymen of any **Protestant Episcopal Church**, on certifying their name or style as provided in § 101 or 103 of this title, shall be a corporation with the franchise, rights and powers therein vested in trustees of other **religious societies.** (26 Del. Laws, c. 89, § 10; Code 1915, § 2173; Code 1935, § 2480; 27 Del. C. 1953, § 114.)

SECTION 115. Formation of **Roman Catholic Church** corporations. In every **congregation** of the **Roman Catholic Church**, the ordinary of the **diocese**, the **pastor** of the **congregation** for the time being, according to the **practice** and **discipline** of the **Church**, 1 other person annually designated by the ordinary, and 2 other persons annually elected by the members of the **congregation** from among their number...shall be constituted a body politic and corporate, under such title as may be assumed by the corporation, and recorded in a certificate under the hands and seals of the corporators first chosen...The certificate shall be acknowledged before any person entitled to take acknowledgments of instruments to be used in this State and recorded among the corporation records of the county wherein the **congregation** has or possesses a **place of worship**. (19 Del. Laws, c. 599, § 1; Code 1915, § 2716; Code 1935, § 2483; 27 Del. C. 1953, § 115; 59 Del. Laws, c. 29.)

SECTION 116. Additional powers of **Roman Catholic Church** corporations; records; **pastor** as president. Every **Roman Catholic Church** corporation, in addition to the powers now possessed by **religious** corporations by virtue of the laws of this State, may appoint the hour and place of the meeting at which the 2 of its members annually elected shall be chosen and the manner in which such election shall be held and shall provide a good and sufficient record book wherein shall be registered from time to time all of its proceedings, which record shall at all times be open to inspection by any member of the **congregation** or any **ecclesiastical** officer of the **denomination** of **Christians** having, according to the **discipline** and **practice** thereof, authority over the **congregation** or the right to be informed concerning its management and interests of the corporation.

The **pastor** of the **congregation** for the time being (if any there be) shall always be present. It may frame such rules and ordinances for the orderly conduct of **Divine**

worship and the advancement of the interests of the **congregation** as a majority of the corporation may from time to time deem necessary, provided that the same shall not conflict with the constitution or laws of the United States or of this State, or with the **discipline** and **practice** of the **denomination**. (19 Del. Laws, c. 599, § 2; Code 1915, § 2177; Code 1935, § 2484; 27 Del. C. 1953, § 116.)

SECTION 117...(a)(1) If at any time 1 of the annually elected corporators of a **Roman Catholic Church** corporation dies, resigns or becomes disqualified by ceasing to be a **pewholder** of the **Church**, it shall be competent for the remaining members of the corporation to appoint a successor...

(2) If at any time the member annually appointed by the ordinary of the **diocese** dies or resigns, it shall be competent...to fill the vacancy in the corporation by appointing another person to serve for the remainder of the term... (19 Del. Laws, c. 599, § 3; Code 1915, § 2178; Code 1935, § 2485; 27 Del. C. 1953, § 117.)

SECTION 118...Any person...holding land...in trust for any particular **Church** or **congregation**, **Church society**, **congregation** of the **denomination** wherein a **Roman Catholic Church** corporation is formed...who conveys the same to the corporation as soon as possible after its formation under the terms of this chapter...any gift...made to any such **congregation**...shall inure to the benefit of the corporation...whether the corporation is or is not accurately described in such gift...provided that the intention of the donor or testator is clear that the same should inure to the benefit of the **congregation**. (19 Del. Laws, c. 599, § 4; Code 1915, § 2179; Code 1935, § 2486; 27 Del. C. 1953, § 118.)

TITLE 27, **Religion**, CHAPTER 3. **SUNDAY** SCHOOLS AND YOUNG MEN'S **CHRISTIAN** ASSOCIATIONS, SECTION 301...Any 10 or more persons associated together for the promotion of the interests of **Sunday schools**, or as a **Young Men's Christian**

Association for the promotion of **religious** knowledge and improvement, may become incorporated by the election of managers, not less than 3 nor more than 12, and by taking a corporate name and certifying the same, together with the object of the incorporation, under the hands and seals of the managers, to the Recorder of the county, who shall record such certificate. (13 Del. Laws, c. 419, § 1; Code 1915, § 2186; Code 1935, § 2493; 27 Del. C. 1953, § 301.)

TITLE 27, **Religion**, CHAPTER 5. **SABBATH SCHOOLS**, SECTION 501...In Sussex County, the **teachers** or persons having charge of a **Sabbath school** shall return to the County Council in March, annually, the manner in which any appropriation has been applied and the vouchers therefore...(Code 1852, § 703; Code 1915, § 2191; Code 1935, § 2498; 27 Del. C. 1953, § 502.)

TITLE 27, **Religion**, CHAPTER 7. MISCELLANEOUS PROVISIONS, SECTION 701. Permit for **religious camp meetings**. No person, association of persons, **Church** or **religious** corporation shall hold or conduct a **camp meeting or outdoor religious meeting** without first obtaining a permit authorizing the holding of such meeting. (29 Del. Laws, c. 263, § 1; Code 1935, § 4110; 27 Del. C. 1953, § 701.)

SECTION 703 (a) Whenever application is made to the commission of any county for permission to hold a **camp meeting or outdoor religious meeting,** the commission shall investigate and ascertain whether or not the granting of such permit would be detrimental to the peace and good order of the community in which it is desired to hold such meeting and in making such investigation due regard shall be had to petitions or remonstrances of the citizens of such community.

(b) If...the commission is satisfied that it is proper to do so, a permit may be issued authorizing the holding of such **camp meeting or outdoor religious meeting**; otherwise, such permit shall be refused. Each permit so issued shall specify clearly the place and time for holding such meeting. The commissions provided for in this chapter may make such reasonable rules... in relation to the holding of **camp meetings or outdoor religious meetings** as they deem wise...(29 Del. Laws, c. 263, § 3; Code 1935, § 4112; 27 Del. C. 1953, § 703.)

SECTION 704...(a) Whoever holds or conducts, or assists in holding or conducting, a **camp meeting or other outdoor religious meeting** without first obtaining the permit...shall be fined in such amount or imprisoned...as the court in its discretion may determine. (b) No permit shall be required in order to hold a **camp meeting or outdoor religious meeting** within any incorporated town...(29 Del. Laws, c. 263, § 4; Code 1935, § 4113; 27 Del. C. 1953, § 704.)

DELAWARE RELIGIOUS AFFILIATION

The Encyclopedia Britannica, 11th edition, published in 1911, stated:

> The principal **Churches**, in order of their membership were, in 1890, the **Methodist Episcopal**, **Presbyterian**, **Protestant Episcopal**, **Baptist**, **Roman Catholic**, **Quaker** and **Lutheran**.

http://www.1911encyclopedia.org/
Delaware#Population

The Catholic Encyclopedia, Volume XV, Copyright 1912 by Robert Appleton Company, stated as of 1908, a census listed **Delaware's** active **Church** membership and the **Sunday**-school membership of the leading **denominations** as:

Methodist Episcopal - 40,000
Protestant Episcopal - 6,280

Baptist - 5,000
Presbyterian - 12,700
Catholic - 25,000, with 20 **Churches** with 34 **priests** and 12 **parochial schools** with an attendance of 3,100.

Among the African American **Church** membership in 1908, **Methodist** and **Baptist** were predominate. Other **creeds** in the State as of 1908, were: **Lutheran, Unitarian, Swedenborgian, Christian Science, Methodist Protestant**, various divisions of the **Baptist Church, Seventh Day Adventist**, and **Hebrew**.

http://www.newadvent.org/cathen/04692a.htm

The Wikipedia Online Encyclopedia, as of 2006, listed **Delaware** as:

Christian - 79 percent, consisting of:
- **Methodist** - 22 percent
- **Baptist** - 21 percent
- **Lutheran** - 4 percent
- **Presbyterian** - 3 percent
- **Pentacostal** - 3 percent
- **Other Protestant** - 15 percent
- **Catholic** - 10 percent
- **Other Christian** - 1 percent

Other Religions - 2 percent
Non-Religious/Non-Reporting - 19 percent

http://en.wikipedia.org/wiki/Delaware#Religion

The U.S. Religious Landscape Survey, conducted by The Pew Forum on Religion & Public Life, 2007, published in the USA Today, listed **Delaware** as:

Christian - 75.5 percent, consisting of:
- **Evangelical Protestant** - 15 percent
- **Mainline Protestant** - 18 percent

Black Protestant - 14 percent
Catholic - 27 percent
Orthodox - 1 percent
Other Christian - <0.5 percent

Mormon - <0.5 percent
Jehovah's Witnesses - <0.5 percent
Jewish - 2 percent
Muslim - <0.5 percent
Buddhist - <0.5 percent
Hindu - <0.5 percent
Other World Religions - <0.5 percent
Other Faiths - 4 percent
Unaffiliated - 19 percent
Did not answer - <0.5 percent

www.pewforum.org
www.usatoday.com/news/graphics/pew-religion-08/flash.htm

THE GREAT SEAL OF THE STATE OF NORTH CAROLINA
MAY 20. 1775
APRIL 12. 1776
ESSE QUAM VIDERI

NORTH CAROLINA

In 1584 Queen Elizabeth granted to Sir Walter Raleigh the right to discover and hold any lands not inhabited by **Christian people**. This charter was England's first attempt to colonize America.

In 1629 King Charles I granted land to Sir Robert Heath, but he made no attempt to colonize it, though a few settlers from Virginia, New England and the Barbados, found their way there.

When Charles II returned to the throne, he wanted to reward eight friends who supported him, so in 1663, he separated Carolina from Virginia and granted a charter to Sir George Carteret and seven others for land on the Atlantic coast between Virginia and Florida. They were "absolute lords proprietors" of the province of Carolina, with full powers to make and execute such laws as they deemed proper.

Though originally given the name Carolina by the Frenchman Ribaut in honor of King Charles IX of France, the Englishmen who took possession of it kept the name in honor of King Charles II of England.

In 1669, the lords proprietors set forth the "Fundamental Constitutions of Carolina" attributed to philosopher John Locke, which **established** the **Church of England** in the colony.

In an effort to attract settlers, the lords proprietors issued a "Declaration and Proposal," declaring: "We will grant, in as ample manner as the undertakers shall desire, freedom and **liberty of conscience** in all **religious** and

spiritual things, and to be kept inviolably with them, we having power in our charter so to do."

In 1664, the proprietaries entered into an "Agreement" with certain "adventurers," desiring to come from Barbados and elsewhere to Carolina, that:

"8. No person...shall be any ways molested, punished, or called in question, for any difference in opinion or practice in **matters of religious concernment**, who do not actually disturb the civil peace,...but all and every person and persons may, from time to time and at all times, freely and fully have and enjoy his and their judgments and **consciences** in **matters of religion** throughout all the Province, they behaving themselves peaceable and quietly, and not using this liberty to Licentiousness, nor to the Civil Injury or outward disturbance of others; **any Law, statute or clause, usage or custom of this realm of England** to the contrary hereof in any wise notwithstanding.

"9. No pretense shall be made from the charter right of advowsons to infringe the liberty above conceded...and we grant unto the General Assembly power to appoint **ministers** and **establish** maintenance. Giving liberty besides to any person or persons to keep and maintain what **Preachers** or **Ministers** they please."

In 1665 Charles issued a second charter in which the concession of **religious liberties** was repeated, though making it clear that that Carolina had **established** the **Church of England**.

Due to the offer of **religious freedom**, **dissenters** of all **denominations** came to Carolina. The earliest being **Quakers** fleeing **Anglican** Virginia, settling mostly in the north. They acquired political power and challenged the proprietaries' **establishment** of the **Church of England**.

Scotch Highlanders, called Covenanters, fled from the ruthless John Graham of Claverhouse, called "Bloody Clavers" who was appointed by Charles II to suppress

Presbyterian meetings, known as **Conventicles**. Scottish supporters of King James II, called Jacobites, also fled to Carolina. It was the descendants of these Scottish immigrants, who. at the beginning of the Revolutionary War wrote the Mecklenberg Declaration.

Irish **Presbyterians** came fleeing from persecution and famine in Ulster.

In 1709, persecuted Germans **Protestants** of the Rhineland-Palatinate fled from the French, arriving as refugees in England. From there, many were sent to Carolina, of which a large number died in the voyage.

Swiss settlers, led by Christoph von Graffenried settled at New Bern, but most were killed by Tuscarora Indians. German **Moravians**, or **Church of the Brethren**, settled Wachovia, Bethabara, Bethania and Winston-Salem.

Protestants of France, called **Huguenots**, were persecuted until King Henry of Navarre protected them by the **Edict of Nantes**. In 1685, King Louis XIV revoked the edict, denied **Huguenots religious freedom,** and forbade them from leaving on pain of death. Some did escape to Holland, England and to America, settling in Carolina on the banks of the Cooper and Santee.

In 1683, Joseph Blake, brother of the great Admiral Robert Blake -"Father of the Royal Navy," settled Charleston with a large company of **Protestant** English **dissenters**, including **Baptists**. In 1684, a **Baptist Church** migrated from Massachusetts under the direction of their **pastor**, William Screven.

After the British took New York from the Dutch and began to enforce the **Church of England**, two shiploads of **Dutch Reformed** left and arrived in Carolina.

In 1674, the population of Carolina was about 4,000. The large number of **dissenting** immigrants in the first 20 years of the colony were greater than the proprietaries had expected.

Dissenters gained such political power that attempts to bring them under the **Church of England** were resisted. The first appointed governor, Sir John Yeamans, was instructed to oberve the promise of **religious liberty** but begin to dissuade **non-conformists**.

The laws to attract new settlers also had provisions allowing settlers to come without having their outstanding debts paid and exempting them from taxes for a year. This resulted in some undesirables, known as "poor whites," arriving, causing some in Virginia to refer to Carolina as "Rogues' Harbor." The slave trade also sprang up, as Africans exhibited greater physical endurance in the hot climate and marshy ground where rice was grown.

Though the **Church of England** was legally **established** in the Carolinas by the "Fundamental Constitutions," it never had popular appeal among the people. Attempts to force **dissenters** to conform to the **Church of England** met resistance.

The colonial law of 1691, relating to the **Sabbath,** forbade all secular work and required "all and every person and persons shall on every **Lord's Day** apply themselves to the observance of the same by exercising themselves of **piety** and **true religion**."

An Act of 1696 giving "liberty of the Province to Aliens," stated that: "All **Christians**...(**Papists** only excepted) shall enjoy the full, free, and undisturbed exercise of their **consciences**, so as to be in the exercise of their **worship** according to the professed rules of their **religion**, without any hindrance, or molestation by any power either **ecclesiastical** or civil whatever."

In 1698, the Legislature passed an act to settle the maintenance of a **minister** at Charleston, Samuel Marshall, the first **clergyman** of the **Church of England** in Carolina. The legislature was moved to the action by its special pleasure in Mr. Marshall's character and conduct, and appropriated to him and his successors forever a yearly salary of £150 out of the public treasury.

In 1704, the Legislature **established the Church of England** and **disfranchised non-conformists**. The resentment to this was so high that the proprietaries had to yield, appointing the **Quaker** Archdale to be governor. Archdale wisely put together a council with only one third of its members being **Church of England**.

After Archdale returned to England, the **Church of England** party passed two acts which caused an outrage. The first, an "Act for the Protection of Government," required all members of the legislature take the **sacrament** in the **Church of England**. The second "for **establishing Religious worship** according to the **Church of England**," gave regulations for the erection of **Churches**, support of **ministers**, **glebes**, **parishes**, and the choice of **ministers**, **vestries, clerks, sextons**, and set up an **ecclesiastical court** having **Episcopal powers** to remove **ministers**.

Other laws were passed requiring French settlers to "conform to the **Church of England** and use a French translation of the **Book of Common Prayer.**"

Commissary Blair of Virginia describe Carolina in 1704: "The country is divided in four sorts: 1st, The **Quakers**, who are the most powerful enemies to **Church government**, but very ignorant of what they profess; 2d, A great many who have **no religion**, but would be **Quakers** if they would not be obliged to lead a more **moral** life; 3d, A sort something like **Presbyterians**, upheld by some idle fellows who have left employment to **preach** and **baptize**, without any orders from any **sect;** and 4th, Those who are zealous for the interest of the **Church**."

Quakers resisted the forced paying of **tithes** to the **Church of England**. In 1711, Governor Spotswood of Virginia wrote that **Quakers** were "not only the principal fomenters of the distractions in Carolina, but made it their business to instill the like pernicious notions into the minds of his majesty's subjects in Virginia."

In 1711, Carolina was divided into two colonies. In 1715, a law required every **vestryman** to take the oath, "I do declare that it is not lawful on any pretense whatever to take up Arms against the King, and that I will not apugne the **Liturgy of the Church of England**."

In 1720, John Hassell was fined £25 for saying that he "had never been beholden to **God** for anything." The court judged the offense worthy of punishment as "to the dishonor of **God Almighty** and his Attributes, and against the **Holy written Profession** and **Religion, now allowed and professed by authority in his now Majesty of Great Britain's Dominions,** and subverting of all the **faithful** and **true believers** and **professors** of the **Protestant Church and Religion now by Law Established and Confirmed.**"

In 1729, the King purchased back the domain and Carolina became a royal province.

The Constitution of 1776 stated: "No person, who shall deny the **being of God** or the truth of the **Protestant religion**, or the **Divine** authority either of the **Old or New Testaments**, or who shall hold **religious principles** incompatible with the freedom and safety of the State, shall be capable of holding any office or place of trust or profit in the civil department within this State."

In 1833, William Gaston, a **Catholic**, was elected associate justice of North Carolina's Supreme Court. While still on the bench, he was elected a delegate to the State Constitutional Convention of 1835. He gave a speech against the clause requiring office holders to be **Protestant**.

The clause was subsequently changed in North Carolina's 1835 Constitution to: "No person, who shall deny the **being of God** or the **truth of the Christian religion**, or the **Divine authority** either of the **Old or New Testaments**, or who shall hold **religious principles** incompatible with the freedom and safety of the State, shall be capable of holding any office or place of trust or profit in the civil department within this State."

In 1868, North Carolina's State Constitution changed the requirement to hold office to its present form: "The following persons shall be disqualified for office: First, any person who shall deny the **being of Almighty God.**"

As of 1910, the Legislature opened with **prayer**, laws required observance of **Sunday**, and punishes any disturbance of **religious congregations**. **Ministers of the Gospel** are exempt from jury duty and their private libraries are exempt from taxation.

Originally, marriages could only be solemnized by **Church of England ministers**. This was extended to justices of the peace in 1741, **Presbyterian ministers** in 1766, and **ministers** of all **denominations** in 1778.

In 1884, **Catholics** in North Carolina erected Belmont Abbey in Gaston County, its first **abbot** being **Right Reverend Leo Haid.** He was appointed **Vicar Apostolic** of North Carolina in 1887.

At Belmont is also a college for the higher education of women under the **Sisters of Mercy**, an orphanage for girls and a preparatory school for boys. As of 1910, North Carolina had approximately 11,000 **Catholics** in 15 **Catholic Churches** with 33 **priests**. There are **parochial schools** at Asheville, Charlotte, Salisbury, Durham, Newton Grove, Raleigh, and Wilmington.

Though not quite one percent of North Carolina's population, the **Jewish** population has had a presence, which the following information attests.

The city of New Bern has a cemetery under Craven Street with at least one **Jew** buried there: **Rabbi Yakov Abroo,** who died before 1790. New Bern has had an active **Jewish congregation** since before 1824. In the 1850's, **Jews** settled in the counties of Jones, Carteret, Pamlico, Craven and New Bern.

In 1865, following the Civil War, the "**Hebrews of New Bern**" purchased land next to the National Cemetery for a **Jewish Cemetery.** Many late 19th-century tombstones are inscribed in both **Hebrew** and English. In 1908, **Temple Chester B'nai Sholem Synagogue** was completed and in 1919, New Bern's **Jewish** population was 99.

In 1867, the first **Jewish Congregation** in North Carolina received a State Charter. In July of 1876, the **Jewish community** of Wilmington built the **Temple of Israel**, the first permanent **Jewish** house of **worship** in North Carolina.

A **Presbyterian cemetery** in Charlotte, N.C., displayed the notation: "All over the Carolinas lie the remains of **Jews** who lived and died long ago in communities with no consecrated burial place for them. They are safe and remembered in **Church cemeteries,** like this grave in a **Charlotte Presbyterian cemetery** of a woman born during the Revolutionary War. The inscription begins, 'In memory of Mrs. Z. Penick who died April 12, 1854, 73rd year of her age, **a mother in Israel...**'"

There is a **Hebrew Cemetery** in Charlotte, N.C., on McCall Street at Statesville Avenue, which is the oldest and only cemetery that is predominantly **Jewish**. **Elmwood Cemetery** in Mecklenburg County has the grave of a **Jewish** Confederate soldier.

The **Durham Jewish community** traces its origins to the 1870's when German and Eastern European immigrants arrived to peddle and open stores in the growing tobacco town. In the early 1880's, their numbers increased with the arrival of Russian-**Jewish** cigarette rollers. The **Durham Hebrew Cemetery, established** in 1882, may be the oldest **Jewish** institution of record in this area. Owned by **Beth El**, it was the only **Jewish** cemetery for the surrounding geographical area. The **Durham Hebrew Congregation** was organized in 1887 and rented a hall on Main Street.

In 1892, the congregants formally chartered the **congregation** and hired a **Rabbi**. In 1905, they purchased a small, wood-framed **Church** on Liberty Street which became **Beth El Synagogue,** Durham's first **synagogue**. In 1919, the **Jewish** population in Durham was 500.

Congregation Oheb Sholom in Goldsboro, North Carolina, noted: "In February 1883, 33 **Jewish** men...united for the purpose of building a **synagogue**" in Goldsboro. The **Jewish community** already owned a **Torah** and was home to a Cemetery Association and a **Ladies' Hebrew Assistance Society**, indicating that **Jewish** life existed in Goldsboro prior to the formal creation of a **congregation**."

In 1891, **Beth-Ha-Tephila Congregation** was the first **synagogue** founded in Ashville, meeting at Lyceum Hall on Biltmore Avenue.

In 1898, the **Bikur Holim Conservative Congregation** was begun. In 1916, **Beth-ha-Tephila**, an **Orthodox Congregation**, built a **synagogue**, but it was unfortunately burned in an anti-Semitic crime.

Raleigh, N.C. has four **Synagogues**: **Beth Meyer, Conservative**, founded in 1875; **Beth Shalom, Reform**, located in Cary; **Sha'arei Israel/Lubavitch, Orthodox;** and **Temple Beth Or, Reform.** Raleigh's only **Jewish** cemetery has approximately 250-300 graves. The 1919 **Jewish** population of Raleigh was 120.

Greensboro, in Guilford County, had its first permanent **Jewish** settlers in the middle 1890's. They organized **Temple Emanuel,** called the **Greensboro Hebrew Congregation**, in 1907.

In 1898, **Temple of Israel** in Wilmington, Brunswick County, founded **B'nai Israel Cemetery**, also called B'nai Yisroel Bur Grd. In 1919 **Jewish** population of Wilmington was 400. The **Gastonia Hebrew Congregation** organized **Temple Emanuel Cemetery** on New Hope Road in 1913.

Temple Emanu-El Congregation in Weldon, Halifax County, was organized in 1912 and had a **Jewish** cemetery in Roanoke Rapids. In the autumn of 2004, **Temple Emanu-El** closed and gave its **Torah scrolls** and other **Judaica** to the **Jewish Heritage Foundation of North Carolina**, who gave them to Havurat Olam, Cabarrus County's first **Jewish congregation**. A new **congregation** in Virginia Beach got one of its **Torah scrolls and memorial plaques**. The Kehillah, a new **congregation** in **Chapel** Hill, got the furniture, books, candelabras and lectern.

The 1919, the **Jewish** population of Statesville, N.C., was 55. They built historic **Temple Israel** and used Oakwood Cemetery.

In 1932, **Temple Emanuel** was **established** at Winston-Salem in Forsyth County. It has **Mount Sinai Cemetery** which adjoins the cemetery of **Union Ridge United Methodist Church**. The original cemetery grounds were purchased through the **Ladies Aid Society of Winston-Salem Hebrew Congregation**.

In 1936, the Pineview Cemetery in Rocky Mount, Edgecombe County, opened a **Jewish** section called Beth-el. In **Chapel** Hill, Orange County, there is the **Judea Reform Congregation Cemetery,** located on Jones Ferry Road. In High Point, Guilford County, there is **Congregation Bnai Israel**, led by **Rabbi** Jerome Fox, which has a cemetery north of town on Kensington Lane. In Lumberton, Robeson County, there is **Temple Israel**, which has not held services since the 1980's and gave its **Torah** to the **congregation** in Foxfire Village. Whiteville, in Moore County, did not have a **synagogue** so families traveled to Wilmington or Myrtle Beach to attend services until **Beth-Israel Center**, North Street was built.

OCTOBER, 30 1629
CHARLES I GRANT TO SIR ROBERT HEATH

Charles by the **Grace of God** of England Scotland France & Ireland King **Defender of the Faith**...

Whereas our beloved and faithful subject and servant Sir Robert Heath Knight...kindled with a certain laudable and pious desire as well of enlarging the **Christian religion** as our Empire & increasing the Trade & Commerce of this our kingdom...in the parts of America...neither inhabited by ours or the subjects of any other **Christian king**...

But some parts of it inhabited by certain Barbarous men who have not any knowledge of the **Divine Deity**, He being about to lead thither a Colony of men large & plentiful, professing the **true religion**...

And furthermore...all **Churches** which shall happen to be built hereafter in the said Region Territory...by the increase of the **religion & worship of Christ** Together with all...these...Rights...To have exercise use & enjoy in like manner as any **Bishop of Durham** within the **Bishopric** or County palatine of Durham in our kingdom of England...

We...think fit to erect the said Region...in...the province of Carolina..And because... seated among so many barbarous nations it is probable that the incursions as well of those Barbarous as of other enemies Pirates & Robbers may cause fear.

Therefore we...have given...Sir Robert Heath... power...to pursue enemies & Robbers aforesaid by land & sea, even beyond the bounds of his province, and then (**with God's blessing**) to overcome & to take, & being taken by right of war to slay, or according to his pleasure to preserve...

And if by chance hereafter some doubts & questions may be framed about the true sense & meaning of any word clause or sentence contained in this our present charter we...command...that no interpretation be made by which the **religion of the Holy God & true Christian**, or the Allegiance due to us our heirs & successors may suffer in the least.

MARCH 24, 1663
CHARTER OF CAROLINA

Whereas our right trusty, and right well beloved cousins and counselors, Edward Earl of Clarendon... George Duke of Albemarle...William Lord Craven, John Lord Berkley...Anthony Lord Ashley...Sir George Carteret...Sir William Berkley...and Sir John Colleton...being excited with a laudable and pious zeal for the **propagation of the Christian faith**, and the enlargement of our empire and dominions, have humbly besought leave of us, by their industry and charge, to transport and make an ample colony of our subjects, natives of our kingdom of England, and elsewhere within our dominions, unto a certain country hereafter described, in the parts of America not yet cultivated or planted, and only inhabited by some barbarous people, who have no knowledge of **Almighty God**...

3. And furthermore, the patronage and advowsons of all the **Churches** and **chapels**, which as **Christian religion** shall increase within the country, isles, islets and limits aforesaid, shall happen hereafter to be erected, together with license and power to build and found **Churches, chapels and oratories,** in convenient and fit places, within the said bounds and limits, and to cause them to be dedicated and consecrated according to the **ecclesiastical laws of our kingdom of England...**

4. To have...in as ample manner as any **Bishop of Durham** in our kingdom of England, ever heretofore have held...paying yearly to us...the yearly rent of twenty marks of lawful money of England, at **the feast of All Saints**, yearly forever, the first payment thereof to begin and to be made on **the feast of All Saints**, which shall be in **the Year of Our Lord** one thousand six hundred and sixty-five...

9. We...grant unto the said Edward Earl of Clarendon, George Duke of Albemarle, William Lord Craven, John Lord Berkley, Anthony Lord Ashley, Sir George Carteret, Sir William Berkley and Sir John Colleton...authority, at any time or times, from and after **the feast of St. Michael the archangel**, which shall be in **the Year of Our Lord Christ**, one thousand six hundred sixty and seven...to import...goods and commodities...

15. And because that in so remote a country...among so many barbarous nations, and the invasions as well of savages as of other enemies, pirates and robbers, may probably be feared; therefore we have given...power...to...muster and train all sorts of men...to make war and pursue the enemies aforesaid, as well by sea as by land, yea, even without the limits of the said province, and by **God's assistance** to vanquish and take them...

16. By this our charter we give...power...in case of rebellion, tumult or sedition, (if any should happen,) which **God forbid**, either upon the land within the province aforesaid, or upon the main sea...to exercise martial law...

18. And because it may happen that some of the people and inhabitants of the said province, cannot in their private opinions, conform to the **public exercise of religion**, according to the **liturgy, form and ceremonies of the Church of England**, or take and subscribe the **oaths and articles**, made and **established** in that behalf, and for that the same, by reason of the remote distances of these places, will, we hope be no breach of the unity and **uniformity established in this nation...**

We do by these presents...grant...to... such...persons, inhabiting and being within the said province...who really in their judgments, and for **conscience sake**, cannot or shall not conform to the said **liturgy and ceremonies**, and take and subscribe the **oaths and articles** aforesaid, or any of them, such indulgencies and dispensations in that behalf, for and during such time and times, and with such limitations and restrictions as they, the said Edward Earl of Clarendon, George Duke of Albemarle, William Lord Craven, John Lord Berkley, Anthony Lord Ashley, Sir George Carteret, Sir William Berkley, and Sir John Colleton...shall in their discretion think fit and reasonable;

And...that such...persons, to whom such indulgencies and dispensations shall be granted as aforesaid, do and shall from time to time declare and continue, all fidelity, loyalty and obedience to us...and be subject and obedient to all other the laws, ordinances, and constitutions of the said province, in all matters whatsoever, as well **ecclesiastical** as civil, and do not in any wise disturb the peace and safety thereof, or scandalize or reproach the said **liturgy, forms and ceremonies,** or anything relating thereunto.

AUGUST 25, 1663
DECLARATION OF CAROLINA PROPRIETOR

His majesty having been graciously pleased, by his charter bearing date the 24th of March, in the 15th year of his reign, out of a pious and good intention for the **propagation of the Christian faith** amongst the barbarous and ignorant Indians, the enlargement of his empire and dominions, and enriching of his subjects, to grant and confirm to us....all that territory...extending from the north end of the island called Lucke Island...to the west as far as the South seas, and so southwardly as far as the river **St. Matthias**, which bordereth upon the coast of Florida...do hereby...make good those ensuing proposals...

5. We will grant, in as ample manner as the undertakers shall desire, freedom and **liberty of conscience** in all **religious** or **spiritual things**, and to be kept inviolably with them, we having power in our charter so to do...

1665
AGREEMENTS OF LORDS PROPRIETORS OF THE PROVINCE OF CAROLINA

8. Item That no person or persons qualified as aforesaid within the Province...at any time shall be any ways molested punished disquieted or called in question for any differences in opinion or practice in **matters of religious** concernment who do not actually disturb the civil peace of the said Province or Counties but that all and every such person and persons from to time and at all times freely and fully have and enjoy his and their judgments....in **matters of religion** throughout all the said Province they behaving themselves peaceably and quietly and not using this Liberty to Licentiousness nor to the Civil Injury or outward disturbance of others, any Law statute or clause contained or to be contained **usage or custom of this realm of England** to the contrary hereof in anywise notwithstanding.

9. Item That no presence may be taken by us...to infringe thereby ye General clause of **Liberty of Conscience** aforementioned We do hereby grant unto the General Assemblies of ye several Counties power by act to constitute and appoint such and so many **Ministers** or **Preachers** as they shall think fit, and to **establish** their maintenance Giving Liberty besides to any person or persons to keep and maintain what **Preachers** or **Ministers** they please...

2. Item To enact and make all such Laws Acts and Constitutions as shall be necessary for the well Government of ye County...that they be not against the Article for **Liberty of Conscience** above mentioned...

7. Item...trained...soldiers for the...defense of the said...Province and of the Forts Castles Cities &c to suppress all mutinies and Rebellions.

To make war offensive and defensive with all Indians Strangers and Foreigners as they shall see cause and to pursue any Enemy by sea as well as by land.

JUNE 30, 1665
CHARTER OF CAROLINA

Charles the Second, by the **Grace of God**, of Great Britain, France and Ireland, King, **Defender of the Faith**...We were graciously pleased to grant unto our right trusty and right well-beloved Cousin and Counselor Edward Earl of Clarendon...all that province, territory, or tract of ground, called Carolina...

Know ye, That We, at the humble request of the said grantees, in the aforesaid Letters Patents named, and as a further mark of our especial favor to them, we are graciously pleased to enlarge our said grant unto them...

And furthermore, the patronage and advowsons of all the **Churches** and **chapels**, which, as **Christian religion** shall increase within the province, territory, isles, and limits aforesaid, shall happen hereafter to be erected; together with license and power to build and found **Churches, chapels and oratories**, in convenient and fit places, within the said bounds and limits; and to cause them to be dedicated and consecrated, according to the **ecclesiastical laws of our kingdom of England**; together with all and singular the like and as ample rights, jurisdictions, privileges, prerogatives, royalties, liberties, immunities, and franchises of what kind soever, within the territory, isles, islets and limits aforesaid: To have, hold, use, exercise, and enjoy the same, as amply, fully and in as ample manner, as any **Bishop of Durham**, in our kingdom of England, ever heretofore had, held, used, or enjoyed, or of right ought or could have, use, or enjoy...

And because that in so remote a country, and situate among so many barbarous nations, the invasions of savages and other enemies, pirates and robbers, may probably be feared; therefore, we have given...power...to levy, muster, and train up all sorts of men, of what condition soever, or wheresoever born...to make war, and pursue the enemies aforesaid, as well by sea, as by land; yea, even without the limits of the said province, and, by **God's assistance**, to vanquish, and take them; and being taken, to put them to death, by the law of war, and to save them at their pleasure, and to do all and every other thing, which to the charge and office of a Captain-General of an army, hath had the same.

Also, our will and pleasure is, and by this our charter, we do give...full power, liberty, and authority, in case of rebellion, tumult, or sedition, (if any should happen, which **God forbid**) either upon the land within the province...full power and authority, to exercise martial law against any mutinous and seditious persons...

And because it may happen that some of the people and inhabitants of the said province cannot, in their private opinions, conform to the **public exercise of religion** according to the **liturgy, forms, and ceremonies of the Church of England**, or take and subscribe the **oaths and articles made and established** in that behalf; and for that the same, by reason of the remote distances of those places, will, as we hope, be no breach of the unity and conformity **established** in this nation...

We do, by these presents...grant...indulgences and dispensations, in that behalf...

And that no person or persons unto whom such liberty shall be given, shall be any way molested, punished, disquieted, or called in question, for any differences in opinion, or practice in **matters of religious concernments**, who do not actually disturb the civil peace of the province, county or colony, that they shall make their abode in:

But all and every such person and persons may, from time to time, and at all times, freely and quietly have and enjoy his and their Judgments and **consciences**, in **matters of religion**, throughout all the said province or colony, they behaving themselves peaceably, and not using this liberty to licentiousness, nor to the civil injury, or outward disturbance of others: Any law, statute, or clause, contained or to be contained, usage or **custom of our realm of England**, to the contrary hereof, in any-wise, notwithstanding.

MARCH 1, 1669
CHARTER OF CAROLINA

ARTICLE 95. No man shall be permitted to be a freeman of Carolina, or to have any estate or habitation within it, that doth not acknowledge **God**, and that **God** is **publicly** and **solemnly** to be **worshipped**.

ARTICLE 96. It shall belong to the parliament to take care for the building of **Churches**, and the public maintenance of **Divines**, to be employed in the exercise of **religion**, according to the **Church of England**; which being the **only true and orthodox** and the **national religion of all the King's dominions**, is so also of Carolina; and, therefore, it alone shall be allowed to receive public maintenance, by grant of parliament.

ARTICLE 97. But since the natives of that place, who will be concerned in our plantation, are utterly **strangers to Christianity**, whose idolatry, ignorance, or mistake gives us no right to expel or use them ill; and those who remove from other parts to plant there will unavoidably be of different opinions concerning **matters of religion**, the liberty whereof they will expect to have allowed them, and it will not be reasonable for us, on this account, to keep them out, that civil peace may be maintained amidst diversity of opinions, and our agreement and compact with all men may be duly and faithfully observed; the violation whereof, upon what presence soever, cannot be without great offense to **Almighty God**, and great scandal to the **true religion** which we profess;

And also that **Jews, heathens**, and **other dissenters** from the **purity** of **Christian religion** may not be scared and kept at a distance from it, but, by having an opportunity of acquainting themselves with the truth and reasonableness of its **doctrines**, and the peaceableness and inoffensiveness of its **professors**, may, by good usage and **persuasion**, and all those convincing methods of gentleness and meekness, suitable to the rules and design of the **Gospel**, be won ever to embrace and unfeignedly receive the truth;

Therefore, any seven or more persons agreeing in any **religion**, shall constitute a **Church** or **profession**, to which they shall give some name, to distinguish it from others.

ARTICLE 98. The terms of admittance and **Communion** with any **Church** or **profession** shall be written in a book, and therein be subscribed by all the members of the said **Church** or **profession**; which book shall be kept by the public register of the precinct wherein they reside.

ARTICLE 99. The time of every one's subscription and admittance shall be dated in the said book or **religious record.**

ARTICLE 100. In the terms of **Communion** of every **Church** or **profession**, these following shall be three; without which no agreement or **Assembly** of men, upon **presence of religion**, shall be accounted a **Church** or **profession** within these rules:

1. "That there is a **God**."
2. "That **God** is **publicly** to be **worshipped**."
3. "That it is lawful and the duty of every man, being thereunto called by those that govern, to bear witness to truth; and that every **Church** or **profession** shall, in their terms of **Communion**, set down the external way whereby they witness a truth as in the **presence of God**, whether it be by **laying hands on or kissing the Bible**, as in the **Church of England**, or by holding up the hand, or any other sensible way."

ARTICLE 101. No person above seventeen years of age shall have any benefit or protection of the law, or be capable of any place of profit or honor, who is not a member of some **Church** or **profession**, having his name recorded in some one, and but one **religious** record at once.

ARTICLE 102. No person of any other **Church** or **profession** shall disturb or molest any **religious Assembly**.

ARTICLE 103. No person whatsoever shall speak anything in their **religious Assembly irreverently** or seditiously of the government or governors, or of state matters.

ARTICLE 104. Any person subscribing the terms of **Communion**, in the record of the said **Church** or **profession**, before the precinct register, and any five members of the said **Church** or **profession**, shall be thereby made a member of the said **Church** or **profession.**

ARTICLE 105. Any person striking out his own name out of any **religious** record, or his name being struck out by any officer hereunto authorized by each **Church** or **profession** respectively, shall cease to be a member of that **Church** or **profession**.

ARTICLE 106. No man shall use any reproachful, reviling, or abusive language against any **religion** of any **Church** or **profession**; that being the certain way of disturbing the peace, and of hindering the **conversion** of any to the truth, by them in quarrels and animosities, to the hatred of the **professors** and that **profession** which otherwise they might be brought to assent to.

ARTICLE 107. Since charity obliges us to wish well to the **souls of all men**, and **religion** ought to alter nothing in any man's civil estate or right, it shall be lawful for slaves, as well as others, to enter themselves, and be of what **Church** or **profession** any of them shall think best, and, therefore, be as fully members as any freeman.

But yet no slave shall hereby be exempted from that civil dominion his master hath over him, but be in all things in the same state and condition he was in before.

ARTICLE 108. **Assemblies**, upon what presence soever of **religion**, not observing and performing the above said rules, shall not be esteemed as **Churches**, but unlawful meetings, and be punished as other riots.

ARTICLE 109. No person whatsoever shall disturb, molest, or persecute another for his speculative **opinions in religion**, or his **way of worship**.

1691
COLONIAL SABBATH LAW

Relating to the **Sabbath** forbade all secular work and require "all and every person and persons shall on every **Lord's Day** apply themselves to the observance of the same by exercising themselves of **piety** and **true religion**."

1696
ACT "LIBERTY OF THE PROVINCE TO ALIENS"

All **Christians**...(**Papists** only excepted) shall enjoy the full, free, and undisturbed exercise of their **consciences**, so as to be in the exercise of their **worship** according to the professed rules of their **religion**, without any hindrance, or molestation by any power either **ecclesiastical** or civil whatever.

1698
ACT FOR MAINTENANCE OF A MINISTER AT CHARLESTON, SAMUEL MARSHALL

Support for the first **clergyman** of the **Church of England** in Carolina. The legislature was moved to the action by its special pleasure in Mr. Marshall's character and conduct, and appropriated to him and his successors forever a yearly salary of £150 out of the public treasury.

1704
ACT FOR PROTECTION OF GOVERNMENT

And for **establishing Religious worship** according to the **Church of England**, gave regulations for the erection of **Churches**, support of **ministers, glebes, parishes**, and the choice of **ministers, vestries, clerks, sextons,** and set up an **ecclesiastical** court having **Episcopal powers** to remove **ministers**. Other Acts passed required French settlers to "conform to the **Church of England** and use a French translation of the **Book of Common Prayer.**"

MAY 20, 1775 (AS REPORTED)
THE MECKLENBURGH RESOLUTIONS

2. Resolved: That we do hereby declare ourselves a free and independent people; are, and of right ought to be a sovereign and self-governing association, under the control of no power, other than that of **our God** and the General Government of the Congress: To the maintenance of which Independence we solemnly pledge to each other our mutual cooperation, our Lives, our Fortunes, and our most Sacred Honor...

1776
CONSTITUTION OF NORTH CAROLINA

DECLARATION OF RIGHTS, ARTICLE 19. That all men have a natural and unalienable right to **worship Almighty God** according to the **dictates of their own consciences**.

FORM OF GOVERNMENT, ARTICLE 31. That no **clergyman**, or **Preacher** of the **Gospel**, of any **denomination**, shall be capable of being a member of either the Senate, House of Commons, or Council of State, while he continues in the exercise of **pastoral function**.

ARTICLE 32. That no person, who shall deny the **being of God** or the truth of the **Protestant religion**, or the **Divine authority** either of the **Old or New Testaments**, or who shall hold **religious principles** incompatible with the freedom and safety of the State, shall be capable of holding any office or place of trust or profit in the civil department within this State.

ARTICLE 34. That there shall be no **establishment** of any one **religious Church** or **denomination** in this State, in preference to any other; neither shall any person, on any presence whatsoever, be compelled to attend any **place of worship** contrary to his own **faith** or judgment, nor be obliged to pay, for the purchase of any **glebe**, or the building of any **house of worship**, or for the maintenance of any **minister** or **Ministry**, contrary to what he believes right, of has voluntarily and personally engaged to perform; but all persons shall be at liberty to exercise their own **mode of worship**.-Provided, that nothing herein contained shall be construed to exempt **Preachers** of treasonable or seditious discourses, from legal trial and punishment. (In force till 1876)

JULY 30, 1788
NORTH CAROLINA CONVENTION TO RATIFY FEDERAL CONSTITUTION

Governor Samuel Johnston stated:

I know but two or three States where there is the least chance of **establishing** any particular **religion**.

The people of Massachusetts and Connecticut are mostly **Presbyterians**.

In every other State, the people are divided into a great number of **sects**.

In Rhode Island, the tenets of the **Baptists**, I believe, prevail.

In New York, they are divided very much; the most numerous are the **Episcopalians** and the **Baptists**.

In New Jersey, they are as much divided as we are.

In Pennsylvania, if any **sect** prevails more than others, it is that of the **Quakers**.

In Maryland, the **Episcopalians** are most numerous, though there are other **sects**.

In Virginia, there are many **sects**; you all know what their **religious sentiments** are.

So in all the Southern States they differ; as also New Hampshire. I hope, therefore, that gentlemen will see there is no cause of fear that any one **religion** shall be exclusively **established**.

JULY 30, 1788
NORTH CAROLINA CONVENTION TO RATIFY FEDERAL CONSTITUTION

State delegate Henry Abbott stated: "Many wish to know what **religion** shall be **established**. I believe a majority of the community are **Presbyterians**. I am, for my part, against any exclusive **establishment**; but if there were any, I would prefer the **Episcopal**...If there be no **religious test** required, **pagans, deists, and Mahometans** might obtain office among us, and that the senators and representatives might all be **pagans**."

1835
CONSTITUTION OF NORTH CAROLINA

ARTICLE 32. That no person, who shall deny the **being of God** or the truth of the **Christian religion**, or the **Divine** authority either of the **Old or New Testaments**, or who shall hold **religious principles** incompatible with the freedom and safety of the State, shall be capable of holding any office or place of trust or profit in the civil department within this State.

1868
CONSTITUTION OF NORTH CAROLINA

"The following persons shall be disqualified for office: First, any person who shall deny the **being of Almighty God**..."

1971
CONSTITUTION OF NORTH CAROLINA

PREAMBLE. We, the people of the State of North Carolina, grateful to **Almighty God, the Sovereign Ruler of Nations**, for the preservation of the American Union and the existence of our civil, political and **religious** liberties, and acknowledging **our** dependence upon Him for the continuance of those **blessings** to us and our posterity, do, for the more certain security thereof and for the better government of this State, ordain and **establish** this Constitution...

ARTICLE 1, SECTION 1. We hold it to be self-evident that all persons are created equal; that they are endowed by their **Creator** with certain inalienable rights; that among these are life, liberty, the enjoyment of the fruits of their own labor, and the pursuit of happiness...

ARTICLE 1, SECTION 13. All persons have a natural and inalienable right to **worship Almighty God** according to the **dictates of their own consciences**, and no human authority shall, in any case whatever, control or interfere with the **rights of conscience**...

ARTICLE 1, SECTION 17. Slavery is forever prohibited. Involuntary servitude, except as a punishment for crime whereof the parties have been adjudged guilty, is forever prohibited...

ARTICLE 6, SECTION 7. Before entering upon the duties of an office, a person elected or appointed to the office shall take and subscribe the following oath: "I.....do solemnly swear (or affirm) that I will support and maintain the Constitution and laws of the United States, and the Constitution and laws of North Carolina not inconsistent therewith, and that I will faithfully discharge the duties of my office as....., **So Help Me God**."

ARTICLE 6, SECTION 8. The following persons shall be disqualified for office: First, any person who shall deny the **being of Almighty God**...

ARTICLE 9, SECTION 1. **Religion, morality,** and knowledge being necessary to good government and the happiness of mankind, schools, libraries, and the means of education shall forever be encouraged...

ARTICLE 11, SECTION 4. Beneficent provision for the poor, the unfortunate, and the orphan is one of the first duties of a civilized and a **Christian** state. Therefore the General Assembly shall provide for and define the duties of a board of public welfare.

NORTH CAROLINA RELIGIOUS AFFILIATION

The Encyclopedia Britannica, 11th edition, published in 1911, stated:

The **Baptist** and **Methodist Churches** are the leading **religious denominations** in the state; but there are also **Presbyterians, Lutherans,** members of the **Christian Connection** (**O'Kellyites**), **Disciples of Christ** (Campbellites) **Episcopalians, Friends, Roman Catholics, Moravians** and members of other **denominations.**

http://www.1911encyclopedia.org/North_Carolina

The Catholic Encyclopedia, Volume XV, Copyright 1912 by Robert Appleton Company, stated as of 1906, a census listed **North Carolina** as:

Baptist, white 824,385
Baptist, col. 235,540
Christian 165,503
Congregationalists 15,909
Disciples 2,699
Friends 13,637
Lutheran 6,752
Methodist, white 17,740
Methodist, col. 191,760
Presbyterian 85,522

Reformed 60,555
Protestant 13,890
Episcopal 3,981
Roman Catholic 10,897

http://www.newadvent.org/cathen/11108a.htm

The Wikipedia Online Encyclopedia, as of 2006, listed **North Carolina** as:

Christian - 88 percent, consisting of:
- **Baptist** - 40 percent
- **Methodist** - 10 percent
- **Presbyterian** - 3 percent
- **Other Protestant** - 24 percent
- **Catholic** - 10 percent
- **Greek Orthodox/Other Christian** - 1 percent

Jewish/ Islam/ Hindu/ Buddhist/ Other - 1 percent
Non-Religious/Non-Reporting - 11 percent

http://en.wikipedia.org/wiki/North_carolina#Religion

The U.S. Religious Landscape Survey, conducted by The Pew Forum on Religion & Public Life, 2007, published in the USA Today, listed **North Carolina** as:

Christian - 85 percent, consisting of:
- **Evangelical Protestant** - 41 percent
- **Mainline Protestant** - 21 percent
- **Black Protestant** - 13 percent
- **Catholic** - 9 percent
- **Orthodox** - <0.5 percent
- **Other Christian** - <0.5 percent

Mormon - <0.5 percent
Jehovah's Witnesses - <0.5 percent
Jewish - <0.5 percent
Muslim - <0.5 percent

Buddhist - 1 percent
Hindu - <0.5 percent
Other World Religions - <0.5 percent
Other Faiths - 1 percent
Unaffiliated - 12 percent
Did not answer - 1 percent

www.pewforum.org
www.usatoday.com/news/graphics/pew-religion-08/flash.htm

SOUTH CAROLINA
ANIMIS OPIBUSQUE PARATI
DUM SPIRO SPERO
SPES

SOUTH CAROLINA

South Carolina and North Carolina were one colony until 1711, so parts of its history will not be repeated.

In 1629, England's Charles I granted a patent for the area of the Carolinas, but because it was never acted upon, it was forfeited. In 1653, a small company of **dissenting Quakers** arrived from Virginia and began the Albemarle settlement. A few years later, New Englanders purchased land from the Indians on Cape Fear River, but later abandoned it.

In 1663, Charles II granted Sir George Carteret and seven others all of Carolina. Cape Fear was then settled by colonists from Barbados.

Though they **established** the **Church of England**, they allowed **freedom of worship** in order to attract settlers. Difficulty arose when the Constitution framed by the Earl of Shaftesbury, with assistance from philosopher Locke, proved impractical.

In 1670, the foundation of South Carolina was laid with a settlement on the Ashley River. In 1673, Charleston became a permanent settlement. A number of Dutch immigrants arrived from New York, as well as a shipload of slaves.

In 1683, Scotch-Irish **Presbyterians** and Germans from the Rhineland arrived, followed by French **Huguenots**, driven out of France when the King revoked the **Edict of Nantes.**

Carolina's self-interested proprietors, stubborn governors, **Quakers dissenting from the established Church of England**, and the dangerous proximity of

Spanish settlements, led to a revolt which banished the governor and, in 1689, resulted in martial law.

Only by the appointment of **Quaker** proprietor, John Archdale, as governor, was trouble averted. He made many concessions, as did his successor, Joseph Blake. In 1697, **religious liberty** was accorded to all "except **Papists**." Indeed, there is no record of any **Catholic** in South Carolina prior to the Revolution.

In 1704, **Church of England** settlers attempted to exclude **dissenters** from the Assembly, but the law was annulled by Queen Anne. From the next several decades, the proprietors tried to regain control of the colony, but the dissension culminated in the Crown dividing South Carolina from North Carolina in 1711 and taking complete royal control in 1729.

This contributed to the colony's animosity toward England's monarch prior to the Revolutionary War. In September of 1775, South Carolina's royal governor was forced to abdicate and flee on a British man-of-war.

South Carolina's first State Constitution was adopted March 26, 1776, and the State ratified the U.S. Constitution on May 23, 1788. The population of South Carolina in 1820 was 502,741.

South Carolina jealously guarded its States' Rights, which made it the leader in the south prior the Civil War. The State passed a Nullification Act in 1832 in opposition to the high tariffs imposed by the northern Federal Government. On the day of Lincoln's election as President, both Houses of South Carolina's State Legislature passed a resolution considering withdrawal from the Union.

On December 20, 1861, an ordinance was unanimously adopted declaring the "the union now subsisting between South Carolina and other States under the name of the United States of America is hereby dissolved."

The population of South Carolina in 1840 was 594,398 and in 1860 it was 703,708.

South Carolina insisted on immediate withdraw of Federal troops from Charleston harbor, but Lincoln refused, making clear he would defend Fort Sumter. On April 12, 1861, South Carolinians attacked Fort Sumter and the Civil War began.

After the War, a State convention was held in 1865 to set up a new government. On January 14, 1868, a convention composed of 34 whites and 63 blacks adopted the new Constitution, followed by 85 black men and 73 white men being elected to the State Legislature. On July 13, 1868, the Fourteenth Amendment was ratified guaranteeing rights to freed slaves and on March 11, 1869, the Fifteenth Amendment was ratified guaranteeing former slaves the right to vote.

A generation after the Revolution, with the **disestablishment** of the **Anglican Church**, a **diocese** was created in 1820 for **Catholics** scattered in Georgia and the Carolinas. The Irish **Rev. John England** was consecrated as **Bishop**. He **established** the **Seminary of Charleston** for both **Catholics** and **non-Catholics** and founded America's first **Catholic newspaper**, "**The United States Catholic Miscellany**." In 1830, he organized the **Sisters of Our Lady of Mercy**, wrote a model **Constitution of the Church** and incorporated trustees.

Bishop England delivered the first **Catholic** Sermon in the U.S. Capital in the **Sunday** morning **Church** service that was held in the House of Representatives, January 8, 1826.

The overflow audience included President John Quincy Adams, who had previously stated, July 4, 1821, that **Catholicism** and Republicanism were incompatible. **Bishop England** stated: "we do not believe that **God** gave to the **Church** any power to interfere with our civil rights, or our civil concerns...I would not allow to the **Pope**, or to any **bishop** of **our Church**...the smallest interference with the humblest vote at our most insignificant balloting box."

In 1850, the **Diocese of Charleston** encompassed all the Carolinas, which had a **Catholic** population estimated at 8,000. The Civil War wrought havoc on **Catholics** and **Church property** in the south, culminating in Sherman's destructive march to the sea. After the War, **Bishop Patrick Lynch** helped rebuild the ruined and penniless **diocese.**

In 1868, the **Diocese of Charleston** encompassed all the State of South Carolina. There was an estimated **Catholic** population in the state 9,650, with 12 **Churches** served by 31 **priests**, 17 **missions**, 75 **stations**, 8 **chapels**, 108 **religious women, novices and postulants**, 5 academies for young ladies with 395 pupils, 9 **parishes** with 859 **parochial school** students; one **Catholic** hospital run by the **Sisters of Mercy**, at Charleston, and the **diocese** cared for 72 orphans.

The earliest record of **Jewish** presence in South Carolina dates from 1695. In 1749 the **Jewish community** of **Kehilat Kadosh Beth Elohim** was organized and in 1797 dedicated its first **synagogue** in Charleston. Built in the **Sephardic tradition, Beth Elohim** had men's seating on the ground floor facing the reader's desk in the center with accommodations for women in the upstairs gallery. **American Reform Judaism** traces its origins to the **Beth Elohim congregation** when a group of **synagogue** members withdrew in 1825 to **establish** the **Reformed Society of Israelites**. A 1872 map of Charleston featured "bird's-eye" view showing Charleston's **"Sinagogue"** and **Hebrew Orphan Asylum**, incorporated in 1802 as the first American **Jewish** orphan care agency.

In 1797, author and poet Penina Moise was born in Charleston. She was the first American **Jewish** woman to have her works published. A deeply **religious** woman, she composed hymns for use in **prayer services** and poems on **biblical** themes and on contemporary **Jewish** life.

The population of South Carolina in 1880 was 995,577, in 1900 it was 1,340,316, and in 1910 it was 1,515,400. The 1910 Census listed the State of South Carolina as 26th in population.

In 1910, Beaufort County had the fifth largest African American population of any county in the United States, with 90.5 percent. In 1790, South Carolina was second only to Virginia in the number of slaves, having 107,097. In 1909, there were 2,712 public schools in the State for white children, employing 933 men **teachers** and 3,247 women **teachers** for 153,807 pupils. In 1909, there were 2,354 public schools for African American children, employing 894 men **teachers** and 1,802 women **teachers** for 123,481 pupils. There were 27 institutions of higher education for whites and 11 for African Americans. Of the 27 institutions for whites, 5 were **non-sectarian**, 5 were **Presbyterian**, 3 were **Methodist**, 3 were **Baptist**, and 2 were **Lutheran**.

As of 1910, the State allowed a rectory and two acres of land with building to be exempt from taxation, and no **religious** houses are taxed. **Catholic religious societies** which teach children had their **parochial schools** exempt from taxation.

Full **liberty of conscience** was granted in South Carolina, but not as to legalize willful or profane swearing or scoffing or prevent legislation prohibiting the conduct of secular business on **Sunday**. Sessions of the State Legislature are opened with **prayer**.

MARCH 26, 1776
CONSTITUTION OF SOUTH CAROLINA

Whereas the British Parliament, claiming of late years a right to bind the North American colonies by law in all cases whatsoever, have enacted statutes for raising a revenue in those colonies and disposing of such revenue as they thought proper, without the consent and against the will of the colonists.

And whereas it appearing to them that (they not being represented in Parliament) such claim was altogether unconstitutional, and, if admitted, would at once reduce them from the rank of freemen to a state of the most abject slavery; the said colonies, therefore, severally remonstrated against the passing, and petitioned for the repeal, of those acts, but in vain,

And whereas the said claim being persisted in, other unconstitutional and oppressive statutes have been since enacted by which

The powers of admiralty courts in the colonies are extended beyond their ancient limits, and jurisdiction is given to such courts in cases similar to those which in Great Britain are triable by jury; persons are liable to be sent to and tried in Great Britain for an offense created and made capital by one of those statutes, though committed in the colonies;

The harbor of Boston was blocked up; people indicted for murder in the Massachusetts Bay may, at the will of a governor, be sent for trial to any other colony, or even to Great Britain;

The chartered constitution of government in that colony is materially altered;

The English laws and a free government, to which the inhabitants of Quebec were entitled by the King's royal proclamation, are abolished and French laws are restored; the **Roman Catholic religion** (although before **tolerated** and freely exercised there) and an absolute government are **established** in that province, and its limits extended through a vast tract of country so as to border on the free **Protestant** English settlements, with design of using a whole people differing in **religious principles** from the neighboring colonies, and subject to arbitrary power, as fit instruments to overawe and subdue the colonies.

And whereas the delegates of all the colonies on this continent, from Nova Scotia to Georgia, assembled in a general Congress at Philadelphia, in the most dutiful manner laid their complaints at the foot of the throne, and humbly implored their sovereign that his royal authority and interposition might be used for their relief from the grievances occasioned by those statutes, and assured His Majesty that harmony between Great Britain and America, ardently desired by the latter, would be thereby immediately restored, and that the colonists confided in the magnanimity and justice of the King and Parliament for redress of the many other grievances under which they labored.

And whereas these complaints being Only disregarded, statutes still more cruel than those above mentioned have been enacted, prohibiting the intercourse of the colonies with each other, restricting their trade, and depriving many thousands of people of the means of subsistence, by restraining them from fishing on the American coast.

And whereas large fleets and armies having been sent to America in order to enforce the execution of those laws, and to compel an absolute and implicit submission to the will of a corrupt and despotic administration, and in consequence thereof, hostilities having been commenced in the Massachusetts Bay, by the troops under command of General Gage, whereby a number of peaceable, helpless, and unarmed people were wantonly robbed and murdered, and there being just reason to apprehend that like hostilities would be committed in all the other colonies.

The colonists were therefore driven to the necessity of taking up arms, to repel force by force, and to defend themselves and their properties against lawless invasions and depredations.

Nevertheless, the delegates of the said colonies assembled in another Congress at Philadelphia, anxious to procure a reconciliation with Great Britain upon just and constitutional principles, supplicated His Majesty to direct some mode by which the united applications of his faithful colonists might be improved into a happy and permanent reconciliation, that in the mean time measures might be taken for preventing the further destruction of their lives, and that such statutes as immediately distressed any of the colonists might be repealed.

And whereas, instead of obtaining that justice, to which the colonists were and are of right entitled, the unnatural civil war into which they were thus precipitated and are involved, hath been prosecuted with unremitted violence, and the governors and others bearing the royal commission in the colonies having broken the most solemn promises and engagements, and violated every obligation of honor, Justice, and humanity, have caused the persons of divers good people to be seized and imprisoned, and their properties to be forcibly taken and detained' or destroyed, without any crime or forfeiture; excited domestic insurrections; proclaimed freedom to servants and slaves, enticed or stolen them from, and armed them against their masters; instigated and encouraged the Indian nations to war against the colonies; dispensed with the law of the land, and substituted the law martial in its stead; killed many of the colonists; burned several towns, and threatened to burn the rest, and daily endeavor by a conduct which has sullied the British arms, and would disgrace even savage nations, to effect the ruin and destruction of the colonies;

And whereas a statute hath been lately passed, whereby, under presence that the said colonies are in open rebellion, all trade and commerce whatsoever with them is prohibited; vessels belonging to their inhabitants trading in, to, or from the said colonies, with the cargoes and effects on board such vessels, are made lawful prize, and the masters and crews of such vessels are subjected by force to act on board the King's ships against their country and dearest friends; and all seizures and detention or destruction of the persons and properties of the colonists which have at any time been made or committed for withstanding or suppressing the said pretended rebellion, and which' shell be made in pursuance of the said act, or for the service of the public, are justified, and persons suing for damages in such cases are, on failing in their suits, subjected to payment of very heavy expenses.

And whereas large reinforcements of troops and ships have been ordered and are daily expected in America for carrying on war against each of the united colonies by the most vigorous exertions.

And whereas in consequence of a plan recommended by the governors, and which seems to have been concerted between them and their **ministerial** masters to withdraw the usual officers and thereby loosen the bands of government and create anarchy and confusion in the colonies.

Lord William Campbell, late governor, on the fifteenth day of September last, dissolved the general Assembly of this colony, and no other hath been since called, although by law the sitting and holding of general Assemblies cannot be intermitted above six months, and having used his utmost efforts to destroy the lives, liberties, and properties of the good people here, whom by the duty of his station he was bound to protect, withdrew himself from the colony and carried oft the great seal and the royal instructions to governors.

And whereas the judges of courts of law here have refused to exercise their respective functions, so that it is become indispensably necessary that during the present situation of American affairs, and until an accommodation of the unhappy differences between Great Britain and America can be obtained, (an event which, though traduced and treated as rebels, we still earnestly desire,) some mode should be **established** by common consent, and for the good of the people, the origin and end of all governments, for regulating the internal polity of this colony.

The congress being vested with powers competent for the purpose, and having fully deliberated touching the premises, do therefore resolve...

11...Members of the general Assembly shall be chosen...each **parish** and district having the same representation as at present, viz:

parish of **Saint Philip** and **Saint Michael**, Charlestown, thirty members;

parish of **Christ Church**, six members;
parish of **Saint John**, Berkeley...six members;
parish of **Saint Andrew**, six members;
parish of **Saint George** Dorchester, six members;
parish of **Saint James** Goose Creek, six members;
parish of **Saint Thomas** & **Saint Dennis**, six members;
parish of **Saint Paul**, six members;
parish of **Saint Bartholemew**, six members;
parish of **Saint Helena**, six members;
parish of **Saint James Santee**, six members...
parish of **Saint John**, Colleton...six members;
parish of **Saint Peter**, six members...
parish of **Saint Stephen**, six members...
parish of **Saint Mathew**, six members;
parish of **Saint David**, six members...

And...where there are no **Churches** or **Church wardens** in a district or **parish**, the General Assembly at some convenient time before their expiration, shall appoint places of election and persons to receive votes and make returns...

33. That all persons who shall be chosen and appointed to any office or to any place of trust, before entering upon the execution of office, shall take the following oath:

"I, A. B., do swear that I will, to the utmost of my power, support, maintain, and defend the constitution of South Carolina, as **established** by Congress on the twenty-sixth day of March, one thousand seven hundred and seventy-six, until an accommodation of the differences between Great Britain and America shall take place, or I shall be released from this oath by the legislative authority of the said colony: **So Help Me God.**"

MARCH 19, 1778
CONSTITUTION OF SOUTH CAROLINA

PREAMBLE. We, the people of the State of South Carolina...grateful to **God** for our liberties, do ordain and **establish** this Constitution for the preservation and perpetuation of the same.

ARTICLE 3. That as soon as may be after the first meeting of the Senate and House of Representatives, and at every first meeting of the Senate and House of representatives thereafter, to be elected by virtue of this Constitution, they shall jointly in the House of Representatives choose by ballot from among themselves or from the people at large a governor and commander-in-chief, a lieutenant-governor, both to continue for two years, and a privy council, all of the **Protestant religion**, and till such choice shall be made the former president or governor and commander-in-chief, and vice-president or lieutenant-governor, as the case may be, and privy council, shall continue to act as same.

ARTICLE 11. And whereas the **ministers** of the **Gospel** are by their **profession** dedicated to the **service of God** and the **care of souls**, and ought not to be diverted from the great duties of their function, therefore no **minister of the Gospel** or **public Preacher** of any **religious persuasion**, while he continues in the exercise of his **pastorial function**, and for two years after, shall be eligible either as governor, lieutenant-governor, a member of the senate, house of representatives, or privy council in this state.

ARTICLE 12. That each **parish** and district throughout this State shall...elect by ballot one member of the senate, except the district of **Saint Philip** and **Saint Michael's parishes**, Charleston, which shall elect two members...except the **parishes** of **Saint Matthew** and Orange, which shall elect one member...except the **parishes** of Prince George and **All Saints**, which shall elect one member; and the election of senators for such **parishes**...shall...be at the **parish** of Prince George for the said **parish** and the **parish** of **All Saints**, and at the **parish** of **Saint Matthew** for that **parish** and the **parish** of Orange; to meet on the first Monday in January...

And that no person shall be eligible to a seat in the said senate unless he be of the **Protestant religion**, and hath attained the age of thirty years...

13...Each **parish** and district within this State shall send members to the general Assembly in the following proportions...

parish of **Saint Philip** & **Saint Michael's**, Charleston, thirty members;

parish of **Christ Church**, six members;
parish of **Saint John's**, Berkley...six members;
parish of **Saint Andrew**, six members;
parish of **Saint George**, Dorchester, six members;
parish of **Saint James**, Goose Creek, six members;
parish of **Saint Thomas** & **Saint Dennis**, six members;
parish of **Saint Paul**, six members;
parish of **Saint Bartholomew**, six members;
parish of **Saint Helena**, six members;

parish of **Saint James**, Santee, six members...
parish of **All Saints**, two members...
parish of **Saint John**...six members;
parish of **Saint Peter**, six members...
parish of **Saint Stephen**, six members...
parish of **Saint Matthew**, three members...
parish of **Saint David**, six members...

And where there are no **Churches** or **Church-wardens** in a district or **parish**, the house of representatives...shall appoint places of election and persons to receive votes...

The qualification of electors shall be that every free white man, and no other person, who acknowledges the **being of a God**, and believes in **a future state of rewards and punishments...**

No person shall be eligible to sit in the house of representatives unless he be of the **Protestant religion**...

21. And whereas the **ministers** of the **Gospel** are by their **profession** dedicated to the **service of God** and the **care of souls**, and ought not to be diverted from the great duties of their function, therefore no **minister of the Gospel** or **public Preacher** of any **religious persuasion**, while he continues in the exercise of his **pastoral function,** and for two years after, shall be eligible either as governor, lieutenant-governor, a member of the senate, house of representatives, or privy council in this State...

36. That all persons who shall be chosen and appointed to any office or to any place of trust, civil or military, before entering upon the execution of office, shall take the following oath:

"I, A. B., do acknowledge the State of South Carolina to be as free, sovereign, and independent State, and that the people thereof owe no allegiance or obedience to George the Third, King of Great Britain, and I do renounce, refuse, and abjure any allegiance or obedience to him. And I do swear (or affirm, as the case may be) that I will, to the utmost of my power, support, maintain, and defend the said State against the said King George the Third, and his heirs and successors, and his or their abettors, assistants, and adherents, and will serve the said State, in the office of, with fidelity and honor, and according to the best of my skill and understanding: **So Help Me God.**"...

38. That all persons and **religious societies** who acknowledge that there is one **God**, and **a future state of rewards and punishments**, and that **God** is **publicly to be worshipped**, shall be freely **tolerated**. The **Christian Protestant religion** shall be deemed, and is hereby constituted and declared to be, the **established religion** of this State.

That all **denominations** of **Christian Protestants** in this State, demeaning themselves peaceably and faithfully, shall enjoy equal **religious** and civil privileges. To accomplish this desirable purpose without injury to the **religious property** of those **societies of Christians** which are by law already incorporated for the purpose of **religious worship**, and to put it fully into the power of every other **society of Christian Protestants**, either already formed or hereafter to be formed, to obtain the like incorporation, it is hereby constituted, appointed, and declared that the respective **societies of the Church of England** that are already formed in this State for the purpose of **religious worship** shall still continue incorporate and hold the **religious property** now in their possession.

And that whenever fifteen or more male persons, not under twenty-one years of age, professing the **Christian Protestant religion**, and agreeing to unite themselves in a **society** for the purposes of **religious worship**, they shall, (on complying with the terms hereinafter mentioned,) be, and be constituted a **Church**, and be esteemed and regarded in law as of the **established religion** of the State, and on a petition to the legislature shall be entitled to be incorporated and to enjoy equal privileges.

That every **society of Christians** so formed shall give themselves a name or **denomination** by which they shall be called and known in law, and all that associate with them for the purposes of **worship** shall be esteemed as belonging to the **society** so called.

But that previous to the **establishment** and incorporation of the respective **societies** of every **denomination** as aforesaid, and in order to entitle them thereto, each **society** so petitioning shall have agreed to and subscribed in a book the following five articles, without which no agreement for union of men upon **presence of religion** shall entitle them to be incorporated and esteemed as a **Church** of the **established religion** of this State (See Locke's Constitution, Article 97-100):

1. That there is **one eternal God**, and **a future state of rewards and punishments.**

2. That **God** is **publicly** to be **worshipped**.

3. That the **Christian religion** is the **true religion**

4. That the **Holy Scriptures** of the **Old and New Testaments** are of **Divine inspiration**, and are the rule of **faith** and **practice**.

5. That it is lawful and the duty of every man being thereunto called by those that govern, to bear witness to the truth.

And that every inhabitant of this State, when called to make an appeal to **God** as a witness to truth, shall be permitted to do it in that way which is most agreeable to the **dictates of his own conscience**.

And that the people of this State may forever enjoy the right of electing their own **pastors** or **clergy**, and at the same time that the State may have sufficient security for the due discharge of the **pastoral office**, by those who shall be admitted to be **clergymen**, no person shall officiate as **minister** of any **established Church** who shall not have been chosen by a majority of the **society** to which he shall **minister**, or by persons appointed by the said majority, to choose and procure a **minister** for them; nor until the **minister** so chosen and appointed shall have made and subscribed to the following declaration, over and above the aforesaid five articles, viz:

That he is determined by **God's grace** out of the **Holy Scriptures**, to instruct the people committed to his charge, and to teach nothing as required of necessity to **eternal salvation** but that which he shall be persuaded may be concluded and proved from the **Scripture**;

That he will use both public and private admonitions, as well to the sick as to the whole within his cure, as need shall require and occasion shall be given, and that he will be diligent in **prayers**, and in reading of the same;

That he will be diligent to frame and fashion his own self and his family according to the **doctrine of Christ,** and to make both himself and them, as much as in him lieth, wholesome examples and patterns to the **flock of Christ;**

That he will maintain and set forwards, as much as he can, quietness, peace, and love among all people, and especially among those that are or shall be committed to lids charge.

No person shall disturb or molest any **religious Assembly**; nor shall use any reproachful, reviling, or abusive language against any **Church**, that being the certain way of disturbing the peace, and of hindering the **conversion of any to the truth**, by engaging them in quarrels and animosities, to the hatred of the **professors**, and that **profession** which otherwise they might be brought to assent to.

To person whatsoever shall speak anything in their **religious Assembly irreverently** or seditiously of the government of this State. No person shall, by law, be obliged to pay towards the maintenance and support of a **religious**

worship that he does not freely join in, or has not voluntarily engaged to support.

But the **Churches, chapels, parsonages, globes**, and all other property now belonging to any **societies** of the **Church of England**, or any other **religious societies**, shall remain and be secured to them forever.

The poor shall be supported, and elections managed in the accustomed manner, until laws shall be provided to adjust those matters in the most equitable way...

63. That the liberty of the press be inviolably preserved...

1790
SOUTH CAROLINA CONSTITUTION

ARTICLE 1, SECTION 23. And whereas the **ministers** of the **Gospel** are by their **profession** dedicated to the **service of God** and the **care of souls**, and ought not to be diverted from the great duties of their function, therefore no **minister of the Gospel** or **public Preacher** of any **religious persuasion**, while he continues in the exercise of his **pastoral function**, shall be eligible to the office of governor, lieutenant-governor, or to a seat in the senate or house of representatives.

ARTICLE 8, SECTION 1. The free exercise and enjoyment of **religious profession** and **worship**, without discrimination or preference, shall forever hereafter be allowed within this State to all mankind, PROVIDED, That the **liberty of conscience** thereby declared shall not be construed as to excuse acts of licentiousness, or justify practices inconsistent with the peace and safety of this State.

ARTICLE 8, SECTION 2. The rights, privileges, immunities, and estates of both civil and **religious societies**, and of corporate bodies, shall remain as if the constitution of this State had not been altered or amended.

1846
SOUTH CAROLINA SUPREME COURT
CITY OF CHARLESTON V. S.A. BENJAMIN

The case involved an individual who willfully broke the Ordinance: "No person or persons whatsoever shall publicly expose to sale, or sell...any goods, wares or merchandise whatsoever upon the **Lord's Day**." The prosecuting attorney stated:

Christianity is a part of the common law of the land, with **liberty of conscience** to all. It has always been so recognized....If **Christianity** is a part of the common law, its disturbance is punishable at common law. The U.S. Constitution allows it as a part of the common law.

The President is allowed ten days [to sign a bill], with the exception of **Sunday**. The Legislature does not sit, **public** offices are closed, and the Government recognizes the day in all things....The observance of **Sunday** is one of the usages of the common law, recognized by our U.S. and State Governments....The **Sabbath** is still to be supported;

Christianity is part and parcel of the common law....**Christianity** has reference to the **principles** of right and wrong....it is the foundation of those **morals** and manners upon which our **society** is formed; it is their basis. Remove this and they would fall...[**Morality**] has grown upon the basis of **Christianity**.

The Supreme Court of South Carolina delivered its decision: The **Lord's Day**, the **day of the Resurrection**, is to us, who are called **Christians**, the day of rest after finishing **a new creation**. It is the day of the first visible triumph over death, hell and the grave! It was the **birth day of the believer in Christ,** to whom and through whom it opened up the way which, by **repentance** and **faith**, leads unto **everlasting life** and **eternal happiness**!

On that day we rest, and to us it is the **Sabbath of the Lord** - its decent observance, in a **Christian community**, is that which ought to be expected...

What gave to us this noble safeguard of **religious toleration**? It was **Christianity**...But this **toleration**, thus granted, is a **religious toleration**; it is the free exercise and enjoyment of **religious profession** and **worship**, with two provisos, one of which, that which guards against acts of licentiousness, testifies to the **Christian** construction, which this section should receive!

What are acts "of licentiousness" within the meaning of this section? Must they not be such public acts, as are calculated to shock the **moral** sense of the community where they take place? The orgies of Bacchus, among the ancients, were not offensive! At a later day, the Carnivals of Venice went off without note or observation. Such could not be allowed now! Why? **Public** opinion, based on **Christian morality**, would not suffer it!

What constitutes the standard of good **morals**? Is it not **Christianity**? There certainly is none other. Say that cannot be appealed to, and I don't know what would be good **morals**. The day of **moral virtue** in which we live would, in an instant, if that standard were abolished, lapse into the dark and murky night of **Pagan immorality.**

In the Courts over which we preside, we daily acknowledge **Christianity** as the most solemn part of our administration. A **Christian witness**, having no **religious** scruple about placing his hand upon the book, is sworn upon the **Holy Evangelists, the books of the New Testament,** which testify of **our Savior's birth, life, death, and resurrection**; this is so common a matter, that it is little thought of as an evidence of the part which **Christianity** has in the common law.

I agree fully to what is beautifully and appropriately said in Updegraph v. The Commonwealth...

Christianity, general **Christianity**, is, and always has been, a part of the common law: "not **Christianity** with an **established Church**...but **Christianity** with **liberty of conscience** to all men."

1895
(CURRENT)
CONSTITUTION OF SOUTH CAROLINA

INTRODUCTION. At a Convention of the People of the State of South Carolina begun and holden at Columbia on the Tenth day of September, **in the Year of Our Lord** One Thousand Eight hundred and Ninety-five, and thence continued by divers adjournments to the Fourth day of December **in the Year of Our Lord** One Thousand Eight hundred and Ninety-five. (current)

PREAMBLE. We, the people of the State of South Carolina, in Convention assembled, grateful to **God** for our liberties, do ordain and establish this Constitution for the preservation and perpetuation of the same.

ARTICLE I, SECTION 2. The General Assembly shall make no law respecting an **establishment of religion** or prohibiting the free exercise thereof, or abridging the freedom of speech or of the press; or the right of the people peaceably to assemble and to petition the government or any department thereof for a redress of grievances.

ARTICLE 3, SECTION 26. Members of the General Assembly and all officers, before they enter upon the duties of their respective offices, and all members of the bar, before they enter upon the practice of their profession, shall take and subscribe the following oath:

"I do solemnly swear (or affirm) that I am duly qualified, according to the Constitution of this State, to exercise the duties of the office to which I have been elected, (or appointed), and that I will, to the best of my ability, discharge the duties thereof, and preserve, protect and defend the Constitution of this State and of the United States. **So Help Me God**." (1954 (48) 1852; 1955 (49) 23.)

ARTICLE 6, SECTION 2. No person who denies the **existence of the Supreme Being** shall hold any office under this Constitution.

ARTICLE 17, SECTION 4. No person who denies the **existence of a Supreme Being** shall hold any office under this Constitution.

SOUTH CAROLINA RELIGIOUS AFFILIATION

The Encyclopedia Britannica, 11th edition, published in 1911, stated:

In 1906 there were in the state 655,933 members of different **religious denominations**, of whom the **Baptist** bodies were the strongest with 341,456 **communicants**; the **Methodist** bodies had 249,169 members; 35,533 were **Presbyterians**; 12,652 were **Lutherans**; 10,317 were **Roman Catholics**; and 8557 were **Protestant Episcopalians**.

http://www.1911encyclopedia.org/South_Carolina

The Catholic Encyclopedia, Volume XV, Copyright 1912 by Robert Appleton Company, stated as of 1908, a census listed **South Carolina** as:

Baptist-118,217 in 1,003 **Churches** & 410 **ministers**
Methodist Episcopal-85,441 in 798 **Churches** & 357 **ministers**
Presbyterian-23,442 in 275 **Churches** & 121 **ministers**
Lutheran-13,993 in 85 **Churches** & 34 **ministers**
Episcopal-7,620 in 94 **Churches** & 47 **ministers**
Unitarian-117 in 1 **Church** & 1 **minister**
Congregational-71 in 1 **Church** & 1 **minister**
A.R. Presbyterian-4,227 in 45 **Churches** & 36 **ministers**
Catholic-9,650 in 30 **Churches** & 19 **ministers**

http://www.newadvent.org/cathen/14157a.htm

The Wikipedia Online Encyclopedia, as of 2006, listed **South Carolina** as:

Christian - 92 percent, consisting of
- **Baptist** - 45 percent
- **Methodist** - 15 percent
- **Presbyterian** - 5 percent
- **Other Protestant** - 19 percent
- **Catholic** - 7 percent
- **Other Christian** - 1 percent

Other Religions - 1 percent
Non-Religious/Non-Reporting - 7 percent

http://en.wikipedia.org/wiki/South_Carolina#Religion

The U.S. Religious Landscape Survey, conducted by The Pew Forum on Religion & Public Life, 2007, published in the USA Today, listed **South Carolina** as:

Christian - 87.5 percent, consisting of:
- **Evangelical Protestant** - 45 percent
- **Mainline Protestant** - 18 percent
- **Black Protestant** - 15 percent
- **Catholic** - 8 percent
- **Orthodox** - 1 percent
- **Other Christian** - <0.5 percent

Mormon - <0.5 percent
Jehovah's Witnesses - 1 percent
Jewish - 1 percent
Muslim - <0.5 percent
Buddhist - <0.5 percent
Hindu - <0.5 percent
Other World Religions - <0.5 percent
Other Faiths - 1 percent
Unaffiliated - 10 percent
Did not answer - <0.5 percent

www.pewforum.org
www.usatoday.com/news/graphics/pew-religion-08/flash.htm

STATE OF GEORGIA
CONSTITUTION
WIS
DOM
JUSTICE
MODER
ATION
1776

GEORGIA

After the voyage of John Cabot in 1497, England claimed all of America's Atlantic seaboard. In 1565, Spain settled St. Augustine, Florida. For over a century, **Catholic Spanish missions** were along the coast.

When the area of South Carolina began to be populated by **Protestant English settlers** in 1670, Spain plotted with Indians and slaves to harass them. By 1704, the British had driven the Spanish out completely. In the early 1700's, the English Parliament was open to the idea of a buffer colony between the Carolina and Spanish Florida, causing them to be interested in Oglethorpe's proposed colony.

James Oglethorpe was educated at Oxford. At age 17, he joined the Austrian army and fought the invading **Muslim Turks** on the Hungarian frontier, serving as aide-de-camp to Prince Eugene of Savoy. He fought with distinction, especially during the siege and freeing of Belgrade.

At 21 years old, Oglethorpe returned to England where he ended up killing a man in a brawl and spent five months in prison. Upon release in 1722, he was chosen to serve in Parliament, as his father had.

He campaigned to improve the condition of poor in London's prisons and opposed slavery. His first-hand witness of prison atrocities, having had a friend die in debtors' prison, inspired Oglethorpe to found a colony in America where poor and destitute could get a fresh start and people persecuted for **faith** could find refuge.

James Oglethorpe secured the charter for Georgia in 1732, named for King George II, and on January 13, 1733, his ship, "Ann," arrived with 115 settlers in Savannah harbor. **Minister Herbert Henry** offered **prayer** at the ship's arrival.

Georgia's Charter allowed **religious freedom** to any **Protestant**. Oglethorpe brought more immigrants, including **Moravian missionaries. John Wesley**, who would later found **Methodism**, served for a short time as a **minister** in Georgia and his brother, **Charles Wesley,** was Oglethorpe's secretary.

In 1733, London's **Jewish community** numbered 6,000. They funded the **Jewish refugees** of Europe who had come to England on the trip to the new colony of Georgia. A total of 42 **Jews** left, 34 **Portuguese Sephardic Jews** and 8 **German Ashkenazic Jews,** arriving in Savannah on July 11, 1733, just five months after James Oglethorpe. This was the largest group of **Jews** to land in North America prior to the Revolutionary War.

As they had more the a "minyan," a quorum of ten men, and carried with them a **Torah Scroll**, containing the first five books of the **Bible**, the **Jewish** settlers first communal act upon landing was the initiation of **Divine services** in the homes of its members.

This was the beginning of **Kahal Kodesh Mickva Israel**, translated "**Holy Congregation Hope of Israel**," though they did not build a permanent **synagogue** until years later. It is the third oldest **Jewish congregation** in the United States. The oldest **congregation** being founded in New York City in 1654; the second oldest being founded in Newport, Rhode Island, in 1695; the fourth oldest being founded in Philadelphia in 1739 and the fifth oldest being founded in Charleston in 1749.

In a few years more "common" **Ashkenazic Jews** of German and Eastern European descent arrived in Savannah and tensions arose with the "aristocratic"

Sephardic Jews of Spanish and Portuguese decent. The difficulties were related in 1739 letter that **Lutheran minister Reverend Bolzius** of the **Salzburgers**, wrote to a friend in Germany:

"Even the **Jews**, of whom several families are here already, enjoy all privileges the same as other colonists. Some call themselves Spanish and Portuguese, others call themselves **German Jews**. The latter speak High German and differ from the former in their **religious services** and to some extent in other matters as well, as the former do not seem to take it so particular in regard to the **dietary laws** and other **Jewish ceremonies**. They have no **Synagogue**, which is their own fault; the one element hindering the other in this regard. The **German Jews** believe themselves entitled to build a **Synagogue** and are willing to allow the **Spanish Jews** to use it with them in common, the latter, however, reject any such arrangement and demand the preference for themselves."

The large number of settlers that were former debtors and convicts began to cry for rum and slavery and bring accusations against Oglethorpe for his efforts to keep order. Had it not been for the 1734 arrival of industrious **Protestant refugees** from Salzburg, Austria, called "**Salzburgers**," who settled the town of Ebenezer; and the **Swiss German Moravian immigrants** arriving from Fort Argyle in 1735; and the hardy and thrifty **Scotch Presbyterians** arriving from New Inverness in 1736, Oglethorpe's colony would have been wrecked.

On July 5, 1742, some 3,000 Spanish soldiers landed on **St. Simons Island**, intending to capture Georgia in what was called the War of Jenkin's Ear. Fearing the Spanish, many **Sephardic Jews** left the city. By 1774, though, many had returned.

Even **John and Charles Wesley** could not bring a **spiritual** responsibility to Savannah, though in 1738, the eloquent **Rev. George Whitefleld** received a popular welcome and preached an elevated **moral code.**

But neither the Governor, nor the zealous **Preachers** could **establish** the philanthropic or commercial success of the colony of Georgia. Mutiny was spreading and Oglethorpe's life was threatened with actual attempts upon it.

Letters of dissent and accusations against Oglethorpe were written under the pseudonym "The Plain Dealer" and sent to London. In 1743, Oglethorpe had to return to England to face 19 charges before a court martial. Though he was entirely exonerated, he had enough of the colony and never returned. In 1747, the base elements in the colony removed Oglethorpe's prohibition against slavery. In 1751, at the expiration of their charter, the council for Georgia surrendered their charter to the king and Georgia became a royal province.

On January 11, 1758, the King's government passed the **establishment** of the **Church of England**, titled an Act "for **establishing Religious Worship** therein, according to the **Rites and Ceremonies of the Church of England**." The Act set a salary of £25 per annum for every **clergyman** of the **Established Church of England**. Though passed by royal edict, it was not enforced, yet the law excluding **Roman Catholic colonists** was left in effect.

When four hundred **French Catholic Acadian refugees** sought shelter at Savannah, bringing letters from the governor of Nova Scotia to the effect, Governor Reynolds allowed them to stay the winter, then ordered them to leave, most heading for South Carolina.

In 1772, Daniel Marshall **established** the first **Baptist Church** in Georgia.

In the generation before the Revolution Georgia steadily increased in population under royal governors. The cultivation of rice by slaves made the colony economically self-supporting.

The large Tory element in the colony at the outbreak of the Revolution, favored the British. These were mostly wealthy landowners and their 14,000 slaves, who feared commercial ruin in revolution. The revolutionary spirit grew with increased momentum.

In spite of British military successes along the coast, the guerilla incursions of Indians and Florida Rangers to the south and west, and Washington's strained military unable to provide for the colony's safety, Georgia produced many heroes, such as Nancy Hart, known as Molly Pitcher, and Polish General Casmir Pulaski, who died fighting the British at Savannah. Georgia served by waiting, and when at last Washington could assign General Nathaniel Greene and Harry Lee to the army of the South, the recapture of Savannah. The last British post had been abandoned in the colony before the surrender at Yorktown.

During the Revolutionary War, Mordecai Sheftall of Georgia became the highest ranking **Jewish officer** of the American Revolutionary forces. Along with his son Sheftall, he was captured by British forces and imprisoned in Antigua. Eventually they were traded for two captured British officers.

As late as the Revolution, there was scarcely a **Catholic** in the entire State of Georgia, nor was there a **priest** in the State for many years thereafter.

In 1777, Georgia had passed its first State Constitution, The Preamble stated: "We the people of Georgia, **relying upon the protection and guidance of Almighty God**, do ordain and establish this Constitution."

Article 6 stated: Representatives shall be chosen out of the residents in each county...and they shall be of the **Protestant religion**."

In 1786, a building in Savannah at Barnard and Whitaker streets was used as a **synagogue**. Services were held regularly, and attendance numbered "seventy-three males and females."

Upon George Washington's election as first president of the United States, Levi Sheftall, president of the **congregation** wrote, on "behalf of the **Hebrew Congregation**," a congratulatory letter "on you appointment, by unanimous approbation, to the Presidential dignity of the country." President Washington dispatched an immediate answer "To the **Hebrew Congregation of the City of Savannah, Georgia**":

"May the same **wonder-working Deity,** who long since delivered the **Hebrews** from their Egyptian oppressors, planted them in the promised land, whose **Providential Agency** has lately been conspicuous in **establishing** these United States as an independent nation, still continue to water them with the dews of **Heaven**, and make the inhabitants of every **denomination** partake in the temporal and **spiritual blessings** of that people, whose **God** is **Jehovah**."

The population of Georgia in 1790 was 82,548.

A second Constitution, adopted 1789, removed the **Protestant requirement**. A third Constitution, adopted 1798, **established religious toleration**.

In 1788, Georgia was the fourth State to ratify the U.S. Constitution. In the first 34 years of its statehood Georgia had difficulties with Indians and land scandals, which led to the disastrous 1838-1839 removal of the Cherokee Indians to Oklahoma in what has been called the "Trail of Tears."

On November 20, 1790, Georgia Governor Edward Telfair granted the **Mickve Israel congregation** a State Charter. In 1898, the **Mickve Israel's synagogue** on Monterey Square was dedicated. Its museum contains letters from George Washington, Thomas Jefferson, James Madison and several other presidents.

About 1793, a few **Catholics** from Maryland moved to Georgia and settled near Locust Grove. They tried unsuccessfully to get a **clergyman**. Shortly after the French

Revolution, **Catholic priests** fled from the French colony of Santo Domingo and the horrors of the slave revolution. One settled in Augusta and another **priest** in Savannah. The **congregation** was incorporated by the State Legislature and the city granted land and a wooden edifice with a small steeple.

In 1810, the State Legislature incorporated the **Catholic Church** of Augusta. They erected a brick **Church of the Holy Trinity** and an **Augustinian friar, Rev. Robert Browne**, became **pastor**.

In 1818, the first **synagogue** was built in the State of Georgia, promoted by **Dr. Moses Sheftall** and **Dr. Jacob De la Motta**, in Savannah on the northeast corner of Liberty and Whitaker streets. The small wooden building was destroyed by fire on December 4, 1829, though the **Torahs** and **ark** were saved. A new brink build was consecrated on that same site in 1841 by **Reverend Isaac Leeser**.

In 1820, Georgia and the Carolinas were separated from the **Catholic See of Baltimore**, and **Bishop John England** was appointed to the newly formed see, which consisted of only hundred **Catholics** in Savannah and fewer in Augusta.

The population of Georgia in 1830 was 516,823. In 1836, **Emory College** at Oxford, a **Methodist Episcopal** school, was founded.

The same year was founded **Wesleyan Female College** at Macon, a **Methodist Episcopal** school and the first institution of learning for women in America.

In 1839, **Bishop England** listed only 11 **priests** in the State. The **Diocese of Savannah**, which comprises the State of Georgia, was **established** in 1850, at which time **Bishop England** stated that there less than 25 **priests** in the entire State.

Georgia supported the State's Right doctrine before the outbreak of the Civil War, and when Lincoln was elected, politicians moved for secession from the Union.

The war brought havoc and devastation to the State. After the termination of hostilities, Georgia for a time refused to allow former slaves in the State Legislature.

In 1869, **Atlanta University - a non-sectarian school**, was founded and in 1870, **Clark University - a Methodist Episcopal school** founded.

The population of Georgia in 1870 was 1,184,109.

In 1877, **Shorter College** at Rome - a **Baptist school** founded, and in 1881, **Morris Brown College - a Methodist school** founded.

The **Jewish Reform movement** was well under way in America by the middle of the nineteenth century. **Reverend Isaac P. Mendes,** who in 1877 began his twenty-seven years of distinguished service as **Rabbi**, dissuaded against too hasty abandonment of the older **Jewish form of worship**. Not until February 2, 1880, was the use of a **canopy in the marriage ceremony** made optional, and another fourteen years passed before members were permitted to go hatless during services. In 1902, the **Union Prayer Book** was adopted, and on January 10, 1904, membership in the **Union of American Hebrew Congregations** was attained and **Mickve Israel**'s transition to **Reform Judaism**.

The last vestige of its Spanish-Portuguese heritage is proudly maintained in the **Sephardic** melody "**El Norah Ah Lee Lah**" sung by the **congregation** during the closing hour of each **Yom Kippur service.**

In 1881, the Cotton Exposition in Atlanta attested to the growing commercial life of the State.

History was made at the International Exposition in Atlanta, September 18, 1895, when the President of Tuskegee Institute, Booker T. Washington was asked to speak. He stated:

"A ship lost at sea for many days suddenly sighted a friendly vessel. From the mast of the unfortunate vessel was seen a signal, 'Water, water; we die of thirst!' The answer from the friendly vessel at once came back, 'Cast down your bucket where you are.' A second time the signal, 'Water, water; send us water!' ran up from the distressed vessel, and was answered, 'Cast down your bucket where you are.' And a third and fourth signal for water was answered, 'Cast down your bucket where you are.' The captain of the distressed vessel, at last heading the injunction, cast down his bucket, and it came up full of fresh, sparkling water from the mouth of the Amazon River.

"To those of my race who depend on bettering their condition in a foreign land or who underestimate the importance of cultivating friendly relations with the Southern white man, who is their next-door neighbor, I would say: 'Cast down your bucket where you are' – cast it down in making friends in every manly way of the people of all races by whom we are surrounded...

"To those of the white race who look to the incoming of those of foreign birth and strange tongue and habits of the prosperity of the South, were I permitted I would repeat what I say to my own race: 'Cast down your bucket where you are.' Cast it down among the eight millions of Negroes whose habits you know, whose fidelity and love you have tested."

The population of Georgia in 1900 was 2,216,331, including 1,034,813 African Americans, 204 Chinese, 1 Japanese, and 19 Indians. In 1900, the largest city was Savannah, with a population of 54,244.

A 1908 Census listed the **Diocese of Savannah** as having 23,000 **Catholics**, 13 **Churches**, 72 **priests**, 18 **missions** with **Churches**, 81 **stations**, and 14 **chapels**. There were 2 **Catholic hospitals** in Georgia run by the **Sisters of Mercy**.

There were 170 orphans at **St. Joseph's Orphanage** in Washington, run by 6 **Sisters of St. Joseph**; **St. Mary's Home for Female Orphans**, Savannah, run by 7 **Sisters of**

Mercy; and 2 **African American orphanages**; there were 94 residents at a Home for the Aged in Savannah, run by 10 **Little Sisters of the Poor.**

In 1910, the most notable feature of the work of the **Church** in Georgia was the **evangelical** energy directed toward the former slaves, a task which is being undertaken by the **Society of the African Missions**. The population of the State was about equally divided between whites and African Americans, with less than five hundred African Americans being **Catholic**.

In 1910, there were 30,000 African Americans in Augusta, of which were only about 20 **Catholics**. **Catholic colleges** are: **College of Marist Fathers** at Atlanta, **College of the Sacred Heart** at Augusta, and **St. Stanislaus Novitiate of the Society of Jesus** at Macon.

As of 1910, the State of Georgia gave full **liberty of conscience** in **matters of religious opinion and worship**, but did not legalize willful or profane scoffing, or prevent legislative enactment for the punishment of such acts.

It is unlawful to conduct any secular business on **Sunday**. Oaths were administered by using the **Bible** to swear upon, by the uplifted hand, or by affirmation, the form being: "You do solemnly swear in the **presence of the ever living God**" or "You do sincerely and truly affirm, etc." The sessions of the legislature are opened with **prayer**.

A great wave of **German Jews** arrived in Savannah beginning in 1840. Some descendants of **Mickve Israel's** colonial settlers include **Mordecai Manuel Noah**, sheriff of New York, founder of the Tammany Hall political machine and early **Zionist**, who in 1825, sought to **establish** a **Jewish** homeland called "**Ararat**" at Grand Island on the Niagara River. Another descendant was **Commodore Uriah Phillips Levy**, who rescued President Thomas Jefferson's home at Monticello from destruction and abolished the practice of flogging in the U. S. Navy.

JUNE 9, 1732
CHARTER OF GEORGIA

Forasmuch as the good and prosperous success of the said colony cannot but chiefly depend, next under the **blessing of God**, and the support of our royal authority, upon the provident and good direction of the whole enterprise...

We do will, ordain and establish, that the said common council for the time being, of the said corporation...shall...have full power and authority to dispose of...the monies and effects belonging to the said corporation...

We do by these presents, for us, our heirs and successors, grant, **establish** and ordain, that forever hereafter, there shall be a **liberty of conscience** allowed in the **worship of God**, to all persons inhabiting, or which shall inhabit or be resident within our said provinces and that all such persons, except **Papists**, shall have a **free exercise of their religion.**

JANUARY 11, 1758
GEORGIA ASSEMBLY PASSED AN ACT

For constituting the several Divisions and Districts of this Province into **Parishes**, and for **establishing Religious Worship** therein, according to the **Rites and Ceremonies of the Church of England**...[Each **clergyman** of the **Established Church of England** to receive from the government a salary of £25 per annum.]

1776
RULES AND REGULATIONS OF THE COLONY OF GEORGIA

Whereas, the unwise and iniquitous system of administration obstinately persisted in by the British Parliament and Ministry against the good people of America hath at length driven the latter to take up arms as their last resource for the **preservation of their rights and liberties which God and the Constitution gave them.**

1777
CONSTITUTION OF GEORGIA

ARTICLE 6: The representatives shall be chosen out of the residents in each county...and they shall be of the **Protestant religion**.

ARTICLE 14. Every person entitled to vote shall take the following oath or affirmation, if required, viz:
"I, A B. do voluntarily and solemnly swear (or affirm, as the case may be) that I do owe true allegiance to this State, and will support the constitution thereof; **So Help Me God**."

ARTICLE 15. Any five of the representatives elected, as before directed, being met, shall have power to...administer the oath to all other members that attend, in order to qualify them to take their seats, viz: "I, A B. do solemnly swear that I will bear true allegiance to the State of Georgia, and will truly perform the trusts reposed in me; and that I will execute the same to the best of my knowledge, for the benefit of this State, and the support of the constitution thereof, and that I have obtained my election without fraud or bribe whatever; **So Help Me God**."

ARTICLE 24. The governor's oath: "I, A B, elected governor of the State of Georgia, by the representatives thereof, do solemnly promise and swear that I will, during the term of my appointment, to the best of my skill and judgment, execute the said office faithfully and conscientiously' according to law, without favor, affection, or partiality; that I will, to the utmost of my power, support, maintain, and defend the State of Georgia, and the constitution of the same; and use my utmost endeavors to protect the people thereof in the secure enjoyment of all their rights, franchises and privileges; and that the laws and ordinances of the State be duly observed, and that law and justice in mercy be executed in all judgments.

And I do further solemnly promise and swear that I will peaceably and quietly resign the government to which I have been elected at the period to which my continuance in the said office is limited by the constitution.

And, lastly, I do also solemnly swear that I have not accepted of the government whereunto I am elected contrary to the articles of this constitution; **So Help Me God**."

ARTICLE 30. When any affair that requires secrecy shall be laid before the governor and the executive council, it shall be the duty of the governor, and he is hereby obliged, to administer the following Oath, viz: "I, A B. do solemnly swear that any business that shall be at this time communicated to the council I will not, in any manner whatever, either by speaking, writing, or otherwise, reveal the same to any person whatever, until leave given by the council, or when called upon by the house of Assembly; and all this I swear without any reservation whatever; **So Help Me God**."

ARTICLE 56. All persons whatever shall have the **free exercise of their religion**; provided it be not repugnant to the peace and safety of the State; and shall not, unless by consent, support any **teacher** or **teachers** except those of their own **profession.**

1789
CONSTITUTION OF GEORGIA

ARTICLE 4, SECTION 5: All persons shall have the **free exercise of religion**, without being obligated to contribute to the support of any **religious** but their own.

1790
PRESIDENT GEORGE WASHINGTON WROTE TO THE HEBREW CONGREGATION IN SAVANNAH, GEORGIA:

Happily the people of the United States have in many instances exhibited examples worthy of imitation, the salutary influence of which will doubtless extend much farther if gratefully enjoying those **blessings of peace** which (under **the favor of Heaven**) have been attained by fortitude in war, they shall conduct themselves with reverence to the **Deity** and charity toward their fellow-creatures May the same **wonder-working Deity**, who long since delivering the **Hebrews** from their Egyptian Oppressors planted them in the **promised land** - whose **Providential Agency** has lately been conspicuous in **establishing** these United States as an independent Nation - still continue to water them with the dews of **Heaven** and to make the inhabitants of every **denomination** participate in the temporal and **spiritual blessings** of that people whose **God is Jehovah.**

1798
CONSTITUTION OF GEORGIA

ARTICLE 4, SECTION 10: No person within this state shall, upon any pretense, be deprived of the inestimable privilege of **worshipping God** in any manner agreeable to his own **conscience**, nor be compelled to attend any **place of worship** contrary to his own **faith** and judgment; nor shall he ever be obliged to pay **tithes**, taxes, or any other rate, for the building or repairing any **place of worship**, or for the maintenance of any **minister** or **Ministry**, contrary to what he believes to be right, or hath voluntarily engaged...No one **religious society** shall ever be **established** in this state, in preference to another; nor shall any person be denied the enjoyment of any civil right merely on account of his **religious principles.**

1861
CONSTITUTION OF GEORGIA

ARTICLE 1, SECTION 2: **God has ordained that men shall live under government;** but as the forms and administration of civil government are in human, and therefore, fallible hands, they may be altered, or modified whenever the safety or happiness of the governed requires it. No government should be changed for light or transient causes; nor unless upon reasonable assurance that a better will be established.

ARTICLE 1, SECTION 7: No religious test shall be required for the tenure of any office, and no religion shall be established by law, and **no citizen shall be deprived of any right or privilege by reason of his religious belief.**

1877
CONSTITUTION OF GEORGIA
(IN CONSTITUTIONS OF 1945, 1976, 1983)

PREAMBLE: To perpetuate the principles of free government, insure justice to all, preserve peace, promote the interest and happiness of the citizen ("and of the family" -added 1983) and transmit to posterity the enjoyment of liberty, we, the people of Georgia, relying upon the **protection and guidance of Almighty God**, do ordain and establish this Constitution.

ARTICLE ON FREEDOM OF **CONSCIENCE**: All men have the natural and inalienable **right to worship God,**

each according to the dictates of his own conscience, and no human authority should, in any case, control or interfere with such **right of conscience**.

ARTICLE ON **RELIGIOUS OPINIONS:** No inhabitant of this State shall be molested in person or property, or prohibited from holding any public office, or trust, on account of his **religious opinions**; but **the right of liberty of conscience shall not be so construed as to excuse acts of licentiousness**, or justify practices inconsistent with the peace and safety of the State.

GEORGIA RELIGIOUS AFFILIATION

The Encyclopedia Britannica, 11th edition, published in 1911, stated:

The total membership of the **Churches** in 1906 was about 1,029,037, of whom:

Baptist - 596,319
Methodist - 349,079
Presbyterian - 24,040
Catholic - 19,273
Disciples of Christ - 12,703
Episcopal - 9,790
Congregationalists - 5,581

http://www.1911encyclopedia.org/Georgia

Wikipedia Encyclopedia, 2006, listed **Georgia** as:

Christian - 85 percent, consisting of:
- **Baptist** - 39 percent
- **Methodist** - 12 percent
- **Presbyterian** - 3 percent
- **Pentacostal** - 3 percent
- **Other Protestant** - 19 percent

Catholic - 8 percent
Other Christian - 1 percent
Other Religions - 2 percent
Non-Religious/Non-Reporting - 13 percent

http://en.wikipedia.org/wiki/Georgia_percent28U.S._state percent29#Religion
http://en.wikipedia.org/wiki/State_religion

The U.S. Religious Landscape Survey, conducted by The Pew Forum on Religion & Public Life, 2007, published in the USA Today, listed **Georgia** as:

Christian - 83 percent, consisting of:
Evangelical Protestant - 38 percent
Mainline Protestant - 16 percent
Black Protestant - 16 percent
Catholic - 12 percent
Orthodox - <0.5 percent
Other Christian - <0.5 percent
Mormon - <0.5 percent
Jehovah's Witnesses - <0.5 percent
Jewish - 1 percent
Muslim - <0.5 percent
Buddhist - <0.5 percent
Hindu - <0.5 percent
Other World Religions - <0.5 percent
Other Faiths - <0.5 percent
Unaffiliated - 13 percent
Did not answer - <0.5 percent

www.pewforum.org
www.usatoday.com/news/graphics/pew-religion-08/flash.htm

CPSIA information can be obtained at www.ICGtesting.com
Printed in the USA
BVOW08s0254150915

417992BV00001B/1/P